SOCIAL FORCES
IN AMERICAN HISTORY

SOCIAL FORCES
IN AMERICAN HISTORY

BY

A. M. SIMONS

NEW YORK
THE BOOK LEAGUE OF AMERICA
1929

PRINTED IN THE UNITED STATES OF AMERICA

COPYRIGHT, 1911,
BY THE MACMILLAN COMPANY.

All rights reserved, including
the right of reproduction in
whole or in part in any form.

Set up and electrotyped. Published October, 1911. Reprinted
November, 1929.

Special edition published by arrangement with
The Macmillan Company.

Norwood Press
J. S. Cushing Co. — Berwick & Smith Co.
Norwood, Mass., U.S.A.

TO MY WIFE

MAY WOOD SIMONS

WHOSE CONTINUOUS COÖPERATION AND ADVICE

AT ALL STAGES OF THIS WORK

MIGHT WELL ENTITLE HER TO BE NAMED

AS CO-AUTHOR

PREFACE

THAT political struggles are based upon economic interests is to-day disputed by few students of society. The attempt has been made in this work to trace the various interests that have arisen and struggled in each social stage and to determine the influence exercised by these contending interests in the creation of social institutions.

Back of every political party there has always stood a group or class which expected to profit by the activity and the success of that party. When any party has attained to power, it has been because it has tried to establish institutions or to modify existing ones in accord with its interests.

Changes in the industrial basis of society — inventions, new processes, and combinations and methods of producing and distributing goods — create new interests with new social classes to represent them. These improvements in the technique of production are the dynamic element that brings about what we call progress in society.

In this work I have sought to begin at the origin of each line of social progress. I have first endeavored to describe the steps in mechanical progress, then the social classes brought into prominence by the mechanical changes, then the struggle by which these new classes sought to gain social power, and, finally, the institutions which were created or the alterations made in existing institutions as a consequence of the struggle, or as a result of the victory of a new class.

It has seemed to me that these underlying social forces are of more importance than the individuals that were forced to the front in the process of these struggles, or even than the laws that were established to record the results of the conflict. In short, I have tried to describe the dynamics of history rather than to record the accomplished facts, to answer the question, "Why did it happen?" as well as, "What happened?"

An inquiry into causes is manifestly a greater task than the recording of accomplished facts. It is certain that I have made some mistakes, probably a great many, in analyzing the underlying forces of so complex a thing as American social development. The finding of such mistakes will prove nothing as to the method save that the leisure of ten very busy years in the life of one individual is all too short a time in which to trace to their origin the multitude of forces that have been operating in American history.

This work has been the more difficult since only a few, historians, and these only in recent years, have given any attention to this viewpoint. It was, therefore, necessary for me to spend much time in the study of "original documents," — the newspapers, magazines, and pamphlet literature of each period. In these, rather than in the "musty documents" of state, do we find history in the making. Here we can see the clash of contending interests before they are crystallized into laws and institutions.

I have not sought after new or bizarre facts. I have

sought rather to understand the reasons for those whose existence is undisputed. Occasionally I have found things which seemed to be neglected in the familiar histories and have stated these. In my references, also, I have tried to name the most accessible works rather than to multiply references and strain after scholastic effect with many citations of seldom used and almost inaccessible material.

In this connection it should be stated that most of this work was written before the publication of the "Documentary History of American Society," edited by Dr. R. T. Ely and John R. Commons of the University of Wisconsin. Otherwise I should have made more frequent reference to its pages. Thanks to the courtesy of these editors, however, I had an opportunity to consult their notes and the original publications upon which that work is based, and this service is here gratefully acknowledged.

CONTENTS

CHAPTER I
CONDITIONS LEADING TO DISCOVERY 1

CHAPTER II
CAUSES OF COLONIZATION 12

CHAPTER III
WHAT THE COLONISTS FOUND IN AMERICA . . . 21

CHAPTER IV
THE COLONIAL STAGE 30

CHAPTER V
THE GROWTH OF SOLIDARITY 55

CHAPTER VI
CAUSES OF THE REVOLUTION 60

CHAPTER VII
THE REVOLUTION 70

CHAPTER VIII
FORMATION OF THE GOVERNMENT 81

CHAPTER IX

Industrial Conditions at the Beginning of the American Government 100

CHAPTER X

Rule of Commerce and Finance 108

CHAPTER XI

Rule of Commerce and Frontier 120

CHAPTER XII

The Westward March of a People . . . 134

CHAPTER XIII

The Birth of the Factory System 143

CHAPTER XIV

Changing Interests 151

CHAPTER XV

The First Crisis — 1819 160

CHAPTER XVI

Condition of the Workers in the Childhood of Capitalism 170

CHAPTER XVII

The First Labor Movement — 1824–1836 . . 179

CHAPTER XVIII

The Youth of Capitalism — 1830–1850 191

CHAPTER XIX

Why the Civil War Came 216

CHAPTER XX

The Crisis in the Chattel Slave System . . . 222

CHAPTER XXI

Rise of Northern Capitalism 238

CHAPTER XXII

The Armed Conflict of Sectional Interests . . 264

CHAPTER XXIII

Reconstruction 285

CHAPTER XXIV

Triumph and Decadence of Capitalism . . . 304

THE SOCIAL FORCES

OF THE

HISTORY OF THE UNITED STATES

CHAPTER I

CONDITIONS LEADING TO DISCOVERY

AMERICAN history is usually made to begin with the voyage of Columbus. Since all historical beginnings are more or less arbitrary, the especial starting point is of no great importance.

History, like time, its principal element, has neither beginning nor end. American social institutions have their roots far back in the days to which history does not run. With these origins the historian does not deal. Here he gives way to the anthropologist, the biologist, and the geologist.

The stream of social evolution which bore the first germs of American society had its main source in Europe. The social genealogy of America goes back to Greece and Rome, and from these comes down through Germans, French, and English, rather than through Mound Builder, Pequod, and Iroquois.

Since the voyages of Columbus form the first link in the chain that was to bring these European influences to these shores, a knowledge of European society at the time of those voyages and the forces that led to them is essential to an understanding of American history.

The "Age of Discovery," in which the voyages of Columbus were the most striking, though by no means isolated events, came during that period of great social transformation known as the Reformation.

It was the period of the revival of Greek learning, of the Decline of the Roman Empire and the Papacy, of the disappearance of feudalism and chivalry, when towns and nations were growing at the expense of feudal tenures, and commerce and manufacturing were taking on new forms and new life. It was a day not so much of a rebirth of old things as of the birth of those new things whose climax, as capitalism, is the dominant feature of the United States to-day.[1]

A number of revolutionary inventions were primarily responsible for these industrial, political, and religious changes. In navigation the compass had but recently made it possible to guide a ship beyond the sight of landmarks. Without the compass the Mediterranean marked the limit of navigation. The "world" surrounding this sea was the extent of human knowledge. Now the navigator could carry his landmarks with him, and the Atlantic could be crossed with as certain accuracy as if its western shore were visible from the Pillars of Hercules.

The astrolabe now gave the location of a vessel by its relation to astronomical bodies. These inventions broke all boundaries to the possibility of exploration.

The invention of gunpowder and its application to war produced equally far-reaching results. The first crude firearms sufficed to render the humble foot soldier more

[1] Henry Cabot Lodge, "Close of the Middle Ages," pp. 518–519.

than a match for the best equipped and armored knight. The feudal castle was not impregnable even to the very beginnings of artillery. Henceforth military power was with him who could maintain the largest number of soldiers and not to the strongest arm and the most easily defended castle. Gunpowder played a decisive part in military affairs at the battle of Crécy in 1346 and the siege of Constantinople in 1453.

To this period also belong the invention of printing with movable type, and the manufacture of paper on a commercial scale.[1]

These industrial changes tended to bring the merchant class into a position of social supremacy. Hitherto public opinion had despised the merchant. He was fair prey for the ruling class of robber barons. Commerce was looked upon with disdain.[2] The passing merchant was considered a legitimate source of revenue by the nobility and their retainers. What would now be classified as highway robbery was by all odds the most respectable industry in central Europe for some centuries prior to the discovery of America.

The ideas of the dominant industrial class, the landed nobility, became the standard of morality as preached by the Church.

"The Church was very hostile to commerce. The theologians sought to show that it was unproductive, and they especially denounced the trade in money, confusing the taking of interest with usury. For many of

[1] The first French mill for the manufacture of paper was erected in 1189, the first English one in 1330, and the first German one in 1390.

[2] Paul Risson, "Histoire Sommaire du Commerce," p. 156; William Clarence Webster, "General History of Commerce," p. 96.

them, even in the sixteenth century, merchants were liars, perjurers, and thieves."[1]

The inventions to which reference has been made were changing all this. They were promoting the growth of towns, the extension of trade, the knowledge of, and therefore the desire for, luxuries which only commerce and the merchants could provide. The Crusades took many of the nobility away, and left their estates in the hands of merchant princes who had taken this property as security for the expense of a crusading outfit.

As the merchants grew in power they became respectable, and commerce became a virtue. When merchant bankers, like the Fuggers, were able to dictate terms of peace and war to kings and emperors, we no longer hear the merchants referred to as "liars, perjurers, and thieves."

By the fifteenth century the merchants were the ruling class in Europe. The great commercial cities of the Mediterranean and of the north of Europe were more powerful than many nations, and within these cities rich merchants arbitered the political destinies of the known world. Any merchant-ruled society seeks new markets. The pressure for exploration at this period was stronger than perhaps at any period before or since. Moreover, the whole commercial and social life was being transformed in such a manner as to make explorations westward across the Atlantic in search of Oriental markets almost inevitable.[2]

---

[1] William Clarence Webster, "General History of Commerce," p. 96.
[2] Cheney, "European Background of American History," pp. 38–39: "As Europe in the fifteenth century became more wealthy and more familiar with the products of the whole world, as the nobles learned to

CONDITIONS LEADING TO DISCOVERY 5

The commercial life of Europe in the Middle Ages was built up around the trade with the Orient. From the East came spices, tea, coffee, precious stones, rare fabrics, dyes, perfumes, drugs, carpets, and rugs, — nearly all luxuries enjoyed by the rich and the powerful alone. In exchange for these the West sent woolen goods, tin, copper, lead, arsenic, antimony, and other metals, and especially gold and silver, of which large amounts were always flowing east to meet the heavy "balance of trade" that favored the Orient.[1]

Certain Mediterranean cities became the western termini of the long voyage from the East, and distributing points for the goods to the local trade centers. Foremost among these cities were Venice and Genoa.

The stream of goods flowing between these cities and the Orient passed through Asia Minor or down the Red Sea, and through the Arabian Gulf. During the eleventh, twelfth, and thirteenth centuries the Moslems were moving north out of Africa and gradually cutting these trade routes one by one. When in 1453 Constantinople fell into the hands of the Mohammedan Turks, the last great route to the Orient was closed to European traders.[2]

Europe did not sit idle while the arteries of its commercial life were being slowly strangled. How to find

---

demand more luxuries, and a wealthy merchant class grew up which was able to gratify the same tastes as the nobles, the demand of the West upon the East became more insistent than ever. Therefore, the men, the nation, the government that could find a new way to the East might claim a trade of indefinite extent and extreme profit."

[1] Edward P. Cheney, "European Background of American History," pp. 9-19; Aloys Schulte, "Geschichte des Mittelalterlichen Handel und Verkehr.," Vol. I, pp. 674-675.

[2] Helmholt, "History of the World," Vol. VII, p. 8.

or make a trade route between Europe and the Orient was a question that so dominated the life of Europe during this time as to be the principal force in molding its social institutions. Yet for almost three centuries there was scarcely a suggestion of seeking a western route. It is doubtful if geographical ignorance was even the principal cause for the neglect of westward exploration. Knowledge came when it was needed, but no such knowledge was wanted during these centuries. Such a westward route would have overthrown existing trade relations. Those who profited by such relations were in control of society, and could scarcely be expected to seek out such a route.[1]

All efforts were directed toward driving back the Moslems and opening up the eastward route. In this fact we find at least one reason for those tremendous movements of armed men, — the Crusades. The accepted explanation of these expeditions is that they were for the purpose of "rescuing the holy sepulchre from the profane touch of the infidel." It is at least suggestive that crusades were not preached until trade routes were endangered, and that they ceased when commerce underwent a transformation that rendered these particular trade routes of less importance to the ruling merchant class.

It was just these changes that paved the way for the discovery of America.

Oriental products, after their arrival in Europe, flowed along certain well-defined channels. For ages the goods that arrived at Venice and Genoa had moved into northern Europe along routes whose location had largely de-

[1] David Macpherson, "History of European Commerce with India" (London, 1812), pp. 7–8.

termined the placing of population and the existence of many social institutions. One set of routes led northward across France. At certain intervals great fairs were regularly held. These fairs performed the same distributing service for the commerce of the Middle Ages that is performed by the great cities of the present. They were, in fact, temporary cities, dissolving when their annual function had been performed.

Another trunk of this commerce led from the terminal cities on the Mediterranean over the Alps and down the Rhine. Because this route was the feeder of the commerce of all northwestern Europe, the Rhine was sprinkled thickly with the castles of the robber barons. The traveler who passes down the Rhine to-day can measure the wealth of this commerce by the ruins of the retreats of the castled thieves who preyed upon it.

Whatever disturbed these trade routes and centers would change the whole social structure resting upon them,— the merchants and the barons who robbed them, the fairs and the country dependent upon them.

This European trade system was being revolutionized and transformed during the years that the Moslems were cutting the trade arteries that united it with the Orient.

Improvements in navigation and shipbuilding had made the voyage around Gibraltar cheaper and safer than the overland trip across France and Germany. The discovery of rich mineral deposits in Germany and England, and the development of the English and Flemish woolen industry contributed still further to this alteration.[1] The fairs decayed, the castles on the Rhine grew

[1] Brooks Adams, "The New Empire," pp. 50-55.

less profitable, and a new group of commercial cities grew on the Baltic and the North seas.

These cities formed a confederation known as the Hanseatic League. Lübeck, Hamburg, Bremen, and other important trading centers entered into this League, and it grew in power until it possessed its own navy, enacted its own laws governing trade relations, made treaties, and had many of the attributes of a strong nation. The very existence of such a powerful federation composed of mercantile cities is significant of the dominant position of commerce during this period.

The Hanseatic League soon entered into other fields of commerce than those depending upon the Oriental goods brought through the Straits of Gibraltar. Its merchants not only built up an extensive local trade within Europe, but, more significant still in connection with the discovery of America, they were developing a caravan trade direct with the Orient by way of an overland route through Russia and China.

The trade of the Hanseatic League and of England, Holland, and western Europe in general was essentially an ocean trade, developing shipbuilding, training sailors, and offering prizes to navigators. Extraordinary efforts were made to increase the size of ships. Henry V of England experimented in the building of ships that would have been considered large at the beginning of the nineteenth century. Boats of 900 tons burden were built at the Southampton docks in 1449.[1]

A summary of the situation at the close of the fifteenth century will show a combination of forces making for

[1] Cunningham, "Growth of English Industry and Commerce," Vol. I, p. 413.

discovery and exploration. The merchants were the ruling class in society. Commerce was built around the Oriental trade. The principal routes of this trade were closed. Within Europe trade centers and routes had shifted to the Atlantic coast. In so shifting there had come a development of navigation and shipbuilding technique such as was essential to any extensive voyage of discovery. Commercial Europe, after facing for centuries toward the East with its outposts on the Mediterranean, was now looking out across the Atlantic from the shore of western Europe.

This commercial world was devoting all its energies to the search for a route to Asia, and there was a general tendency to seek this *via* the Atlantic. Portugal was already creeping around Africa. In 1445 Dinnis Diaz had sailed beyond Cape Verde, the uttermost point of the great westward bend of the African continent. Further progress would have been rapid had not a new and hitherto unexpected obstacle developed. The explorers had reached the source of slave-supply and found this trade more profitable than hunting for trade routes to India.

"Hence one expedition after another sent out for purposes of discovery, returned, bringing tales of failure to reach further points on the coast, but laden with human booty to be sold. . . . Only the most vigorous pressure, exercised on the choicest spirits among the Portuguese captains, served to carry discoveries further."[1]

These navigators had gone far enough, however, to satisfy the rulers of Portugal that India could be reached

[1] E. P. Cheney, "European Background of American History," pp. 66–70; "Cambridge Modern History," Vol. I, pp. 7–16.

around Africa, and they were consequently indifferent to the plea of Columbus.[1] The merchants of the northern cities hoped much from the routes which they could control through Russia and Siberia, or along the Black Sea to China, and were likewise indifferent to westward sailing explorations. The Italian merchants were trying to bargain with the Moslem whom the Crusades had been unable to crush. A western route would only contribute to their decline, and Columbus found no favor for his plan in his native Genoa.

There were three commercial nations on the Atlantic that would profit directly by a western route. Each could hope to control such a route, and none saw any possibility of similar advantages in any other route. These were England, Spain, and France. Columbus made simultaneous application to the first two. England was suspicious of his Spanish affiliations, had plenty of navigators who were beginning explorations, and therefore rejected his offer, and he sailed under a Spanish flag.

It was an "Age of Discovery." Explorers were pushing out in all directions. Many had already suggested that the road to India lay to the west. Contrary to the popularly accepted legends that have become embalmed in textbooks, the rotundity of the earth was quite generally accepted in scientific circles.

[1] "Cambridge Modern History," Vol. I, p. 21: "The circumnavigation of Africa was nearly accomplished; of this route to the wealthy East the Portuguese would enjoy a practical monopoly, and it could be effectively defended. . . . Even if the westward passage were successfully accomplished, it was manifest that Portugal would be unable to monopolize it, and that discovery must ultimately inure for the benefit of the stronger maritime nations of western Europe."

The discovery of America by Columbus was but the inevitable resultant of the operation of forces that were bound to send some one across the Atlantic at about the close of the fifteenth century.

CHAPTER II

CAUSES OF COLONIZATION

THE movement of the peoples of Europe to the New World was but a part of the strange age-long migration of the race toward the setting sun. Great masses of people, such as came to America in colonial times, do not move without some deep, underlying cause. Men and women do not leave their homes and friends and brave the dangers of such an ocean voyage as was required to reach America before the age of steam without some strong, compelling force.

The greatest admirer of the New World could hardly claim that it possessed any powerful attractions at this time. The best that it could offer to the first comers was a chance to struggle with the forces of nature in a state of society but little removed from savagery. Yet hundreds of thousands of people did come to America during the three centuries after its discovery.

If there were no powerful attractions drawing them on, the cause of their migration must be sought in the land from which they came.

It was a time of social upheaval and revolution in Europe. The merchant class was ruling. It was the first division of the great capitalist army, — the advance guard, whose work it was to explore the world and clear the way for the army of occupation, — the industrial capitalist.

CAUSES OF COLONIZATION

The forces of feudalism were not yet completely conquered, and the new class was compelled constantly to fight to hold its position and gain greater power. It was a time when nations and religions were being born, and when in all fields of social life mighty forces were struggling for the mastery.

As fast as the merchant or the manufacturing class attained to power, its members set about divorcing the former serfs and peasants from the soil, and dissolving all old feudal relations, in order that the workers might be "free" to hunt for employers. So it was that in nearly all the leading European nations the people were being driven out of their ancient homes.

In England, for example, this was a time of great growth in the woolen industry. Tenants were being driven off the old estates that great sheep pastures might be created. Seldom has this process been more vividly depicted than in a famous extract from the "Utopia" of Sir Thomas More. This was written in 1615, and the author makes one of his characters say concerning the condition in contemporary England: —

"Your sheep, which are naturally mild and easily kept in order, may be said now to devour men and unpeople, not only villages, but towns, for, wherever it is found that the sheep of any soil yield a softer and richer wool than ordinary there the nobility and gentry, and even those holy men, the abbots, not contented with the old rents which their farms yielded, nor thinking it enough that they, living at their ease, do no good to the public, resolve to do it hurt instead of good. They stop the course of agriculture, destroying houses and towns, reserving only the churches, and inclosed grounds that they may lodge their sheep in them. As if forests and parks had swallowed up too little of the land, those worthy countrymen turn the best inhabited places into solitudes; for when an insatiable wretch, who is a plague to his country, resolves to inclose many thousands of acres of land, the owners, as well as tenants, are turned out of their possessions, by tricks, or by main force, or, being wearied out with ill-usage, they are forced to sell them. By which means those miserable people, both men and women, married and unmarried, old and young, with their poor but numerous families (since country business requires many hands), are all forced to change their seats, not knowing whither to go; and they must sell almost for nothing their household stuff, which could not bring them much money, even though they might stay for a buyer."

All Europe was in a turmoil. The Hundred Years' War had just ceased when Columbus discovered America. Within the next three centuries nearly every nation of Europe was to be engaged in armed conflict, and for much of that time war was practically epidemic on the continent of Europe. Most of these wars were waged nominally around questions of religion. This was simply because the industrial revolution, which placed the capitalist class in power, necessarily had its religious expression. The Reformation, with its individualism in theology, was as perfect a reflex of capitalism as "free competition" and *laissez faire* in economics. "Every one for himself and the devil take the hindmost" was the motto in industry, economics, religion, and politics, and it is noteworthy that the best authorities in each of these fields agreed that the majority of mankind is condemned to perdition.

Nowhere did these religious wars rage with such fury as in Germany, and it was from the locality in which the fighting was most destructive that the largest number of German emigrants came to the New World. The great and fertile Rhine Valley, once the main highway of commerce from the Mediterranean to northern Europe, and therefore the best hunting ground for the robber barons, was now the seat of war after war. The first of these was the Thirty Years' War, ended by the peace of Westphalia in 1649. Historians vie with one another in describing the horrible devastation of this conflict upon the locality in which it was waged. Says one writer: —

"Not only were horses and cattle carried away by the various armies which shifted back and forth over the length and breadth of the land; not only were houses, barns, and even crops burned; but the master of the house was frequently subjected to fiendish tortures, in order that he might thus be forced to discover the hiding place of his gold; or, as often happened, as a punishment for having nothing to give. At the approach of a hostile army the whole village would take to flight, and would live for weeks in the midst of forests and marshes, or in caves. The enemy having departed, the wretched survivors would return to their ruined homes and carry on a painful existence with the few remains of their former property, until they were forced to fly again by new invasions.

. . . .

"The years 1635 and 1636 mark the period of the most terrible misery. In the years 1636–1638 famine and pestilence came to add to the suffering. The people tried to satisfy hunger with roots, grass, and leaves; even cannibalism became more or less frequent. The gallows and the graveyards had to be guarded; the bodies of children were not safe from their mothers. So great was the destruction that where once were flourishing farms and vineyards, now whole bands of wolves roamed unmolested."[1]

Even yet the cup of misery of this ill-fated land was not filled. The peace signed at Westphalia in 1649 was quickly broken so far as the Palatinate was concerned. In 1674 another war broke out between France and Holland, that lasted with but few interruptions and with slight changes of combatants for several years more. Finally, in 1689 the French determined completely to depopulate this country. The result has been stated in one of Macaulay's striking paragraphs: —

"The commander announced to near half a million human beings that he granted them three days of grace, and that within that time they must shift for themselves. Soon the roads and fields, which then lay deep in snow, were blackened by innumerable multitudes of men, women, and children flying from their homes. . . . The flames went up from every market place, every parish church, every country seat, within the devoted province. The fields where the corn had been sowed were plowed up. The orchards were cut down."

These poor hunted creatures fled by tens of thousands to the valleys and broad fields of Pennsylvania, where they have preserved their language, customs, religion, and traditions even to the present day, presenting the

[1] Oscar Kuhns, "The German and Swiss Settlements of Colonial Pennsylvania," pp. 3-9.

strange paradox of the oldest "Americans" speaking a "foreign" tongue. They fled down the Rhine, crowded into Amsterdam, where they became the victims of a horde of hyena-like shipping agents, who plundered them of their last coin, then shipped them upon overcrowded and unseaworthy ships, with such accommodations that sometimes half of them died upon the passage, and the remainder were landed in America, so indebted to the ship's officers that they were sold into temporary slavery to pay their passage.[1]

Throughout this period, whichever of the warring religious sects gained control of any government promptly used its power to "stamp out the heresy" of its competitors. So there was never a lack of religious refugees seeking an asylum in America, although the number of these has been vastly exaggerated, since the love of religious freedom is ordinarily looked upon as a much higher motive for emigration than economic necessity. It is almost needless to say that each little flock of refugees was no sooner safely settled in the New World than it proceeded to discover new heretics among its own members, who were piously driven into the surrounding wilderness.

During the eighteenth century another important element was added to the stream of immigration. This time it came from Ireland and was composed of that body that was to play such an important part in certain phases

[1] For details of these matters, see Frank R. Diffenderfer, "The German Immigration into Pennsylvania through the Port of Philadelphia from 1700-1775," in Part VII of the "Narrative and Critical History of Pennsylvania"; also same author, "The Redemptioners in Pennsylvania," in German Society Publications, Vol. X; Geiser, "Redemptioners in Pennsylvania."

of American history, the Scotch-Irish. An explanation of this movement is contained in the following extract from Campbell's work on "The Puritan in Holland, England, and America" (Vol. II, p. 427): —

"In 1698, upon the demand of the English manufacturers, the woolen industry of Ireland was utterly destroyed. It was claimed that labor was cheaper there than in England, and that, therefore, the product could be sold at a lower price. This was not to be endured. The interference of Parliament was invoked, and by a series of repressive acts, the Irish looms were closed. As one result of this legislation twenty thousand of the Protestant artisans of Ulster, deprived of employment, left Ireland for America, carrying with them the remembrance of how English faith, plighted to their forefathers, had been broken under the influence of English greed."

The next step was the enactment by Queen Anne's parliament of laws persecuting the Scotch-Irish for their religious belief, and this was followed by the establishment of the "rack-renting" system, under which the native Irish, with a lower standard of living, were enabled to underbid the former tenants. Add to this a famine in 1740, and it is no wonder that this "was by far the largest contribution of any race to the population of America during the eighteenth century."[1]

It is the same story everywhere. It was not because America drew them on, but because Europe drove them out, that the colonists came to America.

Thousands of the poorer colonists sold themselves for a series of years as slaves in order to pay the passage money that had been advanced by the shipowners. In

[1] John R. Commons, "Races and Immigrants in America," pp. 34–36.

fact, John R. Commons estimates that probably one half of all the immigrants of the colonial period landed as "indentured servants."

There were three classes of "white slaves" in colonial times. The larger class, to which reference has just been made, were those who agreed with the masters of some vessel that in return for a passage to the New World the shipowner should have the right to sell the passenger into servitude for a definite number of years. In the majority of cases this sale was made at the wharf, and the newspapers of the time regularly contain advertisements of the arrival of ships with "indentured servants" to be sold. In case no buyers came to the ship the passengers were sold to agents, who chained them together and peddled them through the towns and villages.

Another large class of slaves was made up of criminals, sent here largely from England, and sold to the colonists for a term of years.

As the raising of cotton and tobacco and some other staple crops became more profitable, and the close vicinity of the forest with free land made it difficult to keep employees at the beggarly wages which prevailed, the demand for workmen became so great that a regular trade in the stealing of persons for colonial slavery sprung up in England. So prevalent did this practice become that it added a new phrase to the language. Those who stole these children for export to America were called "spirits," and from this came the phrase to "spirit away":

"Children and adults alike were lured or forced upon vessels in the harbor, or carried to the numerous cookshops in the neighborhood of the wharves in the principal seaports, and here they were kept in close confinement until sold to merchants or masters of ships which were about to sail for the colonies. As a result of this spiriting away, frauds became so common, that in 1664 the Committee for Foreign Plantations decided to interfere. . . . A committee was appointed whose duty it was to register the names and ages of all who wished to emigrate to America. But this did not put a stop to the practice. Ten years after this act became a law, it was stated that 10,000 persons were annually spirited away from England by kidnappers."

Finally more than 200,000 negro slaves were stolen from their homes in Africa by Dutch or New England traders and sold to the planters of the Southern colonies. Historians have told us much of the discomforts of the voyagers on the *Mayflower*, but they have had little to say of the horrors endured by the miserable fugitives from the Palatinate, and still less of the terrible sufferings inflicted upon the helpless children stolen from their homes in London to become the slaves of American planters and farmers.

CHAPTER III

WHAT THE COLONISTS FOUND IN AMERICA

SOCIAL institutions are born of two elements, — the land and the people. In the childhood of society these two elements in action and reaction are almost the only factors to be considered. Later the inertia of social institutions may become a far more powerful factor in social evolution than either of the primary factors.[1] We have seen something of the character of those who peopled this continent. We have learned a little of the society from which they came, and of the forces that sent them across the ocean. They were now to build up a society in a new world. As materials to this end they brought with them a vast store of things that mankind had been countless ages in acquiring: the knowledge of reading, and printing and gunpowder, of making tools of iron and steel, of spinning and weaving and making of clothing, social and governmental institutions, churches, laws, creeds, beliefs, prejudices, superstitions. All these things, developed in the complex civilization of Europe, were now transplanted to a world where they had hitherto been unknown.

It was as if some giant hand had gathered a multitude of seeds of all kinds and manner of plants from all the ends of the earth and had flung them at random upon the

[1] J. Paul Goode, "The Human Response to the Physical Environment," in the *Journal of Geography*, Vol. III, No. 7.

American hills and plains. Some would never sprout; others would die with the first frost, or be shriveled with overmuch heat. Some would be drowned with too much rain, while others would lack the tropical downpour essential to life. Some would find the new conditions so exceptionably favorable that they would grow to giant weeds, choking out other plants of greater intrinsic value.

Let us look upon the land where this plentiful load of old achievements, beliefs, and institutions are to be thrown, that we may see which are most suited to survive and flourish, and where each kind may reach its highest development.

The Atlantic coast is a good colonial seed bed. Contrast its abundant harbors, long tidal rivers, and general open appearance with the smooth, closed wall of the Pacific coast. Here is room for many communities to grow up independent of one another. It is almost an axiom of history that peninsulas form a sort of social hotbeds in which nations grow rapidly to a high stage of maturity. A handful of colonists could scarcely have been thrown at any spot from Maine to Georgia without finding a favorable opening in which to lodge and sprout and grow.

In the days when the colonists came to America, and, indeed, in all the years before that time, rivers were the principal means of communication, even in old countries, while in new countries they were almost the only highways of commerce and travel. The region in which the first American colonies were located was amply provided with these natural highways. Abundant navigable rivers afforded access far into the interior. Only in New England was the "fall line" so close to the ocean as to give

WHAT THE COLONISTS FOUND IN AMERICA

rise to the short swift rivers which confine settlement to the coast and supply power to turn the wheels of industry.

An examination of these rivers will tell us much of the history of the region they drain. The broad deep Hudson and Susquehanna tapped country rich in fur in the beginning, which was later to become a bountiful farming region. These facts suggest that some day an Astor should rise and rule at the mouth of one of these rivers and that both should become the seat of great commercial cities. The Rappahannock and the James ebbed and flowed with the tide for many miles through rich alluvial silt, which was to be marked off into broad plantations, first for tobacco and later for cotton. Ocean vessels could sail up these tidewater streams to the wharves of the rich planters, who ruled over armies of chattel slaves and sold their products directly in foreign markets.

When society was so closely connected with the tilling of the soil, the character of that element played an important part in determining social evolution. The glaciated clay of New England with its coating of ice-brought bowlders was difficult of cultivation but slow of exhaustion. It invited small permanent farms, with such small profits as to require an auxiliary industry like fishing, hunting, or trading to maintain a living. The alluvial silt of the South was the opposite in its characteristics. Easy of conquest in the beginning, it invited the cultivation of staple crops with high profits which quickly exhausted the soil, compelling continuous change of location. Slavery was almost as impossible under the former conditions as it was inevitable under the latter.

Climate plays its part in deciding historical events. It would be as hard to imagine the individualistic, energetic, dogmatic Puritan of New England preaching, fighting, trading beneath the torrid sun of the Carolinas, as to think of the fox-hunting, gambling, slaveholder building his plantation mansion with its broad verandas on the bleak New England hills.

While the various peninsulas and river systems into which the Atlantic coast is divided favored a high development of individual colonies, and tended to produce and emphasize local peculiarities, the ocean which connected all the colonies constituted a broad and ever open highway that bound them together. Whatsoever interests like commerce and fishing required the use of this common means of transportation tended to unite the various colonies, and we shall find these interests playing a prominent part in the formation of a united nation. As each colony crept back from the ocean and away from the river, its peoples came into contact with those of its neighbors. At the headwaters of the rivers there would soon arise a body of people more closely united to each other than to any single colony. This process was hastened by the fact that there extended along the full length of the settlements a broad mountain range that set a limit to western expansion during most of the colonial period. Once the Indians had been driven beyond the Appalachians, these mountain ranges formed a protecting barrier for the colonies against further attacks. This protecting barrier to expansion fostered colonial solidarity. It hastened the evolution of society to that partially self-supporting stage, which rendered possible the common action that resulted in political independence and national existence. To understand what the absence of such a limiting and protecting barrier might have meant, it is only necessary to glance at the French spreading over all Canada and the Mississippi Valley, forming no political organizations, and establishing no social or political unity between their widely scattered settlements. In the first stages of industrial evolution only the "extractive industries" are developed. These are the industries that extract raw material directly from the earth, as contrasted with those that work up such raw material into the finished products used by a more complex civilization. In any such industrial stage the social organization will depend quite largely upon the nature of the raw materials to be "extracted."

Off the coast of New England lay the Newfoundland Banks, the richest fishing grounds in the world. From Cape Cod to the Arctics there stretched away the "green pastures" of the whale. These two facts determined political and military relations, affected treaties, repeatedly threatened war, determined colonial and national legislation for more than three centuries, and set in motion streams of influence that even to-day mightily affect the current of industrial and social life.

The Atlantic coast plain, the Appalachians, and the whole eastern bank of the Mississippi Valley were covered with a dense growth of forest. It is almost impossible to exaggerate the influence which this fact played in colonial history. It was the pine forests of New England, in combination with the near-by fishing grounds, that laid the foundation for the great commercial life of that section. Although the choicest trees were marked with the "broad arrow" of the king to indicate that they were to be cut only in order to be shipped to England for use in the royal navy, yet the colonists were seldom troubled with an overly tender legal conscience, and many a "broad arrow" was removed and the tree which it marked converted into masts for some New England merchantman.

The forest was at once an obstacle to settlement and cultivation, a shelter for the Indian, the home of fur-bearing and meat-carrying animals, and a regulator of climate and flow of water. Just how great a part the forest has played in American history we are only beginning to appreciate when it has almost disappeared.

Hunting, both for food and furs; lumbering; ship-building; and the manufacture of such diverse products as turpentine, charcoal, and pearlash; the blockhouse for defense, and the log cabin for shelter, — all these various and most characteristic features of American life owe their existence to this great forest belt.

To follow but one of these features, and that not the most important, but a little way along its ramifications: The woods teemed with animals, large and small, whose furry coverings were coveted by man — or woman. In pursuit of this fur men explored rivers, founded cities, cut the trails through the forest that marked the lines of a future commerce, and sketched in outline the geographic basis of American social life. The fur trade made and modified Indian policies, directed the course of population, located national boundary lines, laid the foundation of much of our present financial organization, created the first of the race of American millionaires, and in a hundred other ways set its stamp upon our social institutions.

Throughout colonial times agriculture was the basic dominant industry in all the colonies, with the possible exception of some of the fishing communities of New England. A large number of the staple crops of Europe were successful here, including wheat, flax, apples, and grapes. Most of the domestic animals of Europe were transplanted to this country with little change. America gave three new plants to agriculture, — corn, tobacco, and potatoes, — and it far exceeds all the rest of the world in the production of another — cotton. The first two and the last one have made and unmade social systems and governmental policies, and have determined the methods of life for great sections of the population. A complete account of any one of these three would give a far more accurate history of America (though still warped and incomplete) than the biographies of any half-dozen "great men" that have lived on this continent.

Only two animals that are peculiar to America have had any great influence on agriculture, — the turkey and the bison. Until within the last decade the influence of the latter was similar to that of all other wild animals, merely as a competitor in supplying meat, but attempts at domestication and cross breeding with domestic cattle would now indicate that this animal may be destined to play a more important part in the future, unless the slight remnant of his blood is too small to found a new race.

America was not an untrodden land when Englishman and Spaniard first set foot upon its shores. Thinly scattered over its vast reaches there lived a race, just evolving out of the hunting and fishing stage into that of a rude agriculture.

The Indian has exercised a profound influence upon American history. He was the ablest savage fighter the world has ever known. Man for man he has taken his weapons from the white man and yet held his own in the centuries-long battle from the Atlantic to the Pacific. He has retreated before superior numbers. He has never acknowledged defeat. The existence of a relentless watchful foe compelled compactness of settlement, determined the location of towns and villages, and developed a race of frontier fighters that proved the decisive influence in every war in which this nation has been engaged. The Indian trails marked the roads that were followed by the traders, the makers of highways, and the builders of railroads, each in turn. Tobacco and corn had both been domesticated by the Indian, and he taught the white man how to raise them. In the fur trade the Indian was always an important factor, and the trade with Indian tribes was for more than two centuries an important part of American commercial life.

It has been generally accepted by historians, based upon the observation of almost countless examples, that when two unlike nations of unequal strength come into conflict, the succeeding steps will be: invasion, conquest, enslavement, amalgamation. The relation of the Indian to the white race has lacked the last two steps. Although the present population of the United States is the most composite in the world, it contains little more than a trace of the blood of the original inhabitants. Neither was the Indian transformed into a slave, as has been the case with multitudes of conquered peoples. This was not because of any lack of inclination in that direction by the white invaders. From the New England Puritans, who divided up the Pequod women and children after massacring the men, and sold King Philip's son to West

Indian sugar planters, to the Spaniards, who, with whips and hot irons, drove a multitude to a horrible death in the mines of Central and South America, attempts to enslave the Indian were never lacking. Yet so far as the race was concerned these attempts were a striking failure. The Indian would die, but he would not serve. During the time of Southern negro slavery if it became known that ever so little Indian blood flowed in the veins of a slave, his value quickly fell off or entirely disappeared, for it was recognized that it was always but a question of time until either the master or the slave would die a violent death.

Had the Indian not possessed this characteristic, how different American history might have been. With a servile native population, acclimated to all portions of the country, the negro need never have been stolen from Africa; slavery would have been a national instead of a sectional institution; the Indian would have been absorbed by the whites or bred in slavery until his numbers were equal to, or exceeded, those of his masters, and — but when one enters the realm of historical "ifs," there is no place to stop.

We have seen something of what the colonists found when they came to America. We have said nothing of the minerals and the natural wealth that were found at a later time. This chapter is meant only to suggest some of the things that will be discussed at much greater length, as occasion arises. Yet the history of America is just the story of how these raw materials, natural resources, indigenous products, and peoples were used by those who came to this country, and by their descendants in satisfying their wants.

CHAPTER IV

THE COLONIAL STAGE

THERE is much in common in the course of social evolution through which each of the colonies passed. Each was working out the problem of the creation of a new social unit with much the same materials. In the beginning the colony was generally established as an outlying possession of some private trading company. The London Company and the Plymouth Company were private corporations to which nearly all of what is now the United States was assigned as private property. Had the first ships sent out discovered gold, or realized the rich profits to be made in furs, the whole history of this country would possibly have been different. It is within the realm of the possible that these companies might have built up gigantic private enterprises with governmental functions like that of the East India Company in British India. That this idea is by no means fanciful is shown by the history of the Hudson Bay Company in the much less favorable location of northern Canada.

The first expeditions sent out by these companies did not find gold. They did not find profits of any kind. Consequently, the companies soon lost interest and the colonies were permitted to work out their own salvation.

The course of evolution pursued in each colony bears a striking resemblance to the line of development that the race has followed. Caution is needed in applying this or any other historical analogy, because the colonists were not primitive savages, and they did not evolve independent of the remainder of the world.

In the beginning nearly every colony, being confronted with the problem of maintaining a small group, composed of individuals of nearly equal strength, in the midst of a hostile environment, solved that problem as the race solved it at the same stage by the adoption of primitive communism. As soon as the colony advanced to the point where division of labor and the importation of domestic animals with diversified industry made its appearance, communism was naturally discarded. It had not "failed" or "succeeded," or been "rejected" by the colonists any more than the similar stage in race history.[1]

Very early the colonies began to develop important differences, which were destined to have the most far-reaching consequences. It therefore becomes necessary to consider them separately, or at least by sections. This division and the peculiar development of the various sections depends largely upon geographical conditions, some of which already have been considered.

In each stage of social evolution the size of the social unit depends first of all upon the extent and character of the transportation system upon which it rests. During colonial times there were three systems of commercial communication: (1) up and down the rivers within each colony; (2) along the coast between the colonies; (3) for-

[1] Doyle, "English Colonies in America," Vol. I, pp. 55-64, *passim*, where this evolution is traced, but with a complete misunderstanding of its explanation.

eign, across the ocean.[1] All except the last of these have to-day been overshadowed by the public highways and the railroads.

Such a system, or combination of systems, or lack of system, according to the point of view, tended to the creation of a series of almost isolated societies with very different characteristics. Each such society had its own seaport which evolved into the commercial, financial, and political head of the colony. From this city the river reached into the interior, determining the direction and extent of settlement, and acting as the common carrier for the produce of the forest and later of the farms that grew up along its banks. The colony as a whole, in the beginning at least, was constantly recruited from across the ocean and procured many of its necessities from the same source. During this time it was really in much closer touch with Europe than with perhaps its nearest neighbor among the other colonies.[2]

Aside from this individual isolation, the colonies as a whole fell into three well-marked groups. These groups were New England, the Middle Colonies (between the Hudson and the Potomac), and the Southern, lying south of the latter river.

[1] Weeden, "Economic and Social History of New England," Vol. I, pp. 376–377.

[2] "Each of the thirteen original colonies had one or more seaports, and the main current of trade existing during the entire colonial era, and in some respects up to much later periods, was between these ports and the interior districts of the colonies in which they were respectively located, on the one hand, and the outer world, *via* the ocean, on the other. Commerce between the colonies was of limited magnitude, and originally nearly all the movements made from one colony to another were conducted in shallops, sloops, schooners, and other sea-going vessels."—I. L. RINGWALT, "Development of Transportation Systems in the United States," p. 3.

THE COLONIAL STAGE

In each of these colonies a somewhat different group of Europeans was working out the problem of a new society with the peculiar natural environment of its locality.

New England was settled in the beginning largely by the Puritans, the English expression of the Reformation. They belonged mostly to the middle class, were generally fairly well educated, extremely individualistic in their ideas, and bigoted in their religion. These characteristics were rather accentuated than otherwise by being transplanted to a new country, and by the fact that whole congregations came together.

In its physical features New England possessed several points that differentiated her quite sharply from the other colonies. The point where the break comes in the rivers between the tidewater level and the rise of the continental mainland is much closer to the ocean than in the more southern portion of the Atlantic coast. The rivers could be navigated but a short distance. On the other hand, this gave rise to numerous water powers, close to the ocean, at the head of navigation, which later marked the seat of manufacturing cities. "With the exception of the Connecticut, therefore," says Semple,[1] "which added fertile meadow lands to the attraction of the fur trade, the streams of New England, in consequence of their limited basins and rapid, broken courses, scarcely affected early settlement."

There was a negative way in which this absence of navigable rivers affected New England life. In the other colonies there was one river around which the life of the colony was grouped and which formed the main highway

[1] Ellen Churchill Semple, "American History and its Geographic Conditions," p. 24.

into the interior and for commerce within the colony itself. The absence of such rivers in New England kept the settlements close to the coast, and made the ocean the main carrier for all commerce, local or foreign. The geographical isolation from the remainder of the Atlantic coast led to an intensive growth of the New England society.

"Mountains and straggling, rugged hills separated her from the great northern valleys. Until the middle of our century, when iron ways and steam-driven carriages pierced the mountain chains, carrying exchanges into the Hudson, Mohawk, and the St. Lawrence valleys, New England was a coastwise community, physically forced into the economic development of the Atlantic coast." [1]

This peculiar isolated, intensive growth so emphasized industrial and social institutions as to give them a remarkable power of impressing themselves upon aftertime. In this regard New England society was much like carefully bred live stock in that it showed a great power of persistence and capacity of impressing its characteristics upon its descendants even when the degree of relationship is extremely small.

During the first twenty years after the famous landing at Plymouth Rock in 1620, New England life rested almost entirely upon crude agriculture, fishing, and the trade with the Indians. Manufactured articles were brought from England, either in exchange for furs or else as a part of the possessions of the steady stream of immigrants. Agriculture was confined largely to the

[1] Weeden, "Economic and Social History of New England," Vol. I, pp. 15-16.

THE COLONIAL STAGE

raising of Indian corn under the instruction of friendly Indians.

In 1624 the first cattle were brought over by Governor Winslow. These increased rapidly and were augmented by new shipments from England until by "1632 no farmer was satisfied to do without a cow; and there was in New England, not only a domestic, but an export, demand for the West Indies, which led to breeding for sale. But the market was soon overstocked, and the price of cattle went down from fifteen and twenty pounds to five pounds; and milk was a penny a quart."[1] This latter statement about the price of milk means very little, as cows were seldom milked at this time, being raised principally for their hides, and secondly for meat, and only very incidentally for their milk.[2]

During this period the machinery of commercial and industrial life and therefore of society in general was extremely crude. The trade with the Indians was carried on largely by barter, or by the use of the shell money called "wampum," which the colonists adopted from the red men. The very fact that such a primitive currency could be used in common by the two races speaks volumes for the nearness to which they came to living upon the same social stage. In addition to "wampum" various commodities, especially corn and beaver skins, were constituted mediums of exchange by colonial law during this period.[3]

---

[1] Albert S. Bolles, "Industrial History of the United States," p. 115.
[2] *Ibid.*, p. 116.
[3] Weeden, "Economic and Social History of New England," Vol. I, pp. 32–47, is a very full discussion of the function of wampum in colonial commerce with the Indians.

This use of various commodities as "money" is characteristic of an early stage of social organization. It is one through which the white race in other lands passed many centuries ago. There was one feature of the emigration from England that tended to prevent further reversion to lower social stages. The colonists came in groups, generally composed of a single church congregation. This transplanted the nucleus of a social organization directly to the New World.

About 1640 a change took place in England which had direct and far-reaching effects upon New England. The struggle between the Puritans and the Cavaliers broke into open warfare, in which the former, under Cromwell, were victorious. Naturally there was no longer any necessity for emigration on the part of the Puritans. On the contrary, it was now the turn of the Cavaliers to emigrate, but as the majority of these went to the Southern colonies we need not concern ourselves with them just now.

The stoppage of immigration meant many things to the colony. Each new family had brought with it a supply of manufactured articles for its own use at least. The ships which brought them carried similar articles for sale to the other colonists. A ship laden with immigrants could afford to carry freight cheaper and make much more frequent trips than one without passengers.

As a result of this condition Weeden [1] tells us that,—

"There were many sellers, few buyers, and hardly any currency. There was a privation, not from scarcity, but it was enforced in the midst of abundance. Wares would not command wares, money there was none, and prices

[1] *Loc. cit.*, Vol. I, pp. 165–166.

THE COLONIAL STAGE

fell to one half, yea, to a third, and staggered at last at about one quarter of the old standard."

As we shall see many times in the history of this country, when a nation is thus suddenly thrown back upon its own resources, it begins to develop new lines of industry. In this case the colonists were forced forward into a new industrial and social stage. New England now entered upon the road of diversified industry, the next step beyond primitive agriculture. The directions that the energies of the colony took were threefold, — domestic manufacturing, fishing, and shipbuilding.

May 13, 1640, the General Court of Massachusetts, passed an order to ascertain —

"What men and women are skillful in braking, spinning, and weaving; what means for the providing of wheels; and to consider with those skillful in that manufacture, what course may be taken to raise the materials and produce the manufacture."[1]

In 1646 a patent was granted to Joseph Jenks of the same colony for an improvement in the manufacture of scythes for the cutting of grass. He succeeded in producing so perfect a tool for this purpose that little improvement was made in his design for nearly three centuries.[2]

In 1648 an iron furnace in Lynn, Massachusetts, was turning out eight tons of iron a week. During the next ten years furnaces were set up at several other places in New England, all making use of the "bog ore" to be found in the marshes.[3]

---

[1] W. R. Bagnall, "The Textile Industries of the United States," p. 4.
[2] Weeden, "Economic and Social History of New England," Vol. I, p. 183.
[3] A. S. Bolles, "Industrial History of the United States," p. 194.

All these branches of manufacture grew steadily during the next hundred years. But faster than any of them grew fishing and shipbuilding and all manner of industrial life connected with the sea, until one writer declares of the people of New England at this time that, "The world never saw a more amphibious population."[1]

The first sawmill was built at Salmon Falls, New Hampshire, in 1663, and was the beginning of the great shipbuilding industry of New England.[2]

All industrial life centered around the sea. Sometimes a farming, fishing sailor, such as made up much of the population, would, with the aid of his neighbors, build a ship at the mouth of some creek, launch it during the spring freshet, and load it with rum for the African coast, fish for the Canaries, or, more frequently, with pitch, tar, hemp, and long masts for England. Here ship and cargo would both be sold, while the former owner, builder, and captain would ship as a sailor on a return voyage, bringing home the proceeds of his venture.

One of the best established routes of colonial trade was the famous "rum-molasses-slaves" triangular voyage. Loading with rum from one of the host of distilleries that filled the coast towns of Massachusetts and Rhode Island, the good Puritan captain would set sail for the African coast with instructions to "put plenty of water in ye rum, and use short meusure as much as possible," as one letter which has been preserved quaintly reads. In Africa the rum was exchanged for "black ivory," as the poor, entrapped negroes were called. Storing this mer-

[1] Willis J. Abbot, "American Merchant Ships and Sailors," p. 8.
[2] Eleanor L. Lord, "Industrial Experiments in the British Colonies of North America," *John Hopkins Univ. Studies in Hist. and Pol. Sci.*

chandise away in his hold, much as he had previously stored the hogsheads of rum, the ship would set sail for the West Indies or the Carolinas, where such of the cargo as had not died on the terrible "middle passage" would be traded for molasses, from which in turn more rum could be manufactured.

A society built upon such foundations could hardly be expected to attain the perfection which tradition has ascribed to Puritan New England. That it was something quite the reverse from the legendary society of most school histories is shown from the following quotation from Weeden, himself a New England writer: —

"We have seen molasses and alcohol, rum and slaves, gold and iron, in a perpetual and unholy round of commerce. All society was fouled in this lust; it was inflamed by the passion for wealth; it was callous to the wrongs of imported savages or displaced barbarians. . . . Cool, shrewd, sagacious merchants vied with punctilious, dogmatic priests in promoting this prostitution of industry."

With the change in the industrial base the appearance of commerce and manufacture and exchange, the whole social organization was transformed. One of the first signs of this was the adoption of a "money economy." "In the year 1670 Massachusetts repealed her law, 'now injurious,' which made corn, cattle, etc., the equivalent for money."[1] Nearly twenty years before (1652) the same colony had established a mint at which the famous "Pine Tree Shillings" had been coined.

These first signs of industrial self-sufficiency were accompanied by the beginnings of political unrest, and the

[1] Weeden, "Economic History of New England," Vol. I, p. 326.

growth of a general independent feeling. One of the phases of this was the establishment of the New England Confederation in 1643, comprising all the New England colonies, except Rhode Island, which was kept out because of the religious heresy of its founder, Roger Williams, and his followers.

New England has been hailed as the birthplace of social equality, and orators and superficial historians are prone to trace all democratic institutions back to the famous "New England town meeting." The fact is that in the beginning these colonies, so far as local government is concerned, were theocratic autocracies. Only those who were property holders and members of the Established Church had any voice whatever even in these town meetings. The social gradations with their privileges were carefully determined by law, even to the sort of clothing which each social class was permitted to wear, and the places which its members were to occupy in the "meeting-house." As soon as even the beginnings of a wage-working class appeared, the wages of its members were fixed by law, and their position carefully defined.[1]

When this stage had been reached in each of the colonies, they began to have a common development which can be better traced as a whole after considering the course by which the others arrived at this same stage.

[1] Weeden, *loc. cit.*, Vol. I, pp. 98–99; McMaster, "The Acquirement of Political, Social, and Industrial Rights of Man in America," pp. 31–36, on general condition of colonial laborers.

Virginia and the Southern Colonies

When we cross the Potomac, the physical conditions are so different that although the people who came as colonists were practically the same as those of New England, yet the industrial and social organization which they developed was strikingly different. Something has already been said of the physiographic conditions of Virginia. There is one phase, however, that is so strikingly described by John Fiske in his "Old Virginia and Her Neighbors" as to be worth quoting. He says (Vol. I, p. 263): —

"The country known as 'tidewater Virginia' is a kind of sylvan Venice. Into the depths of the shaggy woodland for many miles on either side of the great bay the salt tide ebbs and flows. One can go surprisingly far inland on a seafaring craft, while with a boat there are but few plantations on the old York peninsula to which one cannot approach very near."

This broad alluvial belt was in striking contrast with the narrow strip of glaciated clay that fringed the coast of New England. The "fall line" was distant several hundred miles from the coast; there were no rich fishing banks within easy sailing distance, and the nature and the form of agriculture which arose made for dispersion and not for concentration of population.

In the beginning Virginia was ruled by a trading company seeking profits for its shareholders. For the first few years there was little sign of any profits. In fact the colonists repeatedly came within a narrow margin of starvation. Then came the discovery of the possibilities in the cultivation of a plant that was destined to form the basis of the industrial life of Virginia for many years to come. This was tobacco, of whose influence Henry Cabot Lodge says: —

"Tobacco founded this colony and gave it wealth. It was the currency of Virginia, and as bad a one as could be devised, and fluctuating with every crop, yet it retained its place as a circulating medium despite the most strenuous efforts to introduce specie. The clergy were paid and the taxes levied in tobacco. The whole prosperity of the colony rested upon it for more than a century, and it was not until the period of the Revolution that other crops began to come in and to replace it. The fluctuations in tobacco caused the first conflict with England, brought on by the clergy, and paved the way to resistance. In tobacco the Virginian estimated his income and the value of everything he possessed; and in its various functions, as well as in its methods of cultivation, it had strong effect upon the character of the people.

"Tobacco planting made slaves necessary and profitable, and fastened slavery upon the province. The method of cultivation, requiring intense labor and watching for a short period, and permitting complete idleness for the rest of the year, fostered habits which alternated feverish exertion and languid indolence." [1]

The discovery that the cultivation of tobacco for the European market afforded a means by which the colony could be made to produce a profit at once aroused the interest of the stockholders of the company. So long as the colonists were starving and calling constantly for relief there was little interest on the part of the London owners of the corporation. But now there was the possi-

[1] See also Fiske, "Old Virginia and Her Neighbors," Vol. I, p. 227.

bility of building up a gigantic and powerful commercial monopoly. Just what the result of the exploitation of this crop by a great trading corporation owning the entire southern half of what is now the United States would have been we shall never have an opportunity to know. Political considerations (resting, to be sure, upon economic conditions) in England did not permit the experiment to be tried. King James I was having a hard time to keep down the rising power of the commercial class. He was intriguing with reactionary Spain and threatening and fighting rebellious subjects at home in his efforts to that end. Naturally the founders of the Virginia Company were of the rising commercial class. They were establishing the forms of democracy and representative government in their colony. The first representative body in America was the Virginia "House of Burgesses," which was convened in 1619. James was assured that the London Company was but a "seminary to a seditious Parliament," [1] and he therefore revoked their charter, — the sacredness of corporation property not having as yet become a fundamental principle of jurisprudence.

Virginia, consequently, was left to work out her salvation, like New England, as an almost independent province.

The most striking feature of Southern agriculture was the great size of the individual estates. This rested upon the plantation system, a system inseparable from a one-crop or staple agriculture in an alluvial country. The first members of the London Company were given grants of large extent, and a method was soon provided by which these could be extended to almost any size.

[1] *Ibid.*, Chap. VI.

"Every shareholder who met the cost of importing an able-bodied laborer, man or woman, was entitled to fifty acres in the first division and fifty additional in the second. . . . Unscrupulous planters obtained grants in consideration of passage money paid for members of their own families or for their own journeys to and from England. The land offices grew corrupt, and soon it was not deemed necessary to bring evidence of passage paid. A small fee handed to the secretary insured the solicited grant with no questions asked. This practice became so general that it was finally (1705) sanctioned by law. . . . At the close of the century the average size of a Virginia estate was seven hundred acres, and many a planter owned thousands."[1]

These estates were extremely profitable when worked with the slaves brought by the New England and British traders. A body of wealthy planters arose resting upon a subject population. Tobacco being an export crop, and demanding the entire energies of those raising it, other industries were neglected, and the South became dependent upon the New England shipbuilders and merchants. The exhaustive methods of agriculture compelled frequent abandonment of the old fields and the conquest of new ones from the forest.

Early in the eighteenth century the larger portion of

[1] Coman, "Industrial History of the United States," p. 33. Greene's "Provincial America" says: "Governor Spottswood signed on one occasion several grants of ten, twenty, and forty thousand acres, including an aggregate of over 86,000 acres for himself. Theoretically grants were conditioned upon occupation and improvement, but the land administration was in the hands of the governor and council, or sometimes of the councillors alone, who, being themselves large landholders, were lax in enforcing rules which operated against the interests of their class."

the rich alluvial lands along the coast had become private property. Settlement was therefore pushed back upon what is called the Piedmont plateau. This was the land above the "fall line" of the rivers, and its soil and consequent crops and social organization was so wholly different as to have the most important effects upon the whole history of this region, and indeed upon the history of the whole country.

This physiographic line received a still sharper emphasis through the fact that it chanced to coincide with a racial division. It so happened that when in 1700 the line of westward advance of settlement in Virginia had just reached this Piedmont plateau, and when the rich alluvial tobacco land had all been divided up into privately owned plantations, the great exodus from the north of Ireland, which has already been described, took place.[1] The upland agriculture and the social organization based upon it was from the beginning totally different from that of the tidewater region. The back country people were raisers of corn and live stock, of a very stunted kind to be sure. They were most of all hunters and trappers and explorers of the wilderness. From them sprung a race of frontiersmen and Indian fighters that was to become the social class most characteristic of American society.

The period of the "Commonwealth" in England had an important effect in Virginia as well as in New England. This effect was, however, very different. While in New England the triumph of the Puritan in the mother country stopped immigration almost entirely, it gave a strong impetus to a certain sort of immigration into Virginia.

[1] John Fiske, "Old Virginia and Her Neighbors," Vol. II, pp. 456–461.

A number of the Cavaliers, finding England no longer agreeable as a place of residence, came to the New World.[1] These were men of wealth and power, and they retained their power in Virginia. This was the time when the families of Randolph, Madison, Mason, Monroe, Marshall, Washington, and many others whose names were to be famous in American history came to these shores.

Such a society was bound to develop industrial classes that would struggle for mastery. Throughout colonial times, and indeed for many years to follow, there was always one main line of cleavage. With variations of numerous kinds, some of which occasionally obscured the basic division, this line continued almost until the present generation. This was the conflict between the "back country" and the coast district. The causes of this conflict of interest were numerous. In the first place, the coast population was a trading creditor class to which the back country people were indebted. The frontier always offered an opportunity of escape from industrial servitude, both wage and chattel, and this naturally displeased those who profited by such servitude. The older sections have always opposed further expansion, sometimes openly, but more frequently in an indirect and sometimes secret manner. England long endeavored to restrict settlement to a narrow strip along the coast. The merchants of the coast were often deeply interested in the fur trade, and the advance of settlement wiped out this trade. There was always complaint on the part of the frontiersmen that they were overcharged by the

[1] John Fiske, "Old Virginia and Her Neighbors," Vol. II, pp. 27–28; Phillip Alexander Bruce, "Economic History of Virginia in the Seventeenth Century," Vol. I, p. 246, Vol. II, pp. 487–581.

THE COLONIAL STAGE

coast merchants, while the latter retorted with complaints of the nonpayment of debts. The relations with the Indians proved another constant source of friction. The "back country" men were always crowding the Indian from his hunting grounds and coming into conflict with him. They were therefore continually asking for troops and supplies for military expeditions and fortifications. The coast residents, wishing to use the Indian for trading purposes, or at least indifferent to his depredations, opposed appropriations for protection against his attacks.

In 1676 this conflict in Virginia broke into open war as "Bacon's Rebellion." There were peculiar local and personal conditions in this conflict as in all subsequent ones, but the causes assigned for the struggle are practically those given above. Governor Berkeley had been sent from England and had become the especial representative of the Cavalier class that emigrated at this time. His character may be judged from a famous extract from his report to the Commissioners of Plantations in 1670. In response to the question,

"What course is taken about the instructing of the people within your government in the Christian religion?" he replied:—

"The same course that is taken in England out of towns; every man according to his ability instructing his children. We have forty-eight parishes, and our ministers are well paid, and by my consent should be better, *if they would pray oftener and preach less*. But of all other commodities, so of this, *the worst is sent us*, and we had few that we could boast of, since the persecution in Cromwell's tyranny drove divers worthy men hither.

But, I thank God, *there are no free schools*, nor *printing*, and I hope we shall not have them these hundred years; for learning has brought disobedience and heresy and sects into the world, and *printing* has divulged them, and libels against the best government. God keep us from both!"

Berkeley was a direct representative of the royal party in England. He was parceling out the rich plantation lands of Virginia among his favorites even more recklessly than had been the custom hitherto. He had a subservient House of Burgesses, composed of the rich planters, and he refused to call a new election.[1] He was directly concerned in the fur trade and was reported to have made agreements with the very Indians who were massacring the settlers on the frontier. Finally in 1676 Bacon gathered an army in spite of the orders of the Governor, defeated the Indians, and then marching to Jamestown, compelled the election of a new House of Burgesses, and was a successful candidate in that election. When Berkeley continued to plot against his life Bacon fled to the frontier to gather another army, which he again led first against the Indians who had risen once more, and then back again to Jamestown, which was then burned to the ground.

In the midst of these stirring events he was taken sick and died, and Berkeley took such bloody vengeance as to call forth the historic remark from Charles II: "As I live, the old fool has put to death more people in that naked country than I did for the murder of my father."[2]

---

[1] Wilson, "History of the American People," Vol. I, pp. 256–275.

[2] A contemporary report by a member of the Virginia Council contains some sentences that throw a striking light on the character of Bacon's

The story of Virginia was typical of that of Georgia and the Carolinas. In each there was the same plantation system, the same division of interests between coast and back country. In the Carolinas the fur trade was of even more importance, and it was succeeded by a stage which was of little importance in Virginia, but which was to appear again and again in other portions of the country, — the ranching industry.[1]

The Middle Colonies

In very many senses of the word the term "Middle" applies to the colonies of New York, Pennsylvania, New Jersey, and Delaware. In climate and industrial and social structure they lay between the South and New England. The soil lacked the alluvial richness of Virginia and the

Rebellion: "Bacon gathers about him a Rabble of the basest sort of People, whose Conditions are such as by a change could not admit of worse, with these began to stand in Defyance against the government. . . . These are the men that are sett up for the good of ye Country; who for ye ease of the Poore will have no taxes paied . . . would have all magistracie and government taken away & sett up one themselves & to make their good Intentions more manifest stick not to talk openly of shareing men's Estates among themselves."

[1] "In 1708 it was estimated that over 50,000 skins were shipped from Charleston annually. . . . In 1731 the item of deerskins alone amounted to 225,000. . . . The fur trade was at its best from 1721 to 1743. After that it began to decline. In South Carolina it declined rapidly after the removal of the Cherokees from the larger portion of the up-country in 1755. It had been one of the leading industries of the colony, and even as late as 1748 it ranked next to rice in the value of the amount exported. The total value of the exports from Nov. 1, 1747, to Nov. 1, 1748, amounted to £1,129,560, of which rice supplied £618,750 worth, and the fur trade £252,300. . . . The decline of the fur trade in the decade following indicated that the first phase of frontier life had passed. The trader had started his operations on the coast, and as the frontier receded he followed to make room for the cow-pen keepers."

barren rockiness of Massachusetts and Connecticut. Hence it did not drive its population to the sea in boats nor attract them to great plantations, but built up instead a race of small farmers that was destined for many generations to be the dominant factor in American society. Its rivers were long enough for navigation, but did not partake of the marshy character of the James and the Roanoke. They were preëminently fitted for commerce rather than for agriculture or manufacturing.

New York, like several other colonies, was started as a trading venture by a commercial corporation, in this case by the Dutch West India Company. Holland was crowding Spain for first place in the commercial world, and was to hold that position for a moment before being pushed back by rapidly advancing England. In spite of the great wealth that came from the fur trade in New York, the Dutch West India Company, like all the other proprietary companies that established colonies in America, received but small profits. To the time of the control by this Company is due the establishment of the "patroon" estates. In its efforts to secure a permanent agricultural population the Company granted great tracts of country reaching back for miles on either side of the Hudson, together with certain semi-feudal rights to those who brought over a certain number of settlers. In few cases did this result in establishing permanent settlements such as were intended, but it did succeed in creating a mass of indefinite legal relations that still haunt the New York courts.[1]

Pennsylvania was also a private property in the be-

[1] John Fiske, "Dutch and Quaker Colonies in America," Vol. II, pp. 133-140.

ginning, but was established largely for other reasons than personal profit, although the family of William Penn sought very hard to derive such a profit from it.

Both New York and Pennsylvania contained a large percentage of settlers from Continental Europe. Pennsylvania was especially the refuge of the Palatinate Germans.[1]

None of the Middle colonies endured the periods of general hardship that came near destroying New England and Virginia in the cradle. Almost from the beginning they were fairly prosperous and grew rapidly. From the first the agricultural basis of the country was distinct from that of New England or the South. It was not a supplementary industry wrung from a barren soil to assist in supporting an "amphibious population." Neither was it the plantation production of a great staple for export. It was the small, diversified, self-supporting farming that was destined to be for many years the largest element in American industrial life. Moreover, just because this form of farming is, for the early stages of capitalism at least, the most economical, it was not long until Philadelphia was the leading port in America, passing even Boston in the amount of goods exported. Nor was it so many years before Boston was crowded to third place with New York at the head. The furs, lumber, hides, and other diverse products reached a greater value, and became the foundation of a larger and more stable commerce than cotton, fish, rum, or slaves.

Moreover, if New England and the South were drawing vast profits from rum and slaves and smuggling, New York was not without an even more shady and profitable

[1] See pp. 15-17.

commerce, for this city was the headquarters of seventeenth-century piracy. This was the golden age of piracy. Spain was still rich in commerce. Her ships were bringing valuable cargoes from the New World to the Old. But Spain, in spite of, or on account of, the ease with which she was obtaining certain forms of wealth from America, had lost her place as the foremost commercial nation. She had now been relegated to a position much inferior to either Holland or England.

Spain and Holland having lost the power to protect their still rich commerce, a race of pirates arose who preyed upon the merchant ships of these nations. New York was one of the chief harbors for the disposal of piratical plunder.[1] The entire colonial government became involved in piracy. The pirates were forced to share their booty with the royal governors, and this fact was cited as one of the grievances of the party which opposed these governors. This matter finally climaxed with the notorious affair of Captain Kidd, who was sent out to hunt the pirates, but found piracy more profitable, and was himself finally hung, — not because he was worse than the others, but because his career came just at the close of the period when piracy was almost a legitimate means of livelihood, and when the navies of England and Holland had become sufficiently strong to prevent piracy.

By the close of the seventeenth century the same class distinctions that had arisen in the other colonies were apparent in New York.

"Long-continued arbitrary taxation and the repeated failure to obtain representative government had caused

[1] John Fiske, "Dutch and Quaker Colonies," Vol. II, pp. 222–235.

much popular discontent. Though the population of the little city was scarcely more than 4000 souls, a distinction of classes was plainly to be seen. Without regard to race the small shopkeepers, small farmers, sailors, shipwrights, and artisans were far apart in their sympathies from the rich fur traders, patroons, lawyers, and royal officials."[1]

This antagonism broke into armed rebellion under Jacob Leisler, in 1689. The royal Governor was overthrown, and Leisler ruled for a time in his place. But later came reënforcements from England, and Leisler paid the penalty of his rebellion with his life. "Had things gone as Leisler hoped and expected," says John Fiske, "the name of Leisler would be inseparably associated with the firm establishment of representative government and the first triumph of democracy in the province of New York."

The same political lines existed in Pennsylvania, but did not find violent expression until 1763, when a body of between two and three hundred armed frontiersmen moved upon Philadelphia. Benjamin Franklin was sent to their camp by the Governor, and through him they presented a list of their grievances. They complained of the unfair method of districting the colony by which the back countries were given a much smaller number of representatives in the colonial legislature in proportion to population than the older districts. This was a universal method of maintaining the domination of the commercial classes during the colonial period. The complaint also voiced the old grievance concerning the Indians. Indeed, it was to attack some Indians who had

[1] *Ibid.*, Vol. II, p. 184.

been given shelter in Philadelphia that they had moved upon that city. The paper money controversy was also an issue here as it was in nearly every colony.[1]

Having voiced their complaints, the backwoodsmen disbanded and went home, so that Pennsylvania was spared the bloodshed that had taken place in other colonies.

When a society begins to develop class antagonisms, it is a sign that it has reached a point where independent existence is possible. It has begun to have a social life and method of growth of its own. If it is a colony, it has arrived at a critical stage where only a slight jar will be needed to start separatist tendencies.

We have traced each of the main groups of colonies up to the point where this independent evolution was in progress. For a period their history has much in common, and can therefore be best treated as a whole.

[1] Isaac Sharpless, "Two Centuries of Pennsylvania History," pp. 126, 142–143, 154–155. There were similar uprisings in other colonies. Those of Davis and Pate in Maryland and of the "Regulators" in the Carolinas are the most important of those not mentioned in the text.

CHAPTER V

GROWTH OF SOLIDARITY

THE close of the seventeenth century saw the center of colonial life quite thoroughly transplanted to America. None of the principal colonies had any essential portion of their industrial life across the Atlantic. They still imported much, but they imported it in their own vessels, and under the control and for the profit of their own merchants, and not as a part of European commerce.

The colonies were everywhere drawing closer together. This was true in the simple geographical sense. The appearance of boundary disputes in a half dozen places is significant that populations were now approaching each other and that each colony was no longer a small settlement surrounded by miles of wilderness. The settlement of one of these boundary disputes marked a line that was to run with sinister significance through a succeeding century of American history. This was the line between Pennsylvania and Maryland, which was carefully and ceremoniously surveyed and marked by two English surveyors in 1767, from whom it took the name of "Mason and Dixon's Line."

Household industry had developed to the point where each colony was well-nigh self-supporting, so far as the principal necessities of life were concerned. A laboring class, divorced from land and capital, had appeared in each of the colonies. In the South this was composed largely of negro chattel slaves. These had been brought over by the thousands by the traders of New and old England. Nearly all the colonies at some time or another opposed the importation of slaves, but their importation was a profitable business for the mother country, and she would not listen to any restrictive proposals. Indeed, by the agreement called the "Asiento," signed at the treaty of Utrecht in 1713, the slave trade was confined to a monopoly controlled by Queen Anne and her royal successors and court favorites. After that, all the power of the British government was used to push this traffic.

In the Middle colonies the laboring population was composed largely of "indentured servants" and others who were in a more or less open form of slavery. In New England these forms were also found, and here there were also considerable numbers of wageworkers.

The principal highway of commerce was along the coast, and with increasing population and diversity of productions the coast cities were much more closely connected with each other than with the "back country" of their own colony.

Population increased with great rapidity during the first half of the eighteenth century. In 1700 there were about 250,000 people in the thirteen colonies. By 1750 the population had increased to 1,370,000.[1] This increase of population was forcing settlement back from the seacoast, and it was even beginning to flow down into the Ohio valley. These "back-country" settlements were coming into close proximity, and were finding many common interests.

[1] R. G. Thwaites, "The Colonies," pp. 265–266.

The establishment of a crude postal system in 1693 did much to unify colonial life. This system began under private control, but was placed under royal management in 1707. In 1737, Benjamin Franklin was made colonial postmaster-general, and continued in that position until the outbreak of the Revolution. During this time the system was extended to Canada and regular mail routes established between the principal cities.

Every Indian outbreak drove the colonies closer together. Of even greater importance as a unifying force was the series of wars between England and various nations of continental Europe. The colonies were always involved in these wars, since both France and Spain, who were arrayed against England, had colonies on the American continent. In the War of the Austrian Succession, the New England colonists fitted out an expedition that captured Louisburg, in French Canada. This was supposed to be an impregnable fortress, and the fact that it fell before colonial troops gave a feeling of self-confidence that was to develop into one of independence.

The final grapple between France and England for the mastery of the commercial world came in what was known in America as the "French and Indian War," ending in 1763. In America this war was waged for the possession of the Mississippi Valley. The pressure of an increasing population, that had crowded the colonies together until they were quarreling over boundary lines, had become so great that it was at last breaking over the mighty barrier of the Alleghenies. But here it was meeting with conflicting claims of sovereignty. France had been sending her explorers all up and down the tributaries of the Mississippi and the St. Lawrence, and she claimed, by virtue of their discoveries and subsequent occupation by an army of fur traders, all this great inland empire.

Coming from the Atlantic side, the key to this territory lies at the point where the Allegheny and Monongahela rivers meet to form the Ohio, and where the city of Pittsburg now stands.[1]

Virginia and Pennsylvania land speculators were already plotting this country, and when France suddenly seized the gateway to the Ohio and erected a fort on the present site of Pittsburg, England promptly protested. As her messenger to bear this protest she chose a young surveyor, who had been using his position to the advantage of the land companies with which he was just beginning to be connected, and in which his brother was a prominent figure. The name of this surveyor was George Washington. His efforts to persuade the French to leave were in vain; and when war broke out and British soldiers were sent to America he was chosen to coöperate with the regulars under General Braddock in an attack upon Fort Duquesne.

The result of that attack was to add greatly to colonial self-confidence. Braddock refused to accept the advice of the trained Indian fighters who accompanied him, and moved on through the wilderness with all the pomp and ceremony of an English parade ground. Naturally he was ambushed, and when he tried to meet the craftiest wilderness fighters the world has ever known with the tactics of the European martinet, his forces were wellnigh annihilated. The man who reaped what honors were

[1] Frederick A. Ogg, "The Opening of the Mississippi," p. 251.

gained that day was Washington, who, with the trained frontier fighters, covered the retreat of the British regulars and prevented a wholesale massacre. It did not take long for the story of how untrained frontiersmen outfought British regulars to spread throughout the colonies. The result was to take away the halo of invincibility that had surrounded these troops and to replace it with something like contempt.

The growth of economic unity and the appearance of military necessity caused many plans to be set forth for the political unity of the colonies. Some of these, as the New England Confederation of 1643 to 1660, were quite fully organized. Others, as Leisler's plan of union in 1690, and William Penn's in 1697, never reached farther than the theoretical stage. There were several attempts at union on the part of royal governors. The main unifying effect of these officials, however, was indirect and unintended. The common hostility to them on the part of the various colonies tended to create a bond of sympathy that was to prove of value as a basis of a hostile movement against England at the time of the Revolution.

CHAPTER VI

CAUSES OF THE REVOLUTION

By the middle of the eighteenth century American society had its own industrial basis. It had also developed its own political structure to correspond to this industrial base. In the course of this development the interests of the ruling classes of America and England had grown antagonistic.

The industrial revolution was in full swing in England. The steam engine, the power loom, the spinning jenny, and other great basic revolutionary inventions were just taking form. The French and Indian War had laid the foundation of British imperial capitalism. It had given England dominion over India as well as Canada, and had raised Prussia to the dominant position which made possible modern Germany.

This war had been conducted that English markets might be extended, that gold might flow to the mother country, in short, that the just arising capitalist class might prosper. The economic theory accepted by those who controlled British industry and government was what has been called the "Mercantile System." According to this theory one of the great objects of government was to pass laws that would insure a favorable "balance of trade." For this purpose legislation was shaped with a view of making the mother country the manufacturing center to which all other countries sent

CAUSES OF THE REVOLUTION

raw materials, and from which they were forced to buy manufactured articles. Colonies, in particular, were expected to buy all the things they needed of the mother country. This theory, backed by the interests of the ruling class of England, is the explanation of the Navigation Laws, which are commonly given as one of the principal causes of the Revolution.

The recent war had left England with a crushing debt. This was an added reason for seeking to raise revenue in America and for confining American trade to British ports.

Each of the colonies had some especial interest that came into sharp conflict with the actions of the British government. New England, the head and front of the Revolution, had many very serious grievances, although some of them would hardly be looked upon as purely patriotic by those who fix opinions in present society. We have already seen how completely New England was dominated by commercial and fishing interests. Her "great men" were all merchants. But their trade was not conducted in a manner that is commonly supposed to carry social preëminence. David H. Wells, in his article on "American Merchant Marine" in Lalor's "Encyclopedia of Political and Social Science," describes these merchants and their trade as follows: —

"Nine-tenths of their merchants were smugglers. One quarter of all the signers of the Declaration of Independence were bred to commerce, the command of ships, and the contraband trade. Hancock, Trumbull (Brother Jonathan), and Hamilton were all known to be cognizant of contraband transactions, and approved of them. Hancock was the prince of contraband traders, and, with John Adams as his counsel, was appointed for trial before the admiralty court of Boston, at the exact hour of the shedding of blood at Lexington, in a suit for $500,000 penalties alleged to have been incurred by him as a smuggler."

Like all smugglers, Hancock cared little for the forms of law, and trusted to bribery and violence to secure his ends. When his sloop, *Liberty*, was endeavoring to run the customs, he first tried to bribe the officials, and, this failing, locked up the guard in a cabin and unloaded the sloop under the protection of a gang of thugs secured for the occasion.[1]

For many years this smuggling had been winked at by British officials. The smugglers were not averse to dividing their profits to a limited extent with complaisant officials, and England was a long way off in the days of sailing vessels. Even in England there had been a laxity in the enforcement of smuggling laws, which now suddenly ceased. In England enforcement of the laws caused little more than a suppressed grumbling. In America it led to rioting and then to revolution.

In America the suppression of smuggling meant the suppression of the commercial life of New England. We have already seen that one of the principal items of commerce was the famous three-cornered rum-molasses-slaves trade. One of the first of the new taxes was a prohibitive tariff on the molasses from which the rum was made.

Those citizens of New England who were not concerned with commerce were generally interested in fishing, and here again the new legislation struck fatal blows. The

[1] Charles Stedman, "The History of the Origin, Progress, and Termination of the American War," London, 1794, Vol. I, p. 63.

trade with southern Europe was forbidden, and for a time the New England fishers were not permitted to use the Newfoundland Banks.

Another important and profitable article of smuggled commerce was tea. This was brought from Holland. Here the interests of the English governing classes came into direct and sharp conflict with the American smugglers. The East India Company had a monopoly of the tea trade. This company was owned by court favorites. It was threatened with bankruptcy. It had 17,000,000 pounds of tea stored in English warehouses. On this it was required to pay a shilling a pound before it could sell it in England. The English government proposed a scheme by which this tea could be sold in America for less than it would cost the Englishmen who paid the local tax.

The orthodox schoolbook histories assure us that this offer of cheap tea to Americans was an attempt to "bribe a nation," and that the Americans indignantly rejected the bribe and threw the tea into Boston Harbor in defense of a principle. This high-minded rejection of a bribe by John Hancock, the man who was mainly responsible for the famous Boston Tea Party, is scarcely in accord with what we have learned of his character. The fact is that had the tax not been reduced there would have been little objection. It was the reduction itself and not the principle which raised the famous riot. So long as the East India Company was compelled to pay the English tax, the American smugglers could undersell it and were not worried about questions of taxation, or patriotism. But when the tax was rebated the East India Company could undersell the smugglers. This destroyed the profit in smuggling, something infinitely more effective in checking that crime than a whole fleet of gunboats. No wonder that Hancock, whose popular title was the "prince of smugglers," called a mass meeting and with the aid of Samuel Adams organized that glorious mob that dumped the tea in Boston Harbor and started the Revolution, — at least, so the textbooks tell us.

In the Middle colonies there was another specific grievance in addition to the fact that their trade with the West Indies, upon which they depended for specie, was interfered with when smuggling was restricted. New York and Pennsylvania had at least the beginnings of a manufacturing industry. Bishop, in his "History of American Manufactures," assures us that, "Even at the present day, many countries which were reckoned elders in the family of nations ere the ring of the ax was heard in the forests of America, are essentially less independent in regard to some products of manufacture than were the American colonies at the time of the Revolution."

According to the theory of the mercantile system, these budding manufactures were injurious to the mother country, except as the product was used by the makers, and laws forbidding them were passed by the British Parliament. There is little evidence that the laws against manufacturing were ever enforced, but the fact that the long disused smuggling acts were now being revived showed the possibility of similar action in regard to other laws.

There was another grievance which the Middle colonies shared with the South and which was much more important. In these two sections population was already pressing toward the West. There had been a rapid in-

CAUSES OF THE REVOLUTION

crease in the number of slaves in the South and of workers in the Middle colonies. As a result, western lands were becoming valuable, and men prominent in colonial life were already deeply involved in western land schemes.

Here again English officials came into direct conflict with the interests of the dominant class in the colonies. Great fur trading companies had been organized by English merchants, and these companies naturally opposed western settlement. Furthermore, it was well recognized that the closer the colonies were kept to the seaboard, the easier they could be controlled.

The French and Indian War had been precipitated largely by these land speculators.[1] They embraced the most prominent men in the colonies. Washington was especially active along this line. He had used his position as royal surveyor to locate lands within the limits which he was supposed to preserve from settlement. He had helped to maintain what would now be called a "land lobby" in London to push his schemes. When Parliament, by the Quebec Act, extended the jurisdiction of Canada over the western country, his interests were directly threatened, and had the Revolution not occurred, he would have lost some 30,000 acres of land. It would be foolish to say that Washington became a revolutionist because of his western land interests. On the other hand, it has been worse than foolish to depict him

---

[1] Herbert B. Adams, "Maryland's Influence upon Land Cessions," in *Johns Hopkins' University Studies in History and Political Science*, Vol. III; Winsor, "Westward Movement," pp. 34–61; Sumner, "The Financier and Finances of the Revolution," Vol. II, Chap. XXXIII; "Old South Leaflets," Nos. 16, 27, 163; Hunt, "Life of Madison," pp. 46–50; T. Watson, "Life and Times of Thomas Jefferson," pp. 150–153; Schouler, "History of United States," Vol. I, pp. 216–218.

F

as a whole-souled superman unmoved by human considerations.

There was another cause which was more widespread than any of these, and which undoubtedly did more to make the Revolution a popular movement than any one of those previously mentioned. This was the paper money question. With regard to England all the colonies were debtors, and throughout history the debtor class has sought to depreciate the currency.

All the colonies had issued paper money in large quantities. In all save Pennsylvania it had greatly depreciated in value. In some colonies it had become practically valueless, and there had been successive issues, or "tenors," as they were called, each of which had been used to redeem the previous one, and all of which were almost equally worthless. The English merchants who did business in the colonies were compelled to accept this paper money in payment for the goods they sold, as all of the colonies had enacted most stringent laws enforcing the legal tender character of the bills.

This antagonism reached a climax at the close of the French and Indian War. The British merchants had sent over large quantities of goods during this war, and were now pressing for settlement in something besides the depreciated paper money. The British Parliament backed them up in this demand, and enacted a law forbidding further paper money issues in the New England colonies, and restricting them or providing for early prohibition in the others.

This action served to bring an entirely new set of supporters to the cause of the Revolution. Paper money had already been a cause for continuous quarrels within the colonies. The wealthy creditor class had opposed the paper money, and the country debtor class had favored it. Elections for the colonial legislatures had turned upon this issue, and the country districts with their debtor population had been almost universally victorious. This had also been true of the Southern colonies, which were little affected by the Navigation Acts and the laws restricting manufacture.[1] Now all the fierce partisanship that had often broken out in riots against the "plutocrats" of the coast cities was skillfully turned against the British government. The orthodox histories say very little about this point, although contemporary writers, and especially English ones, place it almost in the front rank of causes of the Revolution. Those who have written our histories have been controlled largely by creditor class sympathies, and they are not particularly proud of the fact that one of the prime causes of the Revolution was the desire of a large number of the colonists to escape paying their debts.

It was especially easy to manipulate the paper money sentiment into revolutionary action. In nearly every colony the legislative council, chosen by a more or less popular vote, was controlled by the debtor class and was in a perpetual fight with the royal governor. This fight usually took on a form that is strongly suggestive of a comic opera plot. Each year the legislature would prepare certain laws providing for paper money, western extension, protection against the Indians, or some other line of action to which there was royal objection. Then

[1] This is treated in full in the thesis, "History of Economic Thought in Relation to Economic Conditions," by May Wood Simons, to which the Harris Prize was awarded by Northwestern University.

the governor would veto the laws. The legislature would then refuse to vote the governor's salary. He would haggle with them until his funds gave out or their desire for legislation was satisfied. Then he would sign the laws agreed upon and would receive his salary. Over and over again in almost every colony this process was repeated. The British government constantly sought to find some method by which the governor's salary would be assured without this bargain and sale process. The colonists steadfastly opposed all proposals to pay him from any income save the colonial treasury controlled by the legislature.

This perennial haggling had naturally divided the colonists into two parties, one of which clung to the governor, while the other followed the legislative body. As the governor was the representative of the king, it was easy to turn the adherents of the legislative body into revolutionists.

These legislatures constituted the germs of an independent government. For the colonists they were the government which represented colonial interests. When the industrial life of the colonies had reached the point where its ruling class needed a government to further its interests, that government was ready to its hand in the colonial legislatures.

The Stamp Act, which provided for the collection of money by a stamp to be placed upon all business papers, was hated, not so much because it was "taxation without representation," as because it provided that the funds obtained through its operation should be used for the payment of the salaries of the royal governors. If this were done, there would be an end to the bargain and sale method of securing the governor's signature. This meant that paper money could no longer be issued, and that "stay laws," which prevented the collection of debts, could no longer be enacted.

Parliament not only forbade the issue of paper money, but aggravated the situation by passing the Navigation Laws at the same time. These closed the West India trade, the principal source of colonial specie.

At every point the industrial life of the colonies had reached the stage where it was hampered and restricted by its connection with England. Large classes of the population required an independent government to further their interests. Evolution along the lines already drawn could proceed only with independence. Those who stood for independence were the most energetic and far-sighted among the colonists. In these great basic facts and fundamental conflicts of interest do we find the causes of the Revolution, and not in petty quarrels over insignificant taxes and abstract principles of politics.

CHAPTER VII

THE REVOLUTION

The Revolution succeeded because it was the American phase of an English civil war. It was not so much a conflict between the colonies and the English government, as it was one aspect of a war between different divisions of the English people on both sides the Atlantic.[1] Indeed, it was, in reality, but one battle of a great worldwide struggle between contending social classes. It was a part of the violent upheaval of society by which the capitalist class overthrew feudalism and came into power.

In England there had been a reaction after the overthrow of the Commonwealth and the restoration of Charles II. Feudalism, kingly prerogative, and privilege had gained a new lease of life. The Georges were seeking to push this reaction still further. In this they were supported by the landed nobility and its followers, who constituted the Tory party. Against this party the Whigs, as the representatives of a still new and un-

[1] Justin Winsor, "Narrative and Critical History of America," Vol. VI, article on "The Revolution Impending," by Mellen Chamberlain, p. 1: "The American Revolution was not a quarrel between two peoples, . . . it was a strife between two parties, the conservatives in both countries in one party, and the liberals in both countries as the other party; and some of its fiercest battles were fought in the British Parliament." Page 2: "The American Revolution, in its earlier stages at least, was not a contest between opposing governments or nationalities, but between two different political and economic systems."

developed capitalism, were struggling. Many of the supporters of the old merchant class remained with the Tories, so that the Whigs were coming more and more to be dominated by and to express the interests of the manufacturers.

As we have already seen, the dominant interests in the revolutionary party in America were those from which sprung the present capitalist class, — smuggling merchants, manufacturers, land speculators, etc. But these had already learned how to draw to themselves and use in their interest the great mass of the laboring and small business classes. They did this through the paper money issue and the appeal to the defenders of the popular local legislative assemblies. We shall see later how these issues were discarded or repudiated when they had served their purpose. It would be foolish to attempt to draw the class lines too clearly at this time. In only a few localities was the factory stage present. All industrial stages from frontier savagery to this beginning of the factory system existed. Class interests could not but be confused in such a society, and their political expression would necessarily confound that confusion.

On the whole, however, it may be roughly stated that in England the Whigs stood for capitalism, constitutional government, freedom of trade, and the powers of Parliament, while the Tories represented feudal landed privileges, kingly prerogative, and increase of the royal power.

In America there was no landed nobility with interests of its own to defend, and no king to exercise a royal power. Nevertheless, the Tories on American soil were at all times, up to the very close of the Revolution, fully as numerous as the revolutionists, and their partisans always insisted that they were in a great majority. We hear much of the "hireling Hessians" whom the British brought to America; but which of our textbooks tell us that there were 25,000 Americans enlisted in the British army, or that at many times there were more Americans under the British than the colonial flag?

As a general thing, the Tories in America came from some of the following classes: (1) the personal, political, and business followers, dependents, and friends of the royal governors; (2) the nonsmuggling merchants of New York and the Middle colonies, whose interests were bound up in the British trade, and who suffered from the competition of the smugglers; (3) the large landholders of the same states; (4) the clergy who were attached to the Church of England, and such of their followers as they could influence. In addition to all these more or less active classes there was that great mass of the population that, having no direct interests at stake in a change, remains indifferent, or clings to things as they are.[1]

Each of these two classes extended its ties across the Atlantic, and some of the most effective blows for American independence were struck by those who fought on English soil.

When we come to consider the actual fighting of the Revolution, we meet with many facts that seem to be of considerable importance, but that are usually omitted

[1] Justin Winsor, "Narrative and Critical History of America," Vol. VII; article on "The Loyalists and their Fortune," by George E. Ellis; M. C. Tyler, "The Royalists in the American Revolution," in the *American Historical Review*, Vol. I; A. C. Flick, "Loyalism in New York," Columbia University Series, Vol. XIV, No. 1.

from our histories. Perhaps this is explained by the statement of S. G. Fisher in his "True History of the American Revolution."

"The people who write histories are usually of the class who take the side of the government in a revolution; and as Americans, they are anxious to believe that our Revolution was different from others, more decorous, and altogether free from the atrocities, mistakes, and absurdities which characterize even the patriot party in a revolution. . . . They have accordingly tried to describe a revolution in which all scholarly, refined, and conservative persons might have unhesitatingly taken part; but such revolutions have never been known to happen."

The truth is that the Revolution was to a large extent started and maintained through methods of mob violence and terrorism, such as civilized war hardly tolerates today. One of the first hostile acts, while the colonists were still loudly protesting their loyalty, was the burning of the revenue frigate *Gaspe*, that had very foolishly and tyrannically dared to interfere with the regular business of the New England smugglers. The first active steps toward organized revolution consisted in the formation of "Committees of Correspondence," a sort of semi-secret network of conspirators extending throughout the colonies. This body had its headquarters in Boston, with Samuel Adams, one of those natural organizers and agitators, skilled in all the arts of arousing the masses that have ever been characteristic of popular leaders.[1] This

[1] J. K. Hosmer, "Sam Adams, The Man of the Town-Meeting," in *Johns Hopkins University Studies in History and Political Science*, 1884, p. 34: "He had no private business after the first years of his manhood,

chain of committees early took up the work of terrorizing those who opposed them. The story of the methods used to accomplish this end does not make nice reading. It tells of the whipping of unarmed men by armed mobs, of the wholesale application of that humorous method of torturing which is peculiarly American, and is supposed to have originated at this time, tarring and feathering, and riding on a rail. It describes the burning of houses, the "confiscation" of property, the hanging of not a few, and the application of nearly all the methods of mob violence that ingenuity could devise.

One of the weapons which was most widely used, both locally and nationally, privately and officially, was the boycott. One of the first acts of the first session of the Continental Congress was to declare a boycott on all English goods. This was two years before the Declaration of Independence, while the colonies were still making a great parade of their loyalty. Yet this resolution provided not simply for what has come to be known as a "primary" boycott against English goods. It went on to describe most elaborately the methods to be used to enforce a boycott upon any merchants who should handle British goods, or who should trade with England in any way.[1] The Committees of Correspondence then saw to it that this boycott was enforced, and they worked to such

was the public servant, simply and solely, in places large and small, — fire-ward, committee to see that chimneys were safe, tax-collector, moderator of town-meeting, representative, congressman, governor. One may almost call him the creature of the town-meeting. His development took place on the floor of Faneuil Hall and Old South, from the time when he stood there as a master figure; and such a master of the methods by which a town-meeting may be swayed the world has never seen," etc.

[1] *Journals of the Continental Congress*, Vol. I, pp. 23–26.

THE REVOLUTION

good effect that importations from England fell off one half almost at once.

When the statement is made that only a minority of the population were revolutionists, the question naturally arises as to how this minority was able to win out. The answer is found in the fact noted by every writer who has studied this period that the revolutionists were much more active, efficient, cohesive, and belligerent, more conscious of their aims and more determined in their pursuit than any other portion of society.[1] This is an invariable characteristic of a rising social class. The capitalist class was then the coming class. It was the class to whom the future belonged. It was the class whose victory was essential to progress. The Tories, with their adherence to the royal governors and to the old system of social castes and legal privileges, were harking back to an already dead society. They had neither ideas nor ideals to inspire them. The economic system to which they belonged was already crumbling into the dust of history.

In so far as the military operations on American soil are concerned, they can best be understood if we recall the geographical features of the Atlantic coast. Throughout history the strategic line of attack and defense on that coast, from either a commercial or a military point of view, has been the valley of the Hudson. If the British could occupy this valley, rebellious New England would be cut off from the other colonies, and a base of supplies and operations created from which other mili-

[1] The revolutionists were also the armed and trained riflemen of society. It was the frontiersmen who captured Burgoyne, won the battle of King's Mountain, and generally furnished the fighters at critical times.

tary movements of conquest would have been comparatively easy. Boston, the center of revolt, and Philadelphia, the largest city, could have been occupied almost at will, and a brief raiding expedition would have sufficed to have subdued the Southern colonies.

At the opening of hostilities Boston was already occupied by a British army under General Gage. He permitted a portion of his force to be drawn away to Lexington in the effort to destroy the military stores that the colonists had accumulated, and saw a large portion of this detachment wiped out by a guerrilla attack. Then came the occupation of Bunker (or Breed's) Hill, which commanded Boston. The British army attacked the American intrenchments, and was successful, but at a terrible cost. However, the British still occupied Boston, and the American army was little more than a disorganized mob, totally incapable of conducting any effective siege.

At this moment a most important change took place in the command of the British troops. General Sir William Howe was given charge. The important fact about General Howe was that he was a most intensely partisan Whig, and that he had been one of the strongest defenders of the colonies in the British Parliament. He was absolutely opposed to any use of force against them; believed them to be in the right and entitled to victory. In other words, the work of conquering the colonists was turned over to a man who was anxious that they should not be conquered.

This was the situation when George Washington was made commander in chief of the American forces. He at once prepared to conduct as much of a siege of Boston as was possible. He had an army without guns, ammunition (Bunker Hill was lost because the American ammunition was exhausted), cannon, or even food and clothing. Some small cannon that had been captured by Ethan Allen at Fort Ticonderoga were hauled by the New England farmers on sleds, and at last preparations were made for actual hostilities.

Howe's conduct, in the meantime, had been most mysterious if we consider it as that of a sincere British general. He was a man of military ability. He was located in a city that had once been rendered untenable by the occupation of a hill that commanded it. It is a first principle of military tactics that all elevations commanding a position must be occupied if the position is to be defended. Yet Howe lay in Boston all winter without occupying Dorchester Heights, which commanded the city, and was apparently very much surprised when Washington at last took the hint and threw up some intrenchments on that position. Howe then discovered the very obvious fact that his position in Boston was endangered. He had plenty of ships in the harbor; and the artillery of that day in the hands of such artillerymen as were to be found among the Continentals was not particularly dangerous to a retreating army. Moreover, there had scarcely been a time during the previous winter when he could not have completely routed the American forces, as these were practically without ammunition.

Then, at a time when the Revolution was languishing for lack of the munitions of war, when New York was unguarded at the mouth of the Hudson, Howe sailed away to Halifax, leaving behind him over two hundred cannon, several tons of powder, and a great stock of other military stores. It is hard to conceive of any greater service he could have extended to the revolutionary cause, unless he had marched his troops directly into Washington's camp and turned them over to the American general, and there were some serious obstacles in the way of doing this. Is it any wonder that this auspicious moment was seized to issue the Declaration of Independence?

A few days before that declaration, however, General Howe came back to New York, which he occupied without resistance, showing that his trip to Halifax was unnecessary. He was accompanied by his brother, Admiral Howe, who was equally partisan to the American cause. Here General Howe sent back requests for reënforcements, which were promptly sent him, until he had between 35,000 and 40,000 well armed, fed, and disciplined troops with which to fight between 5000 and 15,000 ragged, ill-fed, and poorly equipped soldiers under Washington. So small were the resources of the Americans that it is doubtful if their military supplies would have permitted six weeks of active fighting before they would have been completely exhausted and scattered. But Howe conducted no active campaign. On the contrary, he was careful never to follow up any advantage which he gained. He would defeat the army under Washington, but always gave ample time for recuperation. At the same time it must be recognized that Washington showed himself a brilliant general, fully capable of utilizing all the opportunities that Howe so kindly gave him.

The next year, 1777, brought the turning point of the

war. The British occupied New York with many more men under Howe than were really needed to hold the position. If now the Hudson Valley could be occupied throughout its length, the backbone of the colonies would be broken. Accordingly Burgoyne was sent down from Canada, by way of Lake Champlain, to occupy that valley. General Howe was to detach some of his superfluous troops and send them up the Hudson to meet Burgoyne. Howe did not do this. He did not even conduct an energetic campaign against that portion of the American army which was near him. On the contrary, he was so mild in his efforts that the Americans, with a much smaller force than Howe, were permitted by him to divide their forces and to send a portion under Gage to assist in the attack upon Burgoyne. Under these circumstances the latter soon found himself much outnumbered, in a hostile country, without supplies and no prospect of relief, and was compelled to surrender.

By this time the British government had become thoroughly aroused to the attitude of Howe. Criticisms of him became so sharp that he resigned and went back to England, where he was the subject of a Parliamentary inquiry that developed the facts as set forth. He was too powerful politically to be punished, but throughout the Revolution the favorite toast at banquets of American officers was "General Howe"; but, strange as it may seem, no school history considers these facts worthy of mention.

With the fall of Burgoyne and the return of Howe to England the war took on a different aspect. It was more rigorously prosecuted in America, so much so that at times it appeared as if the Revolution would fail and become only a rebellion. Its scope, however, had widened. The old commercial rivals of England had joined hands with the colonies. France, Spain, and Holland extended aid in the form of money, munitions of war, and even troops and battleships. England, beset upon all sides, was unable to send the troops that were needed, and that had been so plentiful when Howe was playing at war. Cornwallis was hemmed in at Yorktown by the allied French and Continental troops, was compelled to surrender, and independence was assured.

CHAPTER VIII

FORMATION OF THE GOVERNMENT

THE surrender of Cornwallis in America was followed by a Whig victory in Parliament. On the 27th of February, 1782, this resolution was carried in the House of Commons: —

"That it is the opinion of this House that a further prosecution of offensive war against America would, under present circumstances, be the means of weakening the efforts of this country against her European enemies, and tend to increase the mutual enmity so fatal to the interests both of Great Britain and America."

One month later the Tory ministry fell, and the English allies of the American army came into power in the home country. In some ways the English Whigs were more consistent and more revolutionary than those who had fought under the Continental flag. They curbed the power of the king and the House of Lords, made the House of Commons supreme, and laid the foundations for a much more truly democratic government than this country has yet enjoyed. One reason for this is to be found in the existence in England of a powerful landed interest which was in such sharp antagonism to the rising industrial capitalists that the latter felt keenly the need of continuous curbing of their opponents.

No such condition existed in America. Here the antagonism of classes was rather between the industrial and mercantile creditors on the coast and the farmer debtors of the interior. These latter were apt to make an alliance with the wageworkers of the larger cities, although these were too little developed to play an important part. Consequently the richer class in the colonies did not feel the need of any democratic measures in order to secure allies from the poorer classes in a fight against a crown and landed nobility, as was the case in England.

We see the effect of this condition in the character of the state governments formed during the Revolution. Practically all of these were supposed to be modeled after the British government. But there was an important difference. Since the colonists had left England the crown and the House of Lords had ceased to hold a dominant position in the English government, and their importance was decreased still further by the parliamentary conflict which was being waged simultaneously with the Revolutionary War in America.

In the state governments which were formed during the war to take the place of the old colonial establishments, the second chamber, corresponding to the House of Lords, was given equal power with the lower House. Moreover, this upper House, instead of being representative of a particular form of property relation, and that a declining one, was made representative of property alone, through very high property requirements for membership and suffrage. Property qualifications for voting were characteristic of all the state constitutions adopted during the Revolution, with the single exception of Pennsylvania. This would seem to show that all the fine talk about the rights of men and "taxation without representation" and "all men are created equal" was intended only to secure popular support with which to pull some very hot chestnuts out of the fire for the ruling class of the colonies.

The nature of these state governments gives an idea of the political forms desired by ruling class interests at the time of the Revolution. The national government was too filmy a thing to tell any story clearly. And yet it is possible that this very indefiniteness tells an equally clear story, for it corresponded very closely to the lack of a general industrial life. There were very few interests common to all the colonies, and these few were not of a kind to overcome the immediate separatist ones.

At the outbreak of the war there was, of course, no central government. For the revolutionary forces its place was taken by the conspiratory "Committees of Correspondence." From these sprang the "Continental Congress," which took to itself more and more power as the Revolution continued.[1]

It was this body that controlled the movements of the army, gave Washington his commission, declared independence, made alliances with France, Spain, and Holland, borrowed money and pledged the credit of the combined colonies for its repayment, issued an inconvertible currency, granted letters of marque and reprisal, built a navy, and carried on peace negotiations when the war was ended. Yet this body had no legal existence, no definite powers, none of the things which are supposed to be the essential foundation of a legislative body until the war was over, its important work completed, and its

[1] John Fiske, "The Critical Period of American History," pp. 92-93.

life about to end. The Articles of Confederation, which for the first time provided these things, were not adopted by the various states until 1781, and by that time the Continental Congress, to which those articles for the first time gave a legal sanction, had ceased to play any important function.

Just as the Confederation was born, however, it was saved from the calamity of complete insignificance by being made a property holder. One of the obstacles to all efforts looking toward even so loose a union as that of the Confederation had been the possession by several of the states of great tracts of western land. This land was claimed under old royal grants, all of which were drawn before anything was known about the internal geography of the country, and several of which read " from sea to sea." Some of the smaller states, Maryland in particular, insisted that these lands must be surrendered as a prelude to any plan of confederation. This was at last agreed to, and Maryland made possible the formation of the Confederation in 1781. This action ultimately assured the existence of a national government. The Confederation now had a territory to govern outside the boundaries of the federated states. This territory, although thinly populated, was almost as large as all the thirteen original states. Finally, when Manasseh Cutler appeared before the Continental Congress with a proposition to purchase large tracts of this land, and it began to appear not simply in the light of a territory to be governed, but also as a source of income, Congress roused from its lethargy to almost its only important action since it had been legally constituted, — the passing of the Ordinance of 1787.

This ordinance providing for the organization and government of the great territory between the Ohio, the Mississippi, the Great Lakes, and the Alleghenies contains some remarkable provisions. There is, of course, the famous one upon which the thirteenth amendment to the national constitution was afterward based, providing that "There shall be neither slavery nor involuntary servitude in the said territory, otherwise than in the punishment of crimes, whereof the party shall have been duly convicted." But there is also a complete "bill of rights," providing for religious liberty, the right of *habeas corpus*, and trial by jury, representative government, bail for all save capital offenses, moderate fines, no cruel and unusual punishments, and also for the foundation of a public school system. This latter provision was to be little heeded until a movement of the working class should force this issue upon the people. These provisions, however, when contrasted with the proceedings of the constitutional convention, show that the Continental Congress had become much more of a popular body than was the one that wrote the present fundamental law of the United States.

During the time of the Revolution, in spite of this one very important action by the Continental Congress, the real governing power in the country had been the group of individuals who were in the midst of events and were making history rather than recording its results in legislation. These were the men who best incarnated the spirit of the rising social class. They were willing that the work of legislation, like the work of fighting in the ranks, should be done by others, providing their hands were upon the levers that moved the social machinery.[1]

The American Revolution, like most wars, was fought by those who had least interest in its outcome. The workers and "embattled farmers," who as "minute men" at Concord "fired the shot heard round the world," and left the imprint of their bleeding feet at Valley Forge and Yorktown, found themselves at the close of the war hopelessly indebted to the mercantile and financial class of the coast cities. The Continental currency, with which the government had paid for supplies, had now become valueless in the hands of the producers of wealth. One hundred and twelve million dollars had been thus extorted from the people. Taxes were most inequitably distributed, the poll tax being one of the most common methods of taxation. In Massachusetts it was proposed to collect over five million dollars by this method from 90,000 taxpayers. The fisheries were almost wiped out during the war and only slowly revived with the coming of peace.[2] McMaster says of Vermont: "One half of the community was totally bankrupt, the other half plunged in the depths of poverty." Of another state he says: "It was then the fashion of New Hampshire, as indeed it was everywhere, to lock men up in jail the moment they were so unfortunate as to owe their fellows a six-

---

[1] Woodrow Wilson, "History of the American People," Vol. III, p. 22: "The common affairs of the country had therefore to be conducted as the revolution had in fact been conducted, — not by the authority or the resolutions of the Congress, but by the extraordinary activity, enterprise, and influence of a few of the leading men in the States who had union and harmonious common effort at heart."

[2] American State Papers, "Commerce and Navigation," Vol. I, pp. 6–21.

pence or shilling. Had this law been rigorously executed in the autumn of 1785, it is probable that not far from two thirds of the community would have been in the prisons."

The burden of debt had been multiplied by the depreciation of currency, and the attempt to collect it in specie. To again quote McMaster: "Civil actions were multiplied to a degree that seems scarcely credible. The lawyers were overwhelmed with cases. The courts could not try half that came before them." [1]

The wealthy citizens who had sent their money to war that it might breed and multiply found their bonds would be of little value unless taxes could be squeezed from the workers. The Confederacy had no power to levy taxes, or to collect money in any way save by the sale of lands and bonds and the issuance of paper money. There were no purchasers for any of these commodities.

The manufacturers who had revolted against British tariffs were now looking for a national government to assist them with tariff legislation. The Revolution, by almost completely stopping importations, had acted on the budding manufacturers like a prohibitive tariff. Moreover, the exigencies of war created an abnormal demand for certain articles, and the Continental Congress devoted no small portion of its energies to efforts to encourage domestic manufactures. The moment the war ended, on the other hand, there was a flood of importations. British manufacturers, especially, were accused of "dumping" goods upon the market at less than London prices for the especial purpose of preventing the

[1] McMaster, "History of the People of the United States," Vol. I, p. 302.

growth of American manufactures. We are not surprised to learn that "By no class of the community was the formation of the new government, and its general adoption by the states, more zealously urged than by the friends of American manufactures."[1]

The paramount interest of the time was commercial, and it was fitting that commerce should play the largest part in the formation of the new government. Commerce demanded a powerful central government. No other could afford protection in foreign ports, provide for uniform regulations throughout the country, make and enforce commercial treaties, and maintain the general conditions essential to profitable trading. As Fisher Ames said in the first Congress: —

"I conceive, sir, that the present constitution was dictated by commercial necessity, more than any other cause. The want of an efficient government to secure the manufacturing interests, and to advance our commerce, was long seen by men of judgment, and pointed out by patriots solicitous to promote the general welfare."[2]

All of these interests were confined to the New England and Middle states. Unless a class could be found in the South that was also interested in a centralized government, there could be little hope of forming a union. In the North the farmers were opposed to a central government and the merchants were its friends. In the South the reverse was true. There the great planters, who were the social rulers, favored the formation of the union. The

[1] Bishop, "History of American Manufactures," Vol. I, p. 422.
[2] Annals of Congress, Vol. I, p. 230. See also "History of Suffolk County, Massachusetts," Vol. II, p. 84; and W. C. Webster, "General History of Commerce," p. 341.

explanation of this is found in the fact that the planters of the South did their own exporting, but did it through English merchants. The latter were driving a profitable trade through their control of importations and the channels of export. The merchants were growing rich and the planters poor. The latter saw a possibility of relief in an internal commerce and in the development of domestic shipping with the opening of the West Indian trade through commercial treaties.[1]

To collect debts, public and private, to levy a tariff for the benefit of "infant industries," to protect the fisheries and pay bounties to the fishers, to assist the Southern planter in marketing his crops, and to secure commercial treaties and guard commercial interests in all parts of the world a centralized government was needed. Those who desired such a government were, numerically speaking, an insignificant minority of the population, but, once more, they were the class whose interests were bound up with progress toward a higher social stage. In advancing their interests this wealthy class of planters, merchants, and manufacturers was really building for future progress.

The wageworking, farming, and debtor class naturally had no desire for a strong central government. These desired above all relief from the crushing burden of debt. They sought this relief in new issues of paper money, in "stay laws" postponing the collection of debts, and in restrictions on the powers of the courts. In regard to government they cried out for economy and low taxes. The ever recurring populistic feud between frontier

[1] McMaster, "History of the People of the United States," Vol. I, pp. 272-273.

debtors and coast creditors made its appearance. The former were in an overwhelming majority, but they lacked cohesion, collective energy, and intelligence, — in short, class consciousness.

It was in Massachusetts that the struggle became especially violent. The populistic debtors elected a legislature pledged to carry out their program. When the legislature met, influences were brought to bear upon it by the creditor class of Boston that caused its members to break their pledges. Angered at this anarchistic defeat of the popular will, the farmers began to defy and intimidate the courts. As almost invariably happens, when a working class rises, collectivist ideas found expression. General Knox, then Secretary of War, who was sent by the Continental Congress to investigate the situation, reported that

"Their creed is that the property of the United States has been protected from the confiscation of Britain by the joint exertions of all, and therefore ought to be the common property of all." [1]

When the courts attempted to force the collection of debts from those who had nothing, the desperate debtors rallied to arms under the leadership of Daniel Shays, a veteran of the Revolution, and captured some of the smaller cities. Although there was no money in the treasury of Massachusetts with which to carry on the functions of government, yet the militia was called out to shoot down these starving veterans of the Revolution, and the wealthy merchants and bankers of Boston advanced the money with which to pay the troops.[2]

[1] Irving, "Life of Washington," Vol. IV, p. 451.
[2] McMaster, "History of the People of the United States," Vol. I,

FORMATION OF THE GOVERNMENT

There was a similar situation in Rhode Island, with the difference that in this state the debtors were able to seize the legislature and force it to do their will. The result was something very like civil war, with the debtors trying to force their creditors to accept the paper money that had been issued. Here, also, we find the collectivist idea, coupled with a crude sort of state socialism which, as populism, became familiar on the western prairies more than a century later.

"A convention of all the towns in Providence county met at Smithfield to consult upon further measures of hostility toward the merchants, whom they accused of exporting specie, and thus causing the distresses of the State. A plan of 'State trade' was proposed, to be submitted to the General Assembly, and the Governor was requested to call a special session for that purpose. The plan was for the State to provide vessels and import goods on its own account, under direction of a committee of the legislature; that produce, lumber, and labor, as well as money, should be received in payment of taxes, and thus furnish cargoes in return for which specie and goods could be obtained. Interest certificates were no longer to be received in payment of duties, but the private importers were to be compelled to pay them in money. The act making notes of hand negotiable was to be repealed, and the statute of limitation shortened to two years." [1]

These uprisings gave the final jar that was necessary to solidify the forces working for a national government.

pp. 318–319; G. R. Minot, "History of the Insurrection in Massachusetts in 1786."

[1] S. G. Arnold, "History of the State of Rhode Island," Vol. II, p. 524.

Until the threat arose of the capture of two or more states by the masses, there were many even of the wealthy classes who were inclined to think that their interests might be best furthered by several separate states.

"But the rebellion of Shays broke out. In an instant public opinion changed completely. Stern patriots, who, while all went well, talked of the dangers of baneful aristocracies, soon learned to talk of the dangers of baneful democracies."[1]

There are few things more striking than this complete change of front by the budding capitalists of Revolutionary times in obedience to material class interests. In 1776 they were all for paper money, restriction of the power of the courts, "natural rights," and the whole string of democratic principles. By 1786 they had rejected all these principles and were defending most of the positions of the English government of King George, while the prerevolutionary principles were left for debt-ridden farmers and workingmen. It is at least interesting to learn that the ruling class had even the same demagogues to secure popular support, and that Sam Adams was now an ardent defender of the creditor class.[2]

The framing of the Constitution under these conditions took on much of the character of a secret conspiratory *coup d'état*, such as most historians congratulate America on having escaped. The little group of individuals who best represented the ruling class, and who had dominated throughout the Revolution, were, to

[1] McMaster, "History of the People of the United States," Vol. I, p. 391.
[2] J. K. Hosmer, "Sam Adams, The Man of the Town-Meeting," p. 51.

a large extent, losing their control. They now set about recapturing it through a secret counter-revolution.

The first step was an invitation from Washington to visit him at his home at Mt. Vernon, extended to commissioners appointed by Maryland and Virginia to consider methods of regulating commerce in Chesapeake Bay. These men arranged for a commercial convention at Annapolis, September 11, 1786, and an address was issued which carefully wove in with the local questions general hints of the need for wider national arrangements. This whole matter is set forth in a report of the French minister, Otto, to his chief, Count Vergennes, and as he was more nearly an impartial observer than almost any one else who has reported these events, it might be well to let him tell the story. He says, writing October 10, 1786:—

"Although there are no nobles in America, there is a class of men, denominated gentlemen, who, by reason of their wealth, their talents, their education, their families, or the offices they hold, aspire to a preëminence which the people refuse to grant them; and although many of these men have betrayed the interests of their order to gain popularity, there reigns among them a connection so much the more intimate as they almost all of them dread the efforts of the people to despoil them of their possessions, and, moreover, they are creditors, and therefore interested in strengthening the government and watching over the execution of the laws. . . . By proposing a new organization of the general government all minds would have been revolted; circumstances ruinous to the commerce of America have happily arisen to furnish the reformers with a pretext for introducing innovations.

· · · · · · ·

"The authors of this proposition (the Annapolis convention) had no hope nor even desire to see the success of this assembly of commissioners which was only intended to prepare a question more important than that of commerce. The measures were so well taken that at the end of September no more than five states were represented in Annapolis, and the commissioners from the northern states tarried several days at New York in order to retard their arrival. The states which assembled after having waited nearly three weeks separated under the pretext that they were insufficient in numbers to enter on the business, and to justify this dissolution they addressed to the different legislatures and to Congress a report."[1]

All this scheme is exposed and its character admitted by Madison in papers written by him and discovered after his death. Delegates to this convention purposely remained away in pursuance of a conspiracy to prevent the action for which it was ostensibly called. It was then possible to go to the Continental Congress with the plea that the commercial arrangements for which it was pretended these two gatherings had been called, were so pressing that a larger body must be convened. The Continental Congress then passed a resolution in February, 1787, saying that it was expedient that a convention of delegates from the several states be held in Philadelphia in May "for the sole and express purpose of revising the Articles of Confederation, and reporting to Congress and

[1] Quoted in H. J. Ford, "The Rise and Growth of American Politics," pp. 40–43. See also Morse, "Life of Hamilton," Vol. I, pp. 212–213; H. Von Holst, "Constitutional History of the United States," Vol. I, pp. 50–51; T. Watson, "Life and Times of Thomas Jefferson," p. 292; Schouler, "History of the United States," Vol. I, pp. 32–33.

the several legislatures such alterations and provisions therein as shall, when agreed to in Congress and confirmed by the states, render the Federal Constitution adequate to the exigencies of government and the preservation of the union."

This was the only form of legality in the calling of the body that formulated the fundamental law of the United States; and no sooner had that body assembled than it proceeded to break this one link which was supposed to give it a legal sanction. It absolutely disregarded the conditions of its existence as fixed by Congress, and proceeded to formulate an entirely new government, and never bothered to report to the Congress to which it was supposed to be subordinate.

After this one short appearance in public, the conspirators again took to darkness. They observed the most elaborate precautions to preserve the secrecy of their deliberations. They forbade the keeping of any notes, and refused to give out any information as to their actions. In spite of this rule James Madison took copious notes, which were published almost a half century later. These notes are almost our only source of information concerning the proceedings, as the only other person who kept notes left the convention in disgust before it had completed its work. As Madison was one of the most conservative members of the convention and the one most responsible for its conspiratory character, we may be sure that if any bias is to be found in his report, it will not be in the direction of the unpopular side.

Nevertheless, these debates, as reported, afford ample evidence that the constitutional convention was little more than a committee of the merchants, manufacturers, bankers, and planters, met to arrange a government that would promote their interests. Only twelve states were represented at the beginning, and one of these dropped out before the end. Of sixty-five delegates elected only fifty-five were ever present, and but thirty-nine signed the final report. Throughout the discussions the utmost contempt for the mass of the people was displayed. Madison and Hamilton, who had most to do with the formation of the constitution, were in favor of placing power as far as possible from the people and giving property especial representation. The attitude of the convention is shown by an expression used by Ellsworth of Connecticut in opposing any action restricting slavery. "Let us not intermeddle," he said. "As population increases poor laborers will be so plenty as to render slaves useless." [1]

It has been pointed out that with the return of peace the wealthy classes, including those who had remained Loyalists during the actual fight, returned to power.[2] The merchants of Boston, frightened at Shays' Rebellion,[3] the manufacturers of Pennsylvania, anxious for protection,[4] and wishing to restrict the growing power of the western districts,[5] the commercial classes of the South, desiring a central government for the settlement of disputes concerning navigable rivers, — all of these were opposed to democracy. All were anxious to secure their

[1] J. Allen Smith, "The Spirit of American Government," pp. 27–39.

[2] "Memorial History of Boston," Justin Winsor (editor), Vol. IV, pp. 74–75.

[3] J. L. Bishop, "History of American Manufacturers," Vol. II, p. 14.

[4] M. Farrand, "Compromises of the Constitution," *American Historical Review*, p. 482, April, 1904.

[5] William C. Webster, "General History of Commerce," p. 341.

privileges against attack by the discontented debtors, frontiersmen, farmers, and wageworkers.

It was from these classes, inspired by these motives, that the delegates were drawn that framed the constitution. "There is no doubt that the new constitution was framed primarily in the interest of the industrial and commercial classes, and was finally ratified largely as a result of their active and intelligent work in its behalf."

Having formulated a constitution, the next step was to secure something that would at least have the appearance of a popular acceptance of the document. Since fully two thirds of the population were opposed to any such adoption, and remained so long after it had become a law, it might have appeared that the framers of the constitution had an impossible task upon their hands. Fortunately for them it was not necessary to take a popular vote. The referendum had not yet been accepted as a principle of political action, and the statement of the Declaration of Independence that "all governments derive their just powers from the consent of the governed" had been relegated to the limbo of political platitudes.

The work of imposing the constitution upon the country was further lightened by the fact that at least three fourths of those who would to-day constitute the electorate were then disfranchised. Moreover, the disfranchised ones were just those who were almost unanimous against the constitution. Property qualifications shut out the working class of the cities and the debtors of the back country. Out of a population of 3,000,000 not more than 120,000 were entitled to even vote for those who were to constitute the state conventions that were to consider the constitution.

H

The delegates to these conventions were generally elected on the same basis as the members of the various state legislatures. This again gave an increased advantage to the defenders of the constitution, as the states had been districted with the definite object in view of discriminating against the back-country districts.

In a monograph on "The Geographical Distribution of the Vote of the Thirteen States on the Federal Constitution," by Orin G. Libby, the economic interest back of the delegates to each of the state conventions is carefully investigated. The result shows a recognition of class interests almost marvelous when we consider the generally undeveloped industrial condition of the time. The frontiersmen, the farmers, the debtors, the people who lived in the country and possessed little property, were almost solidly against the constitution. The merchants, the money lenders, the lawyers, the great landowners, and the planters, and those directly under their influence chose delegates who voted for the constitution.

In spite of gerrymandering and disfranchisement, in spite of the marvelous special pleading of Hamilton and Madison, whose political pamphlets in advocacy of the constitution were destined to become the classic commentaries on that document; in spite of the tremendous influence of its powerful friends, it was long before a sufficient number of the states would indorse it to make possible a further step. Many of those who did indorse it qualified that indorsement with a provision for a "bill of rights," and this was provided for at the first session of Congress. Otherwise there would have been no guarantee of freedom of speech, assemblage, and press, or of trial by jury, or freedom of contract, or of any of those things which constitutions, even at that time, were supposed to be established mainly to secure.

Rhode Island refused even this qualified indorsement. Although the Articles of Confederation provided for unanimous action before any law should be binding, yet steps were taken to organize the new government as soon as ten states had given their agreement, and finally Rhode Island was threatened with force to compel its consent.

To sum up: the organic law of this nation was formulated in secret session by a body called into existence through a conspiratory trick, and was forced upon a disfranchised people by means of a dishonest apportionment in order that the interests of a small body of wealthy rulers might be served. This should not blind us to the fact that this small ruling class really represented progress, that a unified government was essential to that industrial and social growth which has made this country possible. It also should not blind us to the fact that there was nothing particularly sacred about the origin of this government which should render any attempt to change it sacrilegious.

CHAPTER IX

INDUSTRIAL CONDITIONS AT THE BEGINNING OF THE AMERICAN GOVERNMENT

THE industrial foundation for national solidarity was slight when the American government was born in 1789. The ruling classes of the different states had been drawn together by the common fear of a proletarian uprising and the common need for a central government to further a few immediate interests. A decade might easily bring such a divergence in these interests that the central government would disintegrate. The only thing that could prevent this would be the growth of a national industrial life.

The size of any industrial unit and of the political establishment based upon it depend upon the character and extent of the transportation system. The method of transporting goods determines the extent of the market. It is seldom that a political unit is larger than the circle of the market for the great staples of production. There have been exceptions to this rule, but they have usually been short-lived or had some peculiar explanation.

When Washington took the presidential chair, methods of transportation in the United States differed little from those which prevailed in Rome when she was mistress of the then known world. What advantage there might be in such a comparison was with the older civilization.

INDUSTRIAL CONDITIONS

The commerce of Rome in the days of Cæsar moved over roads whose very ruins are the wonder and admiration of modern engineers. American commerce at the close of the eighteenth century was painfully dragged over corduroy roads, through unbridged rivers and morasses of mud, that made a profitable interchange of heavy goods over long distances impossible.

The arrangements for the transmission of intelligence were little more effective than those for the carrying of merchandise. When independence was declared, there were only twenty-eight post offices in all the thirteen colonies. Fourteen years later, when Washington had occupied the presidential chair for a year and the new administrative machinery was fairly well installed, there were still but seventy-five. Yet the population was over three millions. A population of equal number to-day, if as widely dispersed, would have several thousand post offices to minister to its wants.

To maintain even these miserable accommodations, postal rates were so high as to be almost prohibitive for ordinary intercourse among the poorer classes of the population. The minimum charge for a single sheet of paper going less than thirty miles was six cents. Then the rates rapidly increased until to send a single sheet more than four hundred and fifty miles cost twenty-five cents. Additional sheets increased the amount still further. Newspapers were taken only at the pleasure of the mail carriers. Consequently correspondence was largely confined to communications on public matters.

Only four cities had a population of over 10,000. Of these New York led with about 30,000, having but recently pushed into first place above Philadelphia with

28,000. Boston claimed 18,000, Charleston, South Carolina, 16,000, and Baltimore, 13,000.

Four fifths of the population were engaged in agriculture, or perhaps it would be more nearly correct to say that the group of diversified industries which were then included under the name of agriculture embraced four fifths of the industrial life of the time. But these farmers harvested their grain with sickles such as Ruth saw in the fields of Boaz. They threshed their grain with a flail, such as their Aryan ancestors brought from the plains of central Asia when they set forth on that long racial march toward the setting sun, of which the colonization of America was the latest, longest step. Although Jefferson was mathematically calculating a plow that would do its work with the least expenditure of energy, two generations were to come and go before plows constructed upon scientific principles were to appear on American farms. In the meantime, the fields were dug up with sharpened sticks pointed with iron, fashioned much after those of which present-day travelers to Egypt and India and central Russia send postal card photographs to friends at home.

Cattle, horses, hogs, and sheep were of a character that no modern farmer would permit to encumber his fields. Cattle were kept almost exclusively for their hides and meat, and as draft animals. Here and there in New England some butter and cheese were made. But the cow as a machine for the transformation of a "balanced ration" into a definite quantity of milk and cream at the least possible expense had scarcely been dreamed of. She must still be capable of foraging her food in the forest through the greater part of the year and of enduring the rigors of a Northern winter without shelter. "Hollow horn," a disease caused by extreme cold, exposure, and insufficient feed, killed many animals yearly.

Although Messenger, the father of the American Hamiltonian strain of trotting horses, was imported in 1786, and Justin Morgan, the sire of the once famous Morgan horses (a strain that great efforts are now being made to revive), was born in 1793, the horses of this time were few in number and generally miserable in character.

The hog of that day was compelled to live in an environment, one of whose conditions of survival was to hunt his own food in the forest and dodge wild animals while doing so, and then be able to stand a drive of several hundred miles to a distant market.[1] He bore little

[1] Parkinson, who wrote of a tour made about this time, described the hogs that he saw in the following language (p. 290): "The real American hog is what is termed the wood-hog; they are long in the leg, narrow on the back, short in the body, flat on their sides, with a long snout, very rough in their hair, in make more like the fish called a perch than anything I can describe. You may as well think of stopping a crow as those hogs. They will go to a distance from a fence, take a run, and leap through the rails, three or four feet from the ground, turning themselves sidewise. These hogs suffer such hardship as no other animal could endure. It is customary to keep them in the woods all winter, as there are no threshing- or fold-yards; and they must live on the roots of trees, or something of that sort; but they are poor beyond any creature that I ever saw. That is probably the cause why the American pork is so fine. I am not certain with American keeping and treatment if they are not the best; for I never saw any animal live without food, except this: and I am pretty sure they nearly do that. When they are fed, the flesh may well be sweet; it is all young, though the pig be ten years olde and like pigs in general, they only act as a conveyance to carry corn to market." For further information on agricultural conditions at this time see H. E. Alvord, "Dairy Development in the United States" in Report of Bureau of Animal Industry for 1899, p. 245 *et seq.;* Captain Williamson, "Description of the Settlement of the Genesee Country in the State of New York" (1799), pp. 32–41; W. Faux, "Memorable Days in Amer-

resemblance to the highly perfected pork-producing machine of the modern fat stock show.

Considerable effort had been made to improve the breed of sheep because of the pressing need of a domestic supply of wool for weaving. Laws forbidding the slaughter of sheep for mutton had been passed in several states, and premiums were quite generally offered to encourage sheep breeding. The first Merinos were imported in 1793, and frequent importations from Spain followed in spite of the efforts of Spain to prevent such action.

Southern industry still rested primarily upon the tobacco crop, which was less profitable than it had once been. Exhaustive methods of exploiting the soil in its production were driving the plantations farther and farther from the seaboard and the river banks. Cotton was still ginned by hand, although Eli Whitney was working on the model of the first cotton gin. Hand ginning was so expensive that cotton raising was not profitable. We are not, therefore, much surprised to learn that there was a strong abolition sentiment in Maryland and Virginia, where the slaves on the worn-out tobacco plantations were no longer earning their "keep," and where they could be bought for from one to two hundred dollars. The rice industry, too, was just ready for a transformation. The first machine for winnowing rice was invented in 1749. A machine for hulling and another for threshing it from the straw were invented just as the eighteenth century was closing.

ica" (1823), pp. 72–73, 113, 139, 143; Dodge, "West Virginia," p. 43; William H. Smith, "History of the State of Indiana," Vol. II, pp. 661–662; Henry Adams, "History of the United States," Vol. I, pp. 16–17.

Manufacturing was still almost entirely in the household stage. Evidences of a coming change were, however, apparent in many directions. The woolen industry, that had led the industrial revolution just then in progress in England, was the first to enter upon the factory stage on this side the Atlantic. England was well aware of the advantage which the newly invented machinery was giving her manufacturers in the markets of the world, and was seeking in every way to maintain her monopoly. Heavy penalties were directed against those who should seek to export any of the new machinery, and several attempts to evade these prohibitions failed. In 1790 Samuel Slater, who had worked in the Arkwright mills in England, came to the United States, and as he had stowed away the plans only in his head, he was not stopped at the customhouse. He built a complete factory the next year in Pawtucket, Rhode Island.

At the very beginning industrial evolution in the United States showed one peculiarity that was to distinguish it from that of European countries. It was unhampered by traditions and feudal institutions and customs, and struck out boldly in new and characteristic paths. In England the woolen industry had always been divided into several processes, each carried on under a different roof, and this division was kept up even after the factory system was introduced. Carding and combing was one industry, spinning another, and weaving, dyeing, and finishing were each separated from all the others. Each of these had its own building, owner, industrial organization, purchasing and marketing facilities. From the very beginning all this was swept aside in the United States, and all these processes were made a part of one act of production under one roof and one management.[1]

Iron and steel were still produced largely as they had been for centuries. But the new "puddling" method had just been introduced; power was being used to drive the blowers, and everywhere there were signs of a coming change. One of the great "household" industries of New England was the manufacture of nails. Each family had its own little anvil, forge, and simple tools. The iron was distributed at regular intervals, and the completed product purchased by those who, a little later, were to gather these workers together in great factories tending giant machines, each of which would produce more nails than a whole community of household workers.

The shoe trade was already concentrating around Boston. But shoes were still made with lapstone, awl, and waxed end.

Superficially industry was sleeping, as it had slept for centuries. A closer study revealed the first movements that heralded a new awakening.

Fitch's steamboat was making regular trips up and down the Delaware in 1790. His neighbors looked upon him as a half-insane crank. He was to share the fate of a multitude of those who have lightened the labor of the world. He died in poverty, the butt of ridicule, while another man and generation reaped fame and wealth from his ideas.

The great industry of the time was shipbuilding and commerce. New England ships were turning watery

[1] "The New England States," Vol. I. Monograph by S. D. N. North, "New England Woolen Manufacturers," p. 202.

furrows in every ocean highway and harbor. Her merchants were already the most powerful in the world, and were accumulating the capital which, invested in the machinery just then being conceived by the minds of inventors, was destined during the next generation to change the whole social structure.

It was the germinal period of capitalism. The beginnings of the greatest of all social transformations were appearing, but were attracting little attention.

CHAPTER X

RULE OF COMMERCE AND FINANCE

THREE divisions of the ruling class united to form the constitution and establish the new government. These were the merchants, the manufacturers, and the planters. The first two at once formed an alliance against the latter to secure control of government. In this alliance the first dominated, since the carrying trade was by far the most highly developed. Its units of capital were larger, its owners more clearly conscious of their class interests, and better equipped to further those interests than the owners of the essentials of any other industry. In this America was following in the already well-worn track of social evolution. Merchants have generally been the advance guard of the capitalist army, gathering the capital and political power to be later employed and enjoyed by the manufacturers.

Events were especially favorable for the American carrying trade. The year of Washington's inauguration saw the fall of the Bastile and the beginning of the French Revolution. Everywhere the capitalist class was coming into power. Napoleon was to come upon the heels of the Revolution, and for a generation western Europe was to do little besides wallow in its own blood. Unless this fact is kept constantly in mind it is impossible to understand events on this side the Atlantic. While the great commercial nations were fighting one another for the carrying trade of the world America ran away with the bone over which they were quarreling.

The man who best incarnated the interests and ideas of the merchants and manufacturers of this time was Alexander Hamilton of New York. So true is this that the history of the first twelve years after the adoption of the constitution has been very rightfully designated as the "Hamiltonian period."

The constitution had been formulated and foisted upon the people largely by stealth and deception, aided by a closely restricted suffrage. Even this would not have been possible without the support of the plantation owners of the South. The Southern planter, however, belonged to a social stage that was already of the past. He was to make some desperate efforts to control the American government, was to succeed for a time, and to go down finally only after the bloodiest war of the century. At this moment his economic power appeared to be upon the wane. The cotton gin had not yet produced its revolution, and tobacco cultivation had passed its zenith. The manufacturing class, on the contrary, was just beginning to feel its strength, and it was with this class, its own first-born, that the merchant class joined hands. In this alliance we find the key to the legislation of the period.

The first bill introduced into the new Congress was a tariff bill. Its protective features would be considered very mild to-day, but the debate shows that it was considered a protective measure. This discussion brought out all the contending interests, as every such bill since has done. Pennsylvania wanted a tariff on molasses, rum, and steel. Massachusetts opposed the first and was doubtful of the second, because of the part they played in her commerce, but was agreed upon the latter. The South opposed a tax on the last two and favored taxing the first. The West, consisting of Kentucky and Tennessee, both of whom were clamoring for admission to the Union, was cajoled into the protection camp by a tariff on hemp to offset their protests against the tax on salt, levied at the behest of the coast merchants and fishers, and bearing heavily on the back country cattle raisers.

This tariff had hardly been enacted into law before Hamilton came forward with the series of proposals whose comprehensiveness and unity of purpose and far-sighted outlook stamp him as one of the greatest exponents of rising class interests, and therefore one of the greatest of what the world calls statesmen that the century has produced.

These measures were designed to carry still farther the plot which began with the constitution. They proposed an interpretation of that document to which but a small minority of the small body who formed it would have agreed. It had been difficult enough to secure its adoption when it was supposed to leave a large measure of autonomy to the states. Now Hamilton proposed and carried through a program of legislation that well-nigh destroyed this autonomy.

Commerce demands a strong central government capable of extending its influence wherever ships sail and goods are sold. To secure such a government having its own sources of income, exercising direct control over the citizen, and tied tightly to the possessors of financial power, was Hamilton's object.

The three most important measures which went to the

building up of this structure were: first, the funding of the national and state debts with the assumption of the latter by the national government; second, the establishment of a national bank; third, the introduction of a protective tariff and excise tax.

Nothing is so impressive to the bourgeois mind as property relations on a large scale. A government with a great national debt, an interest in a bank, and an independent source of revenue fulfilled all ideals in this respect.

The national debt, domestic and foreign, which was inherited by the new government from the old Confederation amounted to about $42,000,000. Hamilton proposed that this should be increased by the nation assuming the debts incurred by the states during the Revolution and still unpaid, amounting to over $30,000,000. This would give a national debt of nearly $75,000,000. Although there are many individuals at the present time who could undertake the payment of such a debt, it appeared of mammoth proportions to the men of 1790.

The certificates of indebtedness had been steadily depreciating during the Confederation. They were now almost worthless. They were held largely by speculators who had bought them for but a few cents on the dollar. These speculators at once gave their adherence to the proposal to make the national government responsible.

The Southern states were especially opposed to this move to strengthen the national government at the expense of the states. The plantation interests were much more closely united to the states and had little need of a strong central government. Moreover, several of the Southern states had already paid their debts, and this new proposal would simply mean that they would be required to assist in bearing the burdens of other states.[1]

The South was very anxious that the national capital should be located in their section. For this Hamilton and those he represented cared little or nothing. They were interested in more substantial things. So Hamilton arranged a bargain with Jefferson. By its terms enough votes were to be given by Hamilton to secure the location of the capital on the Potomac on condition that Jefferson delivered sufficient Southern votes to carry the measure, providing for the assumption of state debts. After it was all over, Jefferson made a loud complaint about getting the worst of the bargain, seeming to forget that bargains are made with just that object in view.

Hamilton's supporters insisted that the certificates of indebtedness should be paid in full, and this without regard to the amounts paid for such certificates by the present holders. From the point of view of expediency (which is much the same as statesmanship) this was undoubtedly correct. But when this action was defended on ethical grounds, with high-sounding protestations of

[1] J. S. Bassett, "The Federalist System," p. 34: "The states which had the largest unpaid debts were naturally the most anxious for funding. Of these Massachusetts, Connecticut, and South Carolina were most notable. On the other hand, the states having the small debts were against the measure, and among them was Virginia, who had paid much of her Revolutionary debt through the sale of western lands. . . . Those persons, and there were many, who favored a strong central government also declared for assumption. In the wake of Virginia followed the states south of her, save South Carolina, while New England was for assumption. The middle states divided, the commercial parts going for, and the agricultural parts against, the measure."

honesty, one is apt to be reminded of another debt that was being repudiated at the very moment such strenuous efforts were being made to pay this one. This was the debt created by forcing the Continental paper money upon farmers in payment (?) for their produce, upon laborers as wages for their toil, upon soldiers in exchange for their lives and their sufferings. These bills had been forced upon such persons by all the power of civil, criminal, and military law, backed up by every form of social ostracism, mob violence, and public pressure that could be devised.

Those to whom it was owed had given, not of their abundance like the holders of the certificates of indebtedness, but of their poverty. This debt amounted to over $100,000,000. It was absolutely repudiated by the government of Hamilton. That repudiation, and consequent loss by the producing class, was one of the causes of the terrible poverty that prevailed. It is at least possible that some of the "prosperity" that followed the enactment of Hamilton's measures was due to the fact that the workers were permitted to produce for use and exchange instead of for confiscation through a useless currency.[1]

[1] Jefferson has thus described the process of funding and assumption: "After the expedient of paper money had exhausted itself, certificates of debt were given to the individual creditors, with assurance of payment as soon as the United States should be able. But the distresses of these people often obliged them to part with these for the half, the fifth, and even a tenth of their value; and speculators had made a trade of cozening them from their holders, by the most fraudulent practices, and persuasion that they would never be paid. In the bill for funding and paying these Hamilton made no difference between the original holders and the fraudulent purchasers of this paper. Great and just repugnance arose at putting these two classes of creditors on the same footing, and great exertions were used to pay the former the full value, and to the latter

I

The class of bankers was just appearing There were only four banks in the entire country. To supply needed banking facilities and tie this powerful interest to the national government, Hamilton proposed a national bank. He united this proposal to his debt plan in a most skillful manner. The bank was to have a capital of $10,000,000. The national government took $2,000,000 of this, receiving in return a loan of the same amount.

The clever feature of the organization was that the certificates of debt were to be accepted for 75 per cent of the value of any number of shares of stock. As the bank was assured of a monopoly for ten years, its stock, and therefore the certificates of debt, were above par almost from the beginning. Yet it was noticed that although the shares were largely oversubscribed, nearly all the purchasers lived north of the Potomac.

The vote in Congress for its establishment was a direct reflection of the possession of the shares. The measure

the price only which he had paid with interest. But this would have prevented the game which was to be played, and for which the minds of greedy members were already tutored and prepared. When the trial of strength on these several efforts had indicated the form in which the bill would finally pass, this being known within doors sooner than without and especially than to those who were in distant parts of the Union, the base scramble began. Couriers and relay horses by land, and swift sailing pilot boats by sea, were flying in all directions, . . . and this paper was bought up at 5/ and even as low as 2/ in the pound, before the holder knew that Congress had already provided for its redemption at par. Immense sums were thus filched from the poor and ignorant, and fortunes accumulated by those who had been poor enough before. Men thus enriched by the dexterity of a leader would follow of course the chief who was leading them to fortune, and become the zealous instruments of all his enterprises." This passage has been criticized by the defenders of Hamilton who have claimed that it accused Hamilton of dishonesty. That it does not do this is plain to any unbiased reader, and there is every reason to believe that it describes actual facts.

was carried by the solid vote of the Northern commercial and manufacturing states against the solid opposition of the plantation states of the South.

The assumption and funding of the debt by the national government created a bondholding, interest-receiving class who naturally worshiped their creator. It also made necessary a steady national income. If the national government was to pay money regularly and directly to one class of citizens, it must be able to take it directly and regularly from another class.

The next step in Hamilton's program included a protective tariff and an excise tax. His famous "Report on Manufactures," submitted in advocacy of a protective tariff, is admittedly the ablest document produced by more than a century of tariff discussion. There is one essential point in which his argument differs from that offered by high tariff advocates of the present time. Hamilton was not troubled with universal suffrage. It was not necessary for him to placate the "labor vote." He spoke only from the manufacturers' point of view. Therefore he gave as one of the reasons for a tariff the high wages paid in this country, and proceeded upon the basis that such wages were an undesirable handicap which would be overcome as the country grew older.

On the question of child labor also he would scarcely use the language about to be quoted if he were spokesman for the present high tariff. He says: —

"It is worthy of particular remark that, in general, women and children are rendered more useful, and the latter more early useful, by manufacturing establishments, than they would otherwise be. Of the number of persons employed in the cotton manufactories of

Great Britain it is computed that four sevenths are women and children, of whom the greater proportion are children and many of a tender age."

The protective tariff, again, like the bank and the national debt, created a class (the manufacturers) peculiarly dependent upon the national government, and who could be reckoned upon to rally to its support and to demand further favors in return for that support.

The rapid growth of manufactures was hindered by the unwillingness of men to work for wages when a whole great continent of untrodden fertile land lay at the western doors of society ready to yield up its bounty to whomever could get upon it and use his labor. Benjamin Franklin had seen this fact and had expressed an opinion that while free land existed, manufacturing would be impossible because no one would work for wages.

This land was now in the hands of the national government, and we find this taking steps to limit settlement and thereby create a body of wageworkers. Acting upon the advice of Hamilton, it was provided that no land should be sold from the public domain except in plots of not less than nine square miles. To still further debar the small farmer the price of even these great tracts was fixed at a minimum of two dollars an acre. But lest the work of the land speculators should be interfered with, long credit was extended to those who could give satisfactory security.[1]

---

[1] Ugo Rabbeno, "American Commercial Policy," p. 176 *et seq.*, explains the working of this policy in detail and adds: "Thus at an epoch when it was not yet possible to initiate a protective policy, which would only have made for the interest of too small a class of capitalists, a land policy was nevertheless introduced, which favored all the interests of the capitalists, whether manufacturers — by excluding laborers from the

The moderately protective tariff and the land policy combined with a most intense public sentiment in favor of domestic products, amounting to a boycott on foreign products where the domestic was attainable, led to a rapid development of manufactures.

The excise tax filled another rôle in the working out of Hamilton's plan. It had been supposed that the national government would have no direct connection with individuals, but would reach them only through the state governments. It was with this understanding that the constitution had been finally adopted. This did not suit Hamilton's plans, nor the interests of those he represented. He wished to bring the central government into direct contact with the citizens in their homes. This was the principal purpose of the tax upon the production of whisky.

Such a tax was peculiarly fitted to accomplish the purpose in view. It was certain to bring about a conflict with a class already hostile to the central government, and this a class without influence in determining legislation. Corn was the principal crop on the frontier. The range within which it can be marketed in its original form and with crude methods of transportation is extremely limited. It can, however, be changed into two forms that admit of extensive and economical transportation, — pork and whisky. The second of these affords by far the greater profits. It is therefore an invariable rule of historical interpretation that a settlement within the corn belt with imperfect transportation facilities will always have

---

soil and compelling them to work for wages — or agriculturists, by leaving the field open to speculative undertakings on a large scale exclusively. See also Schouler, "History of United States," Vol. I, pp. 215–216.

"moonshine stills." This rule has held good for more than a century, and clear across the continent, without regard to the morality or general law-abiding character of the population.

The frontiersmen of Pennsylvania could see no reason why they should not be permitted to market their corn as a beverage unhindered by a revenue tax. Perhaps some of them had heard of the patriotic smugglers of pre-Revolutionary days, or thought that "taxation without representation" was still a crime, and, since they were nearly all disfranchised by property qualifications, they attempted to resist the law.

This gave Hamilton the opportunity for which he had been waiting. Although the "Whisky Rebellion," as the few isolated attacks upon the revenue officers were called, was of insignificant proportions, Hamilton succeeded in inducing Washington to call upon the troops from the neighboring states, until an army of 15,000 was assembled and marched through the riotous localities. This overwhelming show of force established a precedent for direct interference by the national government with the internal affairs of a state, and gave evidence of the possession of sufficient power to enforce the decrees of the central government.[1]

This completed the revolution begun when that conference was called at Annapolis. The whole character of governmental institutions had been transformed. The

[1] Dewey, "Financial History of the United States," p. 106: "The tax was regarded with hostility, particularly in the agricultural regions of the Middle and Southern States. It was asserted that the commercial and importing interests of New England disliked the tariff, but looked with great complacency upon an excise upon an industry in which they were not greatly concerned."

principles of the Declaration of Independence had long ago been cast aside. The spirit of democracy which was roused to win that struggle had been crushed, and social control had been vested in the class whose lineal descendants have held it until the present time. That such action was essential if a great and powerful nation was to arise upon this continent, few will deny.

Without a strong, central government, controlled by the commercial and manufacturing class at this time, it would have been impossible to have laid the foundation for the great development of subsequent years.

CHAPTER XI

RULE OF PLANTATION AND FRONTIER

COMMERCE had progressed with seven-league strides under Hamilton's régime. Aided by the upheaval in Europe, American foreign trade grew from $43,000,000 in 1791 to $204,000,000 in 1801.[1] Nevertheless, the merchants were driven from power. There were many reasons for this, not all of them directly due to the clash of immediate industrial interests.

The Federalists seem to have become drunk with power. They took the unpopular side in the French Revolution, and sought to suppress all expressions of sympathy with the Revolutionists. The better to do this they passed the "Alien and Sedition Laws," vesting extraordinary powers in the President for the punishment of those who criticized the government, and giving him the power summarily to deport foreigners. There was much opposition to this growing centralization of autocratic power. This brought support to other divisions of the budding capitalist class rather than to the merchants.

The principal industrial divisions of the population struggling for the control of government were the small farmers, the frontiersmen, the manufacturers, the merchants, and the Southern plantation owners. It will be at once noted that these overlap in the actual processes

[1] William C. Webster, "General History of Commerce," p. 352.

of industry. This was still more true of their political interests. Consequently any exact analysis of the play of industrial forces as reflected in political events is almost impossible.

Agriculture in the sense of small, diversified farming was still by far the most common industry. It was much more "diversified" than is advised to-day by even the most enthusiastic opponents of "one-crop" farming. The compilers of the census of 1810 tell us that they have excluded many "doubtful articles" from the manufacturing schedules, which

"... from their very nature were nearly allied to agriculture, including cotton pressing, flour and meal, grain and sawmills, barrels for packing, malt, pot and pearl ashes, maple and cane sugar, molasses, rosin, pitch, slates, bricks, tiles, saltpeter, indigo, red and yellow ochre, hemp and hemp mills, fisheries, wine, ground plaster, etc., all together estimated at $25,850,795, making the aggregate value of manufactures of every description in the United States in 1810 equal to $198,613,484."

Here we are at the very birth of the family of modern industries from the great mother industry of agriculture. The whole process of industrial evolution consists of a gradual separation of the production of more and more "doubtful articles" from farming.

Many children of agriculture were just preparing to leave the farm at this time and to take up their abode in factories. The making of cloth was just passing from the "household" stage, where production is in the family and for the family, to the "domestic" stage, where, while production still goes on in the home, the product seeks an outside market.

This domestic stage, of so much importance in European industrial history, was to be but a short tarrying place for American industry on its road to the factory. The two stages were overlapping at this time. The great bulk of manufacturing was still in the household stage. An important portion had reached the point of domestic production for market. Then we learn that "fifteen cotton mills were erected in New England before the year 1808, working at that time almost 8000 spindles, and producing about 300,000 pounds of yarn a year. Returns had been received of 87 mills erected at the end of the year 1809, 62 of which were in operation, and worked 31,000 spindles."[1]

By 1812 a woolen mill in Middletown, Connecticut, was being run by one of Oliver Evans' engines, invented, designed, constructed, and operated in the United States.[2] The relative importance of the different stages of industrial production of cloth is shown by the report of the census of 1810 that 21,211,262 yards of linen, 16,581,299 of cotton, and 9,528,266 of woolen goods were made in families, out of a total production of about 75,000,000 yards. Note that at this period linen leads, with cotton and woolen following. Soon cotton will press to the front and linen be found dragging far in the rear.

The manufacturing interests were still individualistic, or merged with agriculture. The tariff had aided them, but they were not sufficiently numerous, coherent, nor energetic to become a political factor.[3]

[1] Leander Bishop, "History of American Manufactures," Vol. II, p. 160.

[2] *Niles' Register*, Feb. 1, 1812, p. 406.

[3] Edwin Stanwood, "American Tariff Controversies in the Nineteenth Century," p. 123: "One cannot be surprised that while the foreign

In the closing year of Washington's administration an epoch-making invention had appeared that wrought a revolution throughout a broad section of the country. This was the cotton gin of Eli Whitney. This invention was the last link that made possible the factory system in the cloth industry. It furnished the cheap cotton that laid the foundation of the factory system of England and the world. It increased the production of cotton in the United States one hundred fold in the seven years following its appearance.

By making profitable the cultivation of the short-fibered upland cotton plant it released chattel slavery and the plantation system from the confines of the tide-water region, and sent them on their career of conquest along the foothills of the Alleghenies to Mississippi, Louisiana, and Texas. It wiped out, almost in a day, the glimmering sentiment for abolition which a constantly falling price of slaves had aroused in the breasts of Washington, Jefferson, Madison, and other Virginia tobacco growers. It created a new industrial, and therefore a new political, power, — the slave-owning cotton planter, who was soon to grasp at national domination, to secure it after a short division of power with allied forces, and then to rule su-

trade was growing rapidly and while agriculture was flourishing under the double stimulus of a rapidly increasing and of a profitable foreign vent . . . little attention should be paid to the introduction of manufactures. There was ample employment for all disposable capital in the traffic which gave such large returns; there was no surplus labor to be drawn into new industrial enterprises. Occupation could be found for every man with a mechanical turn in building ships, in building and furnishing the new dwellings and shops required by population and trade, in blacksmithing, shoemaking and other trades connected with the shelter, food and clothing of the people." See also succeeding pages to p. 127.

preme for more than a generation and to be overthrown only when the wage-buying capitalist should wrest the scepter of power by four years of terrible civil war.

This new and vigorous industrial interest, pulsing with power, present and potential, contributed strongly to the overthrow of Hamiltonian Federalism and the installation of Jeffersonian individualism, although, as we shall see, the contrast was not so sharp as is sometimes thought.

It was not the old planters of the seaboard that placed Jefferson in the presidential chair. On the contrary, these were more generally Federalist in their sympathies. They were united by many ties of the past, if not of the present, with the New England merchants.[1]

But the new upland cotton raisers were making common cause with the back country farmers amid whom they were living. With these were allied the great body of frontiersmen who had been pouring through Cumberland Gap, down the Ohio, and out along the Genesee River in New York. These men were always separatist, individualistic, and Jefferson's philosophy appealed to them. Besides they had learned of the opposition of isolated New England to Western expansion and the Western country, and this antagonism had not lost anything in the telling as it traveled to the West, and it was most cordially returned with ample interest.

Jay's treaty with England in 1794 had not provided for the navigation of the Mississippi and had almost raised a rebellion in the West as a consequence. The Southern cotton planters were also apt to remember that John Jay had known so little of that industry that he had

[1] Basset, "The Federalist System," pp. 45, 46.

permitted the inclusion of an article forbidding the export of cotton in American ships, because he did not know that cotton was an American crop.

These new forces, the back country farmers, the frontiersmen, and the new race of upland cotton planters, together with the household manufacturers, made up the elements that overthrew the Federal forces.

Owing to the confusion of interests, the presidential election was extremely close, so close that no one received a majority of the electoral votes. The election, therefore, went to the House of Representatives, where Thomas Jefferson was chosen as President, with Aaron Burr as Vice President. This result was not accomplished without some political intrigue on the part of Hamilton and Aaron Burr, in which a new force was introduced into American politics by the latter. This was the famous Tammany Society of New York which had been founded as a social and philanthropic society in 1789.[1]

Before the Federalists lost control, they took one more long step in the perfection of the program of centralization and removal of the government from democratic control. They had formulated the constitution in secret, secured its adoption by deceit and gerrymandering, extended its provisions by shrewd legislation, and made it clearly an instrument of class government. The next step was to remove the final power of control from the people and vest it in the courts. The first move toward the accomplishment of this was a series of laws passed during the very last days of Federal rule, increasing the

[1] M. Ostrogorski, "Democracy and the Organization of Political Parties," Vol. II, pp. 150–153.

number of courts far beyond the needs of the country at the time. Every place thus created was at once filled with a stanch Federalist. Tradition says that the work of signing the commissions of these judges was stopped only when a messenger from Jefferson stayed the hand of the secretary at midnight, March 3d.

Having thus erected a supreme power beyond the reach of the people, they placed at the head of the judiciary a man who was to carry this usurpation of power to the uttermost limits and to fix it there for a century to come. This man was John Marshall, who occupied the position of Chief Justice of the Supreme Court for thirty-four years, receiving his appointment in 1801. During this time he constantly extended and strengthened the power of his office until it reached proportions undreamed of even by those who founded this government, with the possible exception of Hamilton.[1]

Lest it may be thought that I exaggerate the extent of the revolutionary usurpation of power by Marshall and its influence on subsequent history, I will quote from an authoritative legal work at this point. Joseph P. Cotton, in his "Constitutional Decisions of John Marshall," says: —

"In 1801 one of these 'midnight judges,' Marbury, applied for a mandamus to require the issue of his commission, and in 1803 Marshall delivered his opinion on that application. This opinion is the beginning of American constitutional law. In it Marshall announced

[1] *The Federalist*, No. LXXX, "Extent of the Authority of the Judiciary," by Hamilton, contains a passage that may possibly be understood to imply the existence of such power, but this is doubtful, and it is certain that no one claimed it openly at the time of the adoption of the constitution.

the right of the Supreme Court to review the constitutionality of the acts of the national legislature and the executive, the coördinate branches of the government. Such a power had been spoken of in certain opinions, and, indeed, acted upon in unimportant cases in the state courts, but never in the Federal courts. Common as this conception of our courts now is, it is hard to comprehend the amazing quality of it then. No court in England had such power; there was no express warrant for it in the words of the Constitution; the existence of it was denied by every other branch of the government and by the dominant majority of the country. Moreover, no such power had been clearly anticipated by the framers of the Constitution, nor was it a necessary implication from the scheme of government they had established. If that doctrine were to be law, the Supreme Court was indeed a final power in a democracy, beyond the reach of public opinion."

This completed the process of usurpation of power and destruction of democratic control which was begun with the first arrangements for a constitutional convention. With this power to declare laws unconstitutional in its possession the Supreme Court possessed an absolute veto on all legislation and was itself out of the reach of the voters.

Jefferson, the representative of Southern plantation and frontier farmer interests, has always been hailed as the prophet of democracy. But his democracy, in accordance with the interests he represented, was that of individualism, of philosophic anarchy, rather than of associated effort under common management. The cotton plantation owner, whose working class of chattel slaves was forever debarred from political activity, could easily champion this democracy. He would enfranchise the Northern wageworkers whom he hoped, and rightly, as subsequent events showed, might become his allies against the Northern merchants and manufacturers. The pioneer was always democratic in this individualistic sense. Class distinctions had not yet arisen on the frontier. Ohio, Kentucky, and Tennessee, which were admitted to the Union during this period, were the first states to embody universal suffrage in their constitutions.

This alliance between planter and frontiersman is the key to the political policy of much of this period. This alliance was easier at this time than at any later period. Western emigration was largely from the Southern states. The great stream of peoples was flowing from Virginia and the Carolinas through the Cumberland Gap into Kentucky and Tennessee. The South saw in this movement an extension of its power into the future as well as geographically.

Much of the work of Jefferson was connected with the West. He had been active in formulating the Ordinance of 1787 for the government of the Northwest Territory during the dying days of the Confederation, and his interest in the Western movement had always been close. He devised the system of land survey by townships, ranges, and sections, that has done so much to make American real estate more thoroughly a commodity than the land of any other country. He bought Louisiana, sent Lewis and Clark, and Pike to explore the Far West, and began the famous Cumberland Road as a part of an extensive system of internal improvements. During this period Congress was always willing to appropriate money

RULE OF PLANTATION AND FRONTIER

for the settlement of Indian claims, or for the defense of the frontier in Indian wars.

To all these measures the New England commercial interests were hostile. To a certain extent this was a result of sectional isolation as well as material interests. New England had developed a most intense sectional life, with its own customs, prejudices, dialects, religion, and local patriotism, and because of the intensive character of these ideas and institutions, was to impress them deeply upon large sections of the country.

Such isolation and concentration of thought and interests and policy were bound to become separatist when they were antagonized. When the Federalists under Adams passed the Alien and Sedition Laws, Kentucky and Virginia passed resolutions hinting at secession. Now the South and West were in control, with Virginia dominant, and it was the turn of New England, with Massachusetts at the head, to become "treasonable." For several years this section was openly to advocate and secretly to plot secession until another turn in industrial development should give New England interests the ruling hand, when the doctrine of secession would once more take up its abode in the South.[1]

It was the purchase of Louisiana that particularly aggravated the New England states. This was an application of their own philosophy in regard to the constitution. There was no provision in that instrument for

---

[1] McMaster, "History of the People of the United States," Vol. III, pp. 42-48; Wilson, "A History of the American People," Vol. III, p. 184; Hildreth, "History of the United States," Vol. V, p. 584; Von Holst, "Constitutional History of the United States," Vol. I, pp. 185-186.

the purchase of new territory, and no Federalist had ever given as "liberal construction" to a constitutional question as did Jefferson when he purchased Louisiana, and provided for its government directly from the national capital without the consent of the inhabitants, and with little more than a notification to Congress.

However discontented New England might be, it could not be denied that her merchants were prosperous. The high tide of American commerce was reached in 1810 with a total tonnage of 1,424,783 tons. New England ships were in every harbor. The Oriental trade had become especially profitable. The road to India was at last running through America, though not exactly as Columbus had dreamed.

With the beginnings of a factory system and the rise of a body of wageworkers there appear traces of organized labor and a struggle between employers and employees. The petitions to Congress for higher tariff and for relief and assistance for various industries all complain of the high wages which must be paid. Such a complaint indicates several things in addition to the political impotence of the wageworkers. It is a fairly sure sign that wages were rising, rather than that they were already high. McMaster concludes from his investigations that,[1]

"The rates of wages were different in each of the three great belts along which population was streaming westward. The highest rates were paid in the New England belt, which stretched across the country from Massachusetts to Ohio. The lowest rates prevailed in the southern belt, which extended from the Carolinas to Louisiana.

[1] "History of the People of the United States," Vol. III, pp. 509–515, is a good survey of labor conditions.

In each of these bands again wages were lowest on the Atlantic seaboard, and, increasing rapidly in a western direction, were greatest in the Mississippi Valley."

A contemporary authority furnishes an estimate of the wages paid at this time in the most northern belt, where they were supposed to be the highest. His figures are as follows:[1] —

	1774	1804	1807	1809
Wages per day	$.50	$.75	$.75	$.80
Wheat per bushel	.65	1.55	1.55	1.00

These wages were certainly not high enough to seem to require any action on the part of Congress to enable the employers to pay them. The figures for the last two years given above confirm the general impression that wages were rising at this time. Skilled workmen were beginning to organize unions, and here and there strikes took place.

Strikes and unions were still illegal. When the cordwainers (a branch of the shoemaking trade) went out on strike in Philadelphia in 1805, they were convicted of conspiracy and fined, after which they opened up a shop of their own and appealed to the public for patronage.

In New York the growth of a wageworking class was

[1] *Niles' Register*, Vol. I, p. 79 (quoting from Blodget's "Economics"; McMaster, in *Atlantic Monthly*, Vol. LXXV, p. 22, says of 1800: "Soldiers in the army received three dollars a month. Farm hands in New England were given $4 a month and found their own clothes. Unskilled laborers toiled twelve hours per day for fifty cents. Workmen on turnpikes, then branching out in every direction, were housed in rude sheds, fed coarse food, and given $4 a month from November to May and $6 from May to November. When the road from Genesee River to Buffalo was under construction in 1812, though the region through which it went was frontier, men were hired in plenty for $12 per month in cash, and their board, lodging, and a daily allowance of whisky."

having another effect. Here it was laying the foundations for democracy. During the time of the Revolution, the adoption of the constitution, and the Hamiltonian régime, the property qualifications for office and even for the suffrage were so high that the wageworking class was ignored by the politicians. Nor were the members of this class sufficiently numerous to make any effective protest against this disfranchisement.[1]

During the first decade of the nineteenth century, however, a spirit of rebellion against these restrictions began to be felt in New York. This first germ of a labor movement sought to widen the political powers as well as improve the industrial condition of its members. In New York some success was achieved in this direction, and at once there appeared that other phase of class rule under the form of democracy, — the political machine. Up to this time candidates had been nominated either by informal gatherings of "prominent citizens" or by caucuses of members of the state legislatures or Congress.[2] Now there were signs of so-called "popular" caucuses, and appeals began to be made to labor.

On the whole, this was a period of the beginning of things that are familiar features of the society of three quarters of a century later. It was to be a generation, however, before any of these forces were to become prominent, social features.

Jefferson went into office as the exponent of the idea

[1] "Memorial History of New York," Vol. III, pp. 13–14; McMaster, "History of the People of the United States," Vol. III, Chap. XVII; *Niles' Register*, Vol. I, pp. 80–81, contains table of electoral qualifications in all states.

[2] Ostrogorski, "Democracy and the Organization of Political Parties," Vol. II, p. 12.

that the constitution should be "strictly construed," that the central government should be closely limited in its powers, and, above all, should never be used to serve sectional or class interests. Yet never was the constitution stretched farther than by the purchase of Louisiana and its government direct from the White House. The powers which the Federal government exercised in the preliminary steps to the War of 1812, when an embargo was laid on all commerce and Federal officers were given the right of search and seizure, exceeded anything done by Hamilton. The fact that the possession of centralized power led Jefferson to use and extend that power in the interest of those to whom he owed his election, is noted by nearly all historians. Although he came into office talking of the "revolution" due to his election, yet,

"The great mass of the men, who in 1800 voted for Adams, could in 1804 see no reason whatever for voting against Jefferson. Scarcely a Federal institution was missed. They saw the debt, the bank, the navy, still preserved; they saw a broad construction of the constitution, a strong government exercising the rights of sovereignty, paying small regard to the rights of States, and growing more and more national day by day, and they gave it a hearty support, as a government administered on the principles for which, ever since the constitution was in force, they had contended."[1]

[1] McMaster, *loc. cit.*, Vol. III, p. 198.

CHAPTER XII

THE WESTWARD MARCH OF A PEOPLE

It has been noted that with Jefferson a new political force first made itself felt in national politics. This was the frontier. This ever moving frontier has been the one distinctive feature of American society. A full understanding of its influence unlocks many a difficult problem in that history.

He who would write the history of Greece, Italy, or England has but to describe the life of a body of people occupying a peninsula in the Mediterranean, or an island on the edge of the Atlantic. The scene of his story is fixed. But the history of the United States is the description of the march of a mighty army moving westward in conquest of forest and prairie.

The inundating ocean of population was held for a moment by the great Alleghenian dam. At the period we have been considering, it had just sought out the low places and the unguarded ends and was flowing through and around that dam. Along the buffalo paths, the Indian trails, and down the open rivers it was flowing into the great Mississippi Valley. As it flowed it widened the forest trails for the pack trains, and graded them for turnpikes, and finally leveled the hills and spanned the rivers with bridges on which to lay the iron track of the locomotive.

This army had its scouts, its advance guard, its sappers and miners, its army of occupation. These various battalions reproduced in turn the various social stages through which the race has passed. Biology has taught us that the embryo reproduces in syncopated form the various steps in the evolution of living organisms. The ethnologists and the pedagogue know that in the same manner the child moves through mental stages much like those along which the race has traveled. In the same manner the successive stages of settlement in the march of America's army of pioneers tells again the story of social evolution.

The advance guard of hunters, trappers, fishermen, scouts, and Indian fighters reproduced with remarkable fidelity the social stage of savagery. They lived in rude shelters built of logs or of prairie sod, found their food and clothing by the chase, gathered around personal leaders, were often lawless, brutal, and quarrelsome, though frequently they displayed the even more characteristically savage traits of taciturn silence and fatalistic courage. These men penetrated hundreds of miles into the wilderness ahead of all fixed settlements. They sometimes fraternized and lived with the Indians. Such were the French *coureurs du bois*, who gathered furs from Hudson Bay to the Gulf of Mexico, exploring rivers that have found place upon the maps only within the last few decades.

When these scouts had spied out the land the first body of the main army of conquest appeared. This was composed of the little groups of settlers who clustered along the watercourses and the main lines of advance.

These settlements, drawn together for mutual defense

against the Indians, the wild beasts, and the forest fires, and for mutual coöperation in house-raisings, husking, quilting, and logging "bees," with their "common" pastures in the surrounding forest and their democratic social and political organization, were so much like the Germanic "tuns" described by Tacitus, and the Anglo-Saxon villages of pre-Norman days, that one of the foremost American historians gravely explains the resemblance by the classical reading of New England Puritans.

The people who formed this stage were migratory. No sooner had they carved out a little clearing in the wilderness than they moved on to take up the same task farther west. They too rallied around leaders, generally combined hunting and fishing with farming, and in every war in which the United States has been involved, save the latest, formed its most effective fighters.[1]

With this social stage came the beginnings of agriculture. It was a crude cultivation of the soil that borrowed its methods as well as its only important crop from the Indians. This crop, around which the agricultural life of large sections of the country has centered up to the present time, was Indian corn, or maize. This plant seems to have been especially evolved to meet the conditions of the American frontier. Without it another

[1] T. Roosevelt, "The Winning of the West," Vol. V, p. 128: "The men who settle in a new country and begin subduing the wilderness plunge back into the very conditions from which the race has raised itself by the slow toil of ages. The conditions cannot but tell upon them. Inevitably, and for more than one lifetime, . . . they tend to retrograde instead of advancing. They drop away from the standard which highly civilized nations have reached. As with harsh and dangerous labor they bring the new land up toward the level of the old, they themselves partly revert to their ancestral conditions; they sink back toward the state of their ages-dead barbarian forefathers."

generation or more would have been required for the advancing army of settlement to have reached the Mississippi.

It can be grown in the midst of the forest if the trees be "girdled" by removing a ring of bark, which causes the leaves to fall until the sunlight can filter through. A sharpened stake will do for a planting tool if nothing better is at hand. It will produce a considerable crop from virgin soil with little cultivation, and responds richly to added care. It grows rapidly, and its green ears furnish food early in the season. When ripe, it is easy of storage, is not injured by freezing, contains a great amount of nourishment in small bulk, and, what is perhaps most important of all, can be most easily prepared for food. In no one of the various forms in which it entered into the dietary of the pioneer was any elaborate preparation required. On a pinch an open fire to roast the green ears or the ripened kernels sufficed to satisfy hunger. It took the place of the pastures to which the colonists had been accustomed in Europe. As higher stages of agriculture were reached it became the foundation of the entire livestock industry of the nation.[1]

Following this stage in the East, and preceding it in the West, where the Indians were held back by the regu-

[1] Roosevelt, "Winning of the West," Vol. I, pp. 110–111; Massachusetts Agricultural Report, 1853, p. 485; Stickney, "Use of Maize by Wisconsin Indians," p. 71; Shaler, "The United States of America," Vol. I, pp. 26–27; Census of 1880, volume on "Agriculture," Part I, p. 135; J. H. Salisbury, "History and Chemical Investigation of Maize"; Parkinson, "Tour in North America," pp. 198–199; Drake, "Pioneer Life in Kentucky," pp. 47–57; Michaux, "Travels," etc., Chap. XII. These are some of the works discussing the importance of corn in this stage of American history and describing the methods by which it was cultivated and prepared for consumption.

lar army and not driven out by the frontiersmen, came a third division composed of the cowboys, herdsmen, ranchmen, as they were variously called. Here we find a reproduction of many features of the nomadic stage of social evolution. When the race passed through this period, the large social unit which the care of the herds demands was supplied by the patriarchal family so familiar in the pages of the Old Testament. In America the rancher with his force of cowboys, cooks, etc., formed a very similar self-supporting unit. We are accustomed to think of this stage as having been confined to the second half of the nineteenth century and the Great Plains region.

Like the other social stages, however, it has traveled across the continent. It existed wherever abundant pasture could be found, not yet divided into farms, and not too far from a market to permit the driving of the cattle to the place of slaughter. This stage was found prior to the Revolution in the Carolinas and Virginia, on the eastern slope of the Alleghenies.[1] It came over the

[1] John H. Logan, "History of the Upper Country of South Carolina," speaking of prerevolutionary times, says (pp. 151-152): "Not far from the log hut of the hunter stood that of the cow-driver. . . . The business of stock-raising at this time on the frontier was scarcely less profitable than it is at present (1859) in similar regions of the West. . . . Having selected a tract where cane and pea-vines grew most luxuriantly, they erected in the midst of it temporary cabins and spacious pens. These were used as inclosures in which to collect the cattle at proper seasons, for the purpose of counting and branding them; and from many such places in the upper country, vast numbers of beeves were annually driven to the distant markets of Charleston, Philadelphia, and even New York. . . . These rude establishments became afterwards, wherever they were formed, the great centers of settlements founded by the cultivators of the soil, who followed just behind the cow-drivers in their enterprising search for unappropriated productive lands."

mountains behind the hunters, trappers, and conquerors of the wilderness and flourished in the wild pea pastures along the Ohio. By 1830 this stage was reached on the prairies of Illinois; a decade later it had crossed the Mississippi, where it was to reach its final spectacular efflorescence on the Great Plains at the foot of the Rockies.

Following the ranch came the small farmer, permanent towns, manufacturing, and the general features of the small, competitive system. From here on to the present the course of evolution will be considered under other heads.

Within each of these stages, and more especially the latter, there have been minor divisions that have moved across the country within the general army at approximately the same rate of speed. Some of these divisions have never occupied certain sections. Changes in methods of transportation have fundamentally altered the whole order of progress of the army. Yet in spite of these deviations from the ideal simplicity that has been sketched, the mighty fact of these onward marching battalions of society is the dominant feature of American history, without a grasp of which that history is an almost unintelligible maze.

When we speak of the "frontier," therefore, it is necessary that we say which frontier is meant, for the advancing crest of each of these waves has been the frontier for that social stage. The word is most frequently applied to the stage in which the wilderness was cleared, the prairie sod broken, and the land made fit for agriculture. As it is used henceforth in this work, unless otherwise defined, it will be applied to that whole series of frontiers up to the time of the coming of small industries and competitive capitalism.

While the frontier existed, this was the only country in the world that for many generations permitted its inhabitants to choose in which of the historic stages of social evolution they would live. The competition-crushed, unemployed, or black-listed worker of capitalism moved west into the small, competitive stage with its greater opportunities for self-employment or for "rising." He could move onward geographically and backward historically to the semicommunistic stage of the first permanent settlers who would help him raise his log cabin and clear the ground for his first crop of corn. If he felt himself hemmed in by even the slight restrictions of this stage, he could shoulder his rifle and revert to the wilderness and savagery.

The frontier has been the great amalgamating force in American life. It took the European and in a single lifetime sent him through the racial evolution of a hundred generations. When he had finished, the few peculiar customs he had brought from a single country were gone, and he was that peculiarly twentieth century product, — the typical American. Only since the frontier has disappeared have great colonies grown up in which all the national peculiarities of those who compose them are accentuated by the internal resistance to the seemingly hostile territory about them.

Those individuals who are most commonly instanced as distinctively American are largely born of the frontier and have passed through its successive stages.

The frontier has given rise to the only race of hereditary rebels in history. One strange feature of this westward march has been the remarkable tendency of the same families to remain continuously in the same social stage, moving westward as the succeeding stage encroached upon the one they had chosen. The fathers of those who settled on the Great Plains and in the valleys of the Cordilleras lived in the states of the Mississippi Valley, and their grandparents conquered the forests in Ohio, Kentucky, and Tennessee, while the preceding generation had its home in western New York, Pennsylvania, or Virginia.

This pioneer race had large families, a high death-rate, but a far higher birthright. It has been pointed out that this applied the principle of natural selection in a most pitiless and effective manner.[1] It produced a race physically large and strong, mentally alert, and socially rebellious. It is a race willing to try social experiments. The man who within his own lifetime has seen the whole process of social evolution going on under his eyes is not a believer in the unchangeableness of social institutions.

These social stages have not existed side by side without friction. Each has desired to use the government to further its interests. In this conflict of interest is found an explanation of many political struggles. It was such a clash of interests that made itself felt in the fight over the constitution. It was a factor in the election of Jefferson. It appears again and again throughout American history.

In many respects the description of the frontier and its progress which has been given here applies only to the non-slaveholding states. While slavery existed it

[1] Doyle, "English Colonies in America," Vol. II, p. 56.

changed the method of westward advance in the South fundamentally. The struggle of these two methods of westward movement culminated in the Civil War, and it was the battle for the frontier that brought the slavery question to a climax.

These various general features of the frontier movement are brought together in this chapter, not in order to treat them in full, but in order to emphasize this highly significant phase of American history and make more comprehensible a whole series of questions which must appear in the consideration of that history.[1]

[1] F. J. Turner, "The Significance of the Frontier in American History," is by far the best discussion of this phase of American history. See also Semple, "American History and its Geographic Conditions," Chap. IV; and Gannet, "The Building of a Nation," p. 39 *et seq.*

CHAPTER XIII

THE BIRTH OF THE FACTORY SYSTEM

So far as battles, campaigns, glorious victories, great diplomacy, and other similar paraphernalia with which some historians are mainly concerned, the War of 1812 was insignificant. While jingos boast of "how we licked the Britishers," and it occupies much space in our school histories, yet in a wider and more accurate vision this war is seen to be but a small incident in the great world war in which Napoleon was the central figure. Among the many nicknames that have been applied to this conflict is "The War of Paradoxes." It was waged in defense of maritime interests, but the merchant states threatened to secede to stop it. The alleged cause of the war (the English "Orders in Council") was repealed before war was declared. The most important battle of the war (New Orleans) was fought after the treaty of peace had been signed, and the original subject of dispute (impressment of seamen) was never mentioned in the treaty of peace. Finally, the New England states that were so eager for peace were ruined by its coming, and the South that desired war found its prosperity in peace.

Although many generations of children have been taught that this war was a series of "glorious victories," respect for truth compels the statement that the United States was whipped in nearly every campaign, that the capitol was burned, the coast closely blockaded throughout the war, and in spite of all the stories of how "we humbled the mistress of the seas," the American navy was practically wiped out of existence.

The story of the origin of the war explains some of these contradictions. England was battling with Napoleon for the mastery of Europe and of the world. She was victorious on the seas, and was depending upon that commercial supremacy for resources with which to fight. In this titanic conflict both sides were determined that there should be no neutrals. They could not well make any other decision. The war was so much for commercial supremacy that to admit the existence of a neutral was to give that neutral control of the object for which the struggle was waged.

Napoleon had declared a blockade of England, and England had blockaded nearly all of Europe to ships that had not first cleared from a British port. Napoleon in turn had declared that all ships that did so clear were contraband of war. The result of these "Orders in Council" and "Berlin and Milan Decrees" was that English and French ships preyed upon the commerce of the United States. In spite of this fact, American commerce grew in a most startling manner, until a few New England states were carrying almost one third of the commerce of the world.

In her effort to secure sailors to man the gigantic navy required by the Napoleonic wars, England was in the habit of stopping merchant vessels of the United States and impressing such members of their crews as she desired, with the excuse that they were British deserters. To be sure a large percentage of the men so seized were deserters

THE BIRTH OF THE FACTORY SYSTEM

from the British navy. The great profits of American commerce enabled the shipowners to pay such wages that every British warship anchoring in American waters lost a good portion of its crew.

The plantation interests represented by Jefferson had little understanding or sympathy with the New England merchants. Jefferson was inclined to temporize and experiment. At first the New England merchants were belligerent in their talk and petitions to Congress, but they soon discovered that more money could be made running blockades than in a domestic war, and became the strongest opponents of all retaliatory measures.

The cotton planters, on the other hand, were anxious for war, or at least for some sort of reprisals directed against England.[1] They were selling their cotton to that country. The price was low, and the old antagonism between buyer and seller was being felt. This antagonism, however, was not sufficiently sharp to lead to war. It led rather to a series of peculiar legislative acts based upon the idea that a country could be punished by withholding commerce. The result of this attitude was the passage of the "Embargo" and the "Nonintercourse" acts.

These measures were based upon the idea that the trade of a country is a sort of isolated entity that can be withheld and granted or directed wherever and whenever such action is desired. By withholding the American trade Jefferson thought to punish England. The "Embargo" forbade American ships to leave their harbors save for coast trade. Since a large proportion of

[1] U. B. Phillips, "Georgia and State Rights," in Annual Report of American Historical Association, 1901, Vol. II, pp. 99–100.

American histories have been written by persons with New England prejudices, these histories nearly all declare the "Embargo" to have been a terrible failure. In truth it paralyzed many branches of British industry, sent the price of flour to $19 a barrel in England, caused great petitions to be sent to Parliament begging for relief, and, finally, actually accomplished the object for which it was laid, — secured the repeal of the "Orders in Council," even though the news of that repeal came too late to avert war.[1]

During the war the New England merchants carried their opposition to the farthest point possible without taking up actual hostilities against the national government. They advocated secession, refused to subscribe to the national loan, encouraged their militia to rebel against orders of the national government, sent large sums of specie to Canada for British drafts, supplied food to the British armies and ships, and in general did everything that would bring a profit and injure the national government.[2]

This war has also been called "The Second War for Independence." There is more than a little justice in the name. But that independence was not gained at Lundy's Lane, or New Orleans, by Perry on Lake Erie or by the victory of the *Constitution* over the *Guerrière*. That independence came through developments in a wholly different field. It was a result of the industrial transformation wrought by the war.

---

[1] McMaster, "History of the People of the United States," Vol. IV, pp. 1–2.

[2] Babcock, "Rise of American Nationality," pp. 156–158; Dewey, "Financial History of the United States," p. 133.

THE BIRTH OF THE FACTORY SYSTEM

The most important event of the period was the birth of a royal heir, the last of the long line of ruling classes that have dominated society since the appearance of private property. This last prince of the line of class rule was the machine-owning capitalist class. The United States census of 1900 is authority for the statement that "the factory system obtained its first foothold in the United States during the period of the Embargo and the War of 1812." To be sure, this same authority assures us that,

"The manufacture of cotton and wool passed rapidly from the household to the mill, but the methods of domestic and neighborhood industry continued to predominate, even in these industries down to, and including, the decade between 1820 and 1830; and it was not until about 1840 that the factory method of manufacture extended itself widely to miscellaneous industries, and began rapidly to force from the market the handmade commodities with which every community had hitherto supplied itself."

In spite of the fact that the factory industry had been struggling for a foothold since the beginning of the century, and that much boasting had been made of the extent to which manufacturing was carried on, the opening of the war saw the country in such a dependent condition that the Secretary of War begged that the Embargo be raised temporarily in order that the government might obtain the woolen blankets that were required in the Indian trade, since these could not be produced in the United States.

Any war tends artificially to stimulate manufactures. The purchase of large quantities of uniform articles favors the factory rather than the household producer. Government specifications frequently provided that the goods must be of American manufacture. With no foreign competition, a limited number of domestic producers, and production inadequate to demand, factories yielded several hundred per cent profit.

As had been the case in Europe, the mercantile capitalists had accumulated the capital for the establishment of the factory system. Woodrow Wilson notes that, "The very shipowners of the trading ports had in many instances sold their craft and put their capital into the manufacture of such things as were most immediately needed for the home market." [1]

Another law of historical evolution is illustrated in the way that the rising social class found expression in the social consciousness. Every effort was made to encourage manufactures. Societies were formed, premiums offered, bounties paid, tax exemptions granted, and every possible means for the fostering of manufactures was put into operation.

The most strenuous efforts were made to entice foreign artisans to America. All their effects were exempt from duty. Pennsylvania hastened to grant them especial privileges of citizenship. Many legislatures passed resolutions pledging their members to wear only home-made goods. To encourage the woolen industry, bounties were offered for the importation of merino sheep, and Pennsylvania taxed dogs to raise money with which to import rams of this famous breed.

---

[1] "History of the American People," Vol. III, p. 240; D. B. Warden, "An Account of the United States of America" (1819), pp. 262–263; Matthew Carey, "New Olive Branch," Chap. V.

Manufactures could not fail to flourish under such conditions. In the production of cotton there were 87 mills in 1811 operating 80,000 spindles and producing 2,880,000 pounds of yarn, with 4000 employees. By 1815 there were half a million spindles running, with 76,000 employees, working up 27,000,000 pounds of raw cotton. The iron industry developed to the point where it lacked but 3000 tons of supplying the whole country. It is worthy of note that it now began to center around Pittsburg. Earthenware, glass, cordage, and all manner of wooden ware manufactures shot up into prominence.

The number of patents rapidly increased. The first complete mill for the production of cotton cloth was set up by Francis C. Lowell at Waltham, Massachusetts, in 1815. Elkanah Cobb, of Vermont, invented a machine for weaving blankets that did the work of several men.

Soon the manufacturing capitalist began to develop even more clearly the outlines of a definite class consciousness. *Niles' Weekly Register*, the great organ of the manufacturers during the next forty years, was started in Baltimore, September, 1811. From the beginning it was an active defender of protective tariffs. In 1819 we hear it voicing the jealousy of the manufacturers and shipowners for the favor of the national government.

One of the memorials sent by the manufacturers to Congress at this time makes a suggestive complaint and explanation in these words:[1]—

"The fostering care bestowed on commerce — the various statutes enacted in its favor — the expense incurred for that purpose — the complete protection

[1] *Niles' Register*, July 17, 1819, p. 351.

it has experienced, form a most striking contrast with the situation of manufactures, and the sacrifice of those interested in them. . . . There is but one way to account for the care bestowed on the commercial and the neglect of the manufacturing interests. The former has at all times been well represented in Congress and the latter, never."

The period immediately succeeding the war came near to strangling the infant manufacturing industry in the cradle. As had been the case at the close of the Revolution, European and especially British manufacturers poured a flood of goods upon the American market. They could the more easily do this since the Napoleonic wars ended with the battle of Waterloo in 1815. But the whole fabric of American society was changing, and in that change the factory system was to find new strength and grow until it became the dominant factor in that society.

CHAPTER XIV

CHANGING INTERESTS

In the twenty years immediately following the War of 1812 forces were evolving, institutions arising and changing, centers of social gravity shifting, and deep basic movements of various sorts taking place that have had the most lasting effects upon the whole structure of American life.

It was essentially a time of realignment of interests, and of changes in social attitude.

America had hitherto looked eastward across the Atlantic. Sometimes it looked with anger, but always with interest, and its problems were entangled with those of the older continent. Public questions turned on points located, in part at least, beyond the national boundaries. The dominant economic activity, aside from agriculture, had been commerce, and commerce is always concerned with external affairs. The industrial, social, and political upheavals that had taken place in Europe during the early years of the American Republic were such as to attract attention. The French Revolution and the Napoleonic wars were dramas that compelled the attention of the world.

After the War of 1812 the American social mind became introspective. Henceforth it was not to be concerned primarily with treaties, commercial bounties, impressment, embargoes, and matters of the open sea and distant lands, but with turnpikes and canals, tariffs and manufactures, public lands, currency, banks, crises, poverty, state sovereignty, and chattel slavery.[1]

It was not alone that commerce was declining and manufactures growing. The people themselves were leaving the seaboard and setting their faces toward the West. The dribbling streams of immigrants that had been pressing through the clefts in the Alleghenies now became a mighty flood that poured over and around these barriers and swept down upon the Mississippi Valley. Between 1815 and 1820 western Pennsylvania, with Kentucky, Tennessee, and southern Ohio and Indiana, were filled with a hustling population.

During this period the people of the Ohio Valley reached the small farmer stage. Since each farm was a small household manufacturing establishment, and especially as the beginnings of the factory system were also apparent, this locality developed a protectionist sentiment. Its most pressing need, however, was for better transportation facilities. It is not surprising,

[1] Boston *Yankee*, Nov. 4, 1819: "The time appears to be fast approaching when an important change must take place in the situation of the people of this country. The unexampled success of American commerce during the late troubled state of Europe appears to have fairly intoxicated the population of this country. Every newspaper from N. Orleans to Maine was loud in advocating the commercial policy; but the tranquillity of Europe has wrought such a change in the commercial world that the Americans begin to see and feel that it is not on commerce alone they must depend. New evidence arises every day to prove that we cannot entirely be a commercial people. The prosperity of the U.S. is bottomed upon the success of agriculture and manufactures, which begin to excite interest in proportion to the decline of commerce." See also McMaster, "A Century of Social Service," *Atlantic Monthly*, Vol. LXXIX, p. 23; F. J. Turner, *Atlantic Monthly*, Jan., 1903, p. 84.

therefore, that Henry Clay, "the father of the American protective system" and the great champion of internal improvements, should have been sent to Congress from Kentucky during this period.

The South was also undergoing an industrial transformation. Here it was not the supplanting of one form of industry by another so much as the rise of a new crop that was working the change. The invention of the cotton gin had made the cultivation of upland cotton profitable, and as a consequence the competition of Western lands was ruining the agriculture of the seaboard. The "Virginia dynasty," composed of the Washingtons, Madisons, Jeffersons, Randolphs, and others, whose families came across the Atlantic at the time of the Commonwealth in England, were being impoverished, and losing their industrial power, were being relegated to the rear politically.

So complete was the industrial decline of Virginia that one observer declared that the larger plantations were nearly all plunging their owners deeper and deeper into debt. In 1830 John Randolph prophesied that the time was coming when the masters would run away from the slaves and be advertised for in the public papers.[1] It was during this period that Thomas Jefferson became so impoverished that public subscriptions were raised to relieve him and Congress purchased his library, a transaction from which sprung the present magnificent Congressional Library.[2]

It is not surprising that such an industrial condition should have given rise to considerable antislavery sen-

[1] Frederick J. Turner, "The Rise of the New West," p. 59.
[2] Thomas Watson, "Life and Times of Thomas Jefferson," p. 508.

timent in Virginia. This sentiment was of short duration. In another generation the upland cotton planters and the Louisiana sugar raisers were demanding slaves in such numbers that their production in Virginia became a profitable industry.

In New England, although the old fishing and mercantile rulers were passing off the stage, many of the same families succeeded to the line of power by investing their capital in the rapidly growing manufactures.

Until this period the merchants and the commercial interests, in alliance with the Southern planters, had controlled the national government. The manufacturers who were struggling for influence in that government were quick to point out the extent to which the nation had used its machinery for the benefit of commerce. Matthew Carey, the great spokesman of the manufacturing interests, places upon the title pages of his "Essays on Political Economy" a table comparing the treatment accorded to agriculture, commerce, and manufactures. In his "New Olive Branch" he points out that,

"The second act passed by the first Congress contained clauses which secured to the tonnage of our merchants a monopoly of the whole China trade — and gave them paramount advantages in all other foreign trade. . . .

"The same act gave our merchants an additional decisive advantage by allowing a discount of ten per cent on the duties upon goods imported in American vessels.

"The tonnage duty upon vessels belonging to American citizens was fixed at six cents a ton; on American-built vessels, owned wholly or in part by foreigners, thirty cents; and on all other foreign vessels, fifty cents.

"In order to exclude foreign vessels from the coasting trade they were subjected to a tonnage duty of fifty cents per ton for every voyage; whereas our vessels paid but six cents, and only once a year."

The methods by which these favors for the mercantile interest were secured are very clearly understood by Carey, and he instances them as an example that must be followed by the manufacturers if they are to have the use of the government to defend their interests.

"It is not difficult to account for this parental care," he tells us. "The mercantile interest was ably represented in the first Congress. It made a judicious selection of candidates, and carried the elections pretty generally in the seaport towns. . . . The representation in Congress was divided almost wholly between farmers, planters, and merchants. The manufacturing interest was, I believe, unrepresented; or, if it had a few representatives, they were not distinguished men, and had little or no influence. It shared the melancholy fate of all unrepresented bodies in all ages and all nations."

As fond parents are prone to predict brilliant futures for each new-born infant, so at the time of the birth of the factory system the most extravagant blessings were expected from its development. Even the columns of the Annals of Congress break into peans of promise, singing of the blessings to be brought with the new machinery. In a report submitted by Tench Coxe in 1814 he congratulates the workers of America on "the variety of ingenious mechanisms, processes, and devices, which, while they save labor, manifestly exempt them from the deleterious modes of the old manufacturing system." He proceeds in a strain that has a queer sound in the ears of those who have seen the effects actually produced by these machines: —

"Women, relieved in a considerable degree from their former employments as carders, weavers, and fullers by hand, occasionally turn to the occupation of the weaver, with improved machinery and instruments, which abridge and soften the labor, while the male weavers employ themselves in superintendence, instruction, superior or other operations, and promote their health by occasional attention to gardening, agriculture, and the clearing and improvement of their farms. . . . These wonderful machines, working as if they were animated beings, endowed with all the talents of their inventors, laboring with organs that never tire, and subject to no expense of food, or bed, or raiment, or dwelling, may be justly considered as an equivalent to an immense body of manufacturing recruits enlisted in the service of the country." [1]

Unfortunately for this idyllic picture the machines became instruments of private profit in the hands of a class of non-workers who soon became a power in the national government, while those who operated these instruments were doomed to exploitation, and, to paraphrase the words of Matthew Carey, quoted above, "shared the melancholy fate of all unrepresented bodies in all ages and all nations."

While the old ruling class in the South and in New England was being disrupted by the disintegration of its economic base, the new economic class of manufacturers was gaining political power and influence. By 1816 it was able to carry through Congress a tariff law

[1] Annals, 1814, Appendix, pp. 2601–2602.

with fairly strong protective features. This measure was carried by the votes of the Middle and Western states, with some help from the South. The commercial interests of New England, led by Daniel Webster, a newcomer in Congress, offered the strongest opposition. John C. Calhoun of South Carolina was a supporter of the tariff. Changing economic interests later reversed the positions of these two antagonists.

The South still hoped that it might become the seat of manufactures, or at least that it would find in New England cotton factories a better market than abroad; while the fear of foreign competition in the raising of cotton led Southern planters to desire a market in which they might hope to have at least a great advantage.[1]

Louisiana was beginning to produce sugar, and the interests of the producers of this crop led her representatives in Congress to join with the protectionists.

The decline of New England commercial and Southern tobacco interests was transferring the center of power to the Middle and Western states. Pennsylvania was now becoming the "Keystone state" in more than location. Although it had not yet obtained the domination in manufacturing that it was later to possess, it was advancing toward that position. Its most strikingly strategic position at this time was due to its possession of the principal gateway to the West. Hostile Indians still occupied northern Ohio and Indiana, and the great highway of the Hudson, Mohawk, and Genesee rivers was not being used.

---

[1] Edward Stanwood, "American Tariff Controversies in the Nineteenth Century," p. 106; C. K. Babcock, "The Rise of American Nationality," p. 160; *Niles' Register*, Vol. XXVI, p. 113.

158 SOCIAL FORCES IN AMERICAN HISTORY

The Ohio River was the main artery of trade and travel. Until after 1830 there was to be little settlement west of the Alleghenies that was not dependent upon this river. A map of population prior to that time shows few important settlements in that region bordering on the Great Lakes that is now almost dominant in national life. The principal cities of the West were Cincinnati, Marietta, Louisville, and St. Louis. This trans-Allegheny empire had grown to great importance in American life. Its trade was determining the growth of seaboard states and cities and the direction of future national development. Three cities on the Atlantic coast were contending for the control of the Western trade. These were Baltimore, Philadelphia, and New York. The weapons with which cities fight for trade are usually improved systems of transportation. At this time inland transportation was by canals and turnpikes. There was a perfect craze for the construction of these forms of trade highways.[1] New York was planning the Erie Canal. Baltimore had succeeded in inducing Congress to undertake the Cumberland Road, a great national highway to pass through Cumberland Gap, near Wheeling, West Virginia, and on into and across Ohio, Indiana, and Illinois.[2] Philadelphia was developing a system of internal canals with state help, to secure the advantage possessed by the fact that the principal gate for Western trade was already located at Pittsburg.

[1] For a description of the manner in which the War of 1812, with the Embargo and blockade, had compelled the development of inland transportation, and especially of trade by wagons, see McMaster, "History of the People of the United States," Vol. IV, pp. 218–221.

[2] I. L. Ringwalt, "Development of Transportation Systems in the United States," p. 21.

There was still another contestant for the trade of this Western territory. New Orleans, with all the advantage of a never ceasing river current flowing from the source of the trade past her doors, was the natural outlet for many of the products of this district. In 1811, by the launching of the first steamboat on Western waters at Pittsburg, the advantage of the current was largely lost, and the whole aspect of Western travel began to be transformed.[1]

One of the important sources of Western wealth during this period was the fur trade. The American Fur Company, controlled by John Jacob Astor, was chartered in 1808, and within a dozen years had become a power throughout the upper Mississippi Valley and even on the Pacific coast. The explorations of Lewis and Clark and Pike opened up rich fur territory, which was exploited until settlement invaded its sources a generation later.

Owing to the difficulties of transportation, there was no strong national feeling. It was not alone New England that threatened to secede. The Mississippi Valley was filled with intrigue and with separatist sentiment. The ties that bound the interests of this locality with the Atlantic coast were few and tenuous, and were only tightened when the national government used its power to protect Western interests through internal improvements and a protective tariff, and later when the railroad, steamship, and canal systems laid a firm basis for national unity.

[1] L. J. Bishop, "History of American Manufactures," Vol. II, p. 173; Timothy Flint, "Condensed Geography and History of the Western States," Vol. II, pp. 228–229.

CHAPTER XV

THE FIRST CRISIS — 1819

THE industrial boom created by the Embargo, the war, western land speculation, and the canal and turnpike enthusiasm, and fostered by the tariff of 1816 gave the infant capitalism severe internal pains, climaxing in the first crisis in 1819.

There were as many explanations of the cause of this crisis as of any of the subsequent ones. Senator Thomas H. Benton was positive that it was caused by the new United States Bank, that had been chartered in 1816.[1] Many others were sure it was caused by the tariff enacted in the same year. It was really but the American phase of an almost universal collapse of industry and finance following the readjustments attendant upon the close of the Napoleonic wars. Unfavorable weather in Europe had almost ruined the crops of 1816–1817 in England, France, and Italy, adding a catastrophe of nature to an industrial collapse.[2]

Within the United States the period immediately preceding the crisis had been one of feverish speculation.[3] Although there was still a vast quantity of

[1] Thomas H. Benton, "Thirty Years in the United States Senate," Introduction, pp. 5–6; William H. Gouge, "A Short History of Paper Money and Banking in the United States," pp. 33–35.

[2] H. De Gibbins, "Economic and Industrial Progress Century," in Nineteenth Century Series, Vol. XV, pp. 108–109.

[3] *Niles' Register*, June 12, 1819, p. 257.

THE FIRST CRISIS — 1819

"no-rent" land,[1] there had been a wild struggle to secure possession of western lands, with all the attendant phenomena of excessively high prices, fraudulent purchases and manipulation that became so familiar in later years.[2]

The new manufactures also offered a favorable ground for speculation. Joint stock companies, as corporations were still called, had been organized in great numbers, and their stock floated upon the first battalion of that immense army of "innocent purchasers" who have been absorbing similar issues ever since. These same trusting individuals were given an opportunity to absorb a large quantity of stock in canal and turnpike companies, many of which went bankrupt during the ensuing crisis.

The whole situation was greatly aggravated by a state of financial chaos. The charter of the first Bank of the United States, the one championed by Hamilton, had expired in 1811. At once a multitude of private and state banks sprung up. Frequently the principal asset of these banks consisted of a set of plates from which to print paper money. This money was loaned to

---

[1] Warden, "Statistical, Political, and Historical Account of the United States" (1819), Introduction, p. xliv: "Rent exists in a very limited degree in the United States. . . . Except in the immediate neighborhood of great towns, there is very little land let at lease in the United States, the price being so low that any person who has the capital necessary to enter upon the business of farming finds the purchase money of the land a very small addition to his outlay."

[2] C. F. Emerick, "The Credit System and the Public Domain," p. 6 *et seq.* "The year 1814 witnessed the beginning of a great increase in the sales of public lands. In that year 864,536 acres were sold, or 245,370 more than in any year since 1796. During the succeeding five years the sales assumed vast proportions, in 1819 reaching 5,475,648 acres. These figures were not surpassed until 1835." Flint, "Geography and History of Western States," pp. 348–350.

prospective purchasers of land, the bank being secured by a mortgage on the land.

Capitalism, scarcely in existence, could hardly be expected to evolve any effective system of banking. It fell back upon individual initiative, and turned over the function of printing money to whatever band of clever men might get together and secure the easily obtained sanction of some state government. The Constitution forbids any state to "emit bills of credit," but by some strange twisting of this phrase it was held that the states were free to confer this right upon individuals. It would be impossible to exaggerate the carnival of swindling that followed. Nearly every legislature was besieged with applicants for bank charters, and those best able to influence such legislation were granted practically unlimited power to print and circulate money.

Any sudden shock would tumble such a house of cards about the heads of its builders. The shock came when the second Bank of the United States sought to force the restoration of specie payments that had been suspended during the war. This second bank, unlike the first one, was owned largely outside of New England.[1] For the moment the Middle states, with their growing manufactures, and the Southern states, with a profitable cotton crop, were more prosperous, more directly interested in and favored by the national government, and therefore, more patriotic than the decaying commercial states of New England.

Once more a note should be made of the attitude of three men. John C. Calhoun of South Carolina opened

[1] McMaster, "History of the People of the United States," Vol. IV, pp. 313-314.

the debate in Congress in support of the bank. In this he was strongly assisted by Henry Clay of Kentucky, then Speaker of the House of Representatives. The great opponent of the bill was Daniel Webster of Massachusetts.[1] Each of these men reflected a sectional economic interest in this position. As those interests changed, the beliefs and political principles of these men veered to suit the changing wind.

The earliest beginnings of this bank, that was to be such an important factor in the financial, industrial, and political life of this country, were tainted with fraud. The provisions for a paid-in capital, which had been a part of the law creating it, were evaded. The first subscribers were allowed to borrow money upon their stock with which to purchase more stock, and so on until a most unsteady pyramid was built with no genuine assets at bottom.[2] The operations of the bank were then manipulated to the benefit of the board of directors and stockholders. Among the latter, it was alleged by Niles, who was by no means an enemy of the bank, were forty members of Congress.[3]

The scandals were so great that a Congressional committee was appointed to investigate the bank, and when this committee reported, January 16, 1819, the bank stock fell from near 140 (at which point it had been accepted as collateral for loans up to almost its full market value) to 93.[4] Yet the report was largely a whitewash, and its main effect was to frighten the president of the bank into fleeing from the country. Three

[1] McMaster, *loc cit.*, Vol. IV, pp. 310–311.
[2] Wm. H. Gouge, "History of Paper Money and Banking," p. 27.
[3] *Niles' Register*, Feb. 27, 1819.   [4] Gouge, *loc. cit.*, p. 30.

years later a report was forced from the institution that showed that it was absolutely bankrupt at the time of the Congressional investigation, and that it had been guilty of nearly all the acts of crooked finance that such a still unsophisticated age knew.[1]

Immediately after the Congressional investigation and the flight of the president, a new administration realized that only the most drastic steps would save the institution from actually going through bankruptcy proceedings, with the probable criminal prosecution of its officials. There was an immediate restriction of credits, a sudden demand for collections, and an insistence upon specie payments from other banks.

When the Bank of the United States refused to accept the notes of the insolvent state banks, the latter promptly failed, their securities fell into the hands of the national institution, and the tens of thousands of debtors who had borrowed this money for land speculation and other purposes had their property taken away by foreclosure of mortgages.[2]

At once a great "Populistic" movement swept over Kentucky, Illinois, Tennessee, Indiana, and Ohio. The legislature of Kentucky established a state bank, with little more than wind for assets, and declared war upon the Bank of the United States. Maryland, Tennessee, Georgia, North Carolina, Kentucky, and Ohio, all endeavored to tax the branches of the Bank of the United States. But John Marshall was Chief Justice of the Supreme Court, and in the famous case of McCullough *vs.* Maryland the right of the state to tax the

[1] Gouge, *loc. cit.*, p. 31.
[2] F. J. Turner, "Rise of the New West," pp. 126–127.

bank was denied. But the frontier cared little for Supreme Court decisions, and Ohio proceeded to flaunt the decision and to collect the tax by force of arms, while Kentucky withdrew the protection of state laws from the branches located in that state.[1]

The revolt of the West was not surprising. The bank had obtained possession through mortgages of vast tracts of land, both urban and rural. The suffering everywhere was intense.

Thomas H. Benton introduces his "Thirty Years' View" with this striking description of the situation in 1820: —

"The years 1819 and 1820 were a period of gloom and agony. No money, either gold or silver: no paper convertible into specie: no measure or standard of value left remaining. The local banks (all but those of New England), after a brief resumption of specie payments, again sank into a state of suspension. The Bank of the United States, created as a remedy for all these evils, now at the head of the evil, prostrate and helpless, with no power left but that of suing its debtors, and selling their property, and purchasing it for itself at its own nominal price. No price for property or produce. No sales but those of the sheriff or marshal. No purchasers at the execution sales but the creditor or some hoarder of money. No employment for industry — no demand for labor — no sale for the produce of the farm — no sound of the hammer but that of the auctioneer knocking down property. Stop laws — property

[1] Frederick J. Turner, "The Rise of the New West," pp. 136–140, 300; J. B. McMaster, "History of the People of the United States," Vol. IV, pp. 484–510; Horace White, "Money and Banking," p. 285.

laws — replevin laws — stay laws — loan office laws — the intervention of the legislator between the creditor and debtor: this was the business of legislation in three-fourths of the states of the Union — of all South and West of New England. No medium of exchange but depreciated paper: no change even, but little bits of foul paper, marked so many cents and signed by some tradesman, barber, or inn-keeper: exchanges deranged to the extent of fifty or one hundred per cent. DISTRESS the universal cry of the people: RELIEF the universal demand thundered at the doors of all legislatures, State or Federal."[1]

This process of wholesale exploitation by the bank was one of the steps by which the capital necessary to the establishment of the factory system was gathered from the multitude of small producers and brought together in the large sums needed for the introduction of this new industrial stage.

In August, 1819, *Niles' Register* said, "There are 20,000 persons daily seeking work in Philadelphia — in New York 10,000 able-bodied men are said to be wandering the streets looking for it, and if we add to them the women who desire something to do, the amount cannot be less than 20,000 — in Baltimore there may be about 10,000 persons in unsteady employment, or actually suffering because they cannot get into business."

This panic seems to have marked the beginning of regular relief by charitable bodies. There had been plenty of misery before, but the whole population had been so closely knit together that charitable societies

[1] Thomas H. Benton, "Thirty Years in the United States Senate," p. 5.

were seldom needed. In 1815 Henry Niles, the editor and publisher of *Niles' Register*, estimated that there was one pauper for every 250 persons. He also states that no provision was made for any save for those who were disabled physically, except during a short time in the winter.[1] During the winter of 1819–1820 souphouses were established in several of the larger cities. A little later a committee was appointed to investigate the public charities of Philadelphia, and its report reveals a mass of misery among the workers that foretells the city slum of to-day.

While the national government was being used to collect the last farthing from the little farmers and half starving wageworkers, the same forces that were utilizing that government for debt-collecting purposes were developing a bankruptcy code that should free the merchant, banker, manufacturer, and planter from such of his debts as he was unable to pay. The governors of Louisiana and Rhode Island urged the enactment of bankruptcy legislation in their annual messages in 1816. Several states already had enacted such laws, although the national government had repealed the one enacted in 1800, after an existence of only three years. These laws were quickly taken advantage of, and Niles in 1819 remarks that "Twenty or thirty years ago if a man failed for $100,000, people talked about it as something marvelous. But now," he adds, "it is not considered decent for a man to break for less than $100,000, and if a person would be thought a *respectable bankrupt*, he ought to owe two or three hundred thousand more."

A New York judge before whom some of these bank-

[1] *Niles' Register*, IX, p. 232.

ruptcy cases were brought expressed himself as horrified that people "from the class of society" that composed the bankrupts could commit such crimes. He added that he had "witnessed displays of depravity on the part of the agents of moneyed institutions of the most appalling character."[1]

The pressure of the panic created criminals at both ends of the social scale. A "Bank Director," writing to the *London Courier* for May 11, 1820, states that: "Mail robberies and piracies are quite the order of the day. Two men were hung at Baltimore a few months ago for robbing the mail: two more will experience the same fate in a few days at the same place for the same crime. Two men are to be hung there a week hence for piracy, and five others are under sentence of death."[2]

The reorganization following the panic accelerated the industrial tendencies and social readjustments already noted. By 1828 manufacturing had so dominated over commerce in Massachusetts that Webster announced that since the interests of his constituents had become bound up with protection, he had changed his mind and would now support the tariff.

The whole set of social institutions changed to adjust themselves to this new industrial base. The old Federalist party died out in New England, once its stronghold.[3] The religious reflex of the decline of commerce and the rise of manufactures was so like the religious movement that accompanied the rise of capitalism in Europe that it has been designated as "The New England Reforma-

---

[1] Gouge, *loc. cit.*, p. 51. [2] *Ibid.*, p. 36.
[3] Turner, "Rise of the New West," pp. 16–20; Ostrogorski, "Democracy and the Organization of Political Parties," Vol. I, pp. 26–27.

tion." The orthodox clergy that had so long actively participated in the rulership of society were disturbed by the rise of new sects. In the very stronghold of Puritanism, the old orthodoxy was attacked and overthrown by the most liberal of creeds, — Unitarianism. The Congregational clergy, long a part of the ruling hierarchy, was split into warring sects. William E. Channing wrote his famous letter in defense of Unitarianism to the Rev. Samuel Thatcher in 1815. By the time the lines were clearly drawn it was discovered that the new religious forces had captured Harvard College. There was also a division of a similar character in the ranks of the Quakers, and numerous peculiar and separatist sects rose throughout the West.[1]

A national and independent industrial life could not but have its expression in the beginning of a national literature. Washington Irving, really the first American author of any importance, wrote his "Knickerbocker's History of New York" in 1809, and his next, and much more important work, the "Sketch Book," in 1819. Emerson was graduated from Harvard in 1821, the same year that James Fenimore Cooper published "The Spy." The *North American Review* was founded in 1815, and published "Thanatopsis," by William Cullen Bryant, the next year.[2]

[1] W. B. Cairns, "The Development of American Literature from 1815 to 1833," Bulletin of the University of Wisconsin, pp. 8–9.
[2] *Ibid.*, p. 25.

CHAPTER XVI

CONDITION OF THE WORKERS IN THE CHILDHOOD OF CAPITALISM

Social evolution in America has always moved with accelerated speed, and frequently with syncopated measure as compared with its typical form in western Europe. These features were especially noticeable in the introduction of the factory system. In England the progress of industry was from the "household" stage, in which each family produced for its own consumption, to the "domestic" stage, where the family was still the productive unit and the home the only factory, but where production was for the market.

The "domestic" stage was never general in the United States. The transition was almost direct from the "household" to the factory system.

In still another direction American development displays its accelerated tempo. In the first stage of the factory system in the English cotton trade, only the spinning was done by machinery. Weaving was still done in the homes, even at the time the factory system was gaining a foothold in the United States. This transitional stage, combining the old and the new, never existed here. The first establishment in the world to apply the factory system to the entire process of manufacturing cotton cloth, and to perform all the processes by machinery under one roof, was the factory erected by Francis C. Lowell at Waltham, Massachusetts, in 1815.[1]

There was a lack of hampering tradition in the working out of the factory system on this side the Atlantic. Steam power was early made use of, although the influence of water power in locating the early cotton factories in New England should not be overlooked. Improvements in the application of steam began to be made by American inventors about this time, indicating that industry in this country was henceforth to have an independent evolution.[2]

From the very beginning of the factory system in America, it was based upon the existence of a body of propertyless wageworkers. By 1820 there was a large

[1] C. D. Wright, "Industrial Evolution in the United States," p. 131.

[2] In 1816, Oliver Evans appeals to Congress for an extension of his patents on steam engines, and makes this remarkable and prophetic plea: "What will the annual amount of the benefits be when my Columbian engines shall be applied to work many thousands of mills, manufactories, carriages on railways or smooth roads, boats on the great Atlantic and Western waters, raising the value of western lands 50 per cent, by lessening the time of going to market, tantamount to shortening the distance: can any one calculate within one million of dollars?" A writer in *Niles' Register* for the same year (p. 219), commenting on an engine by David Heath, Jr., of New Jersey says: "An engine of four horse power, charged with fuel, may be comprised in the space appointed to the baggage of a stage, and may be lifted on and off the carriage with greatest ease; which carriage he can drive by experiment at the rate of fifteen miles an hour on the bare road, without the use of railways, being regulated to ascend and descend hills with uniform velocity and the greatest safety." On the same page with this remarkable description is to be found an item telling of a marvelous rotary engine said to be "in operation in Messrs. A. & N. Brown's saw-mill, at Manhattan Island." The large number of such items appearing at this time in a single periodical is indicative of the great interest in mechanical progress and the inventive activity of the country.

class of wage laborers employed in weaving, shipbuilding, shoemaking, iron and steel making, printing, rope and sail manufacturing, the building trades, and the construction of turnpikes and canals.

The misery of early English factory workers has become the classic illustration of vicarious suffering in the cause of social evolution. The similar sufferings of American workers at the same stage are less familiar. In both countries the cradle and the home were robbed to secure victims for the natal sacrifice of newborn capitalism.

A member from New York expressed his gratification upon the floor of Congress in 1816 that "Arkwright's machinery has produced a revolution in the manufacture of cotton; the invention is so excellent, the effect in saving labor so immense, that five or six men are sufficient for the management of a factory of 2000 spindles, spinning 100,000 pounds of twist yarn yearly; the other hands are mere children, whose labor is of little use in any other branch of industry." [1]

A Congressional committee in the same year estimated that of the 100,000 persons then employed in the cloth industry, only 10,000 were men, while 66,000 were "women and female children," and 23,000 were boys. Matthew Carey waxes enthusiastic over the opportunities the factory owners offered to young girls. Of one neighborhood he tells us that the girls were "before the establishment of the factory in a state of idleness, barefooted and living in wretched hovels. But since that period they are comfortably fed and clothed — their habits and manners and dwellings greatly improved —

[1] Benton's "Abridgements of the Debates of Congress," Vol. V, p. 638.

CONDITION OF THE WORKERS

and they have become useful members of society. . . . Judging from the state of other establishments, it is fair to presume that more than half of the whole number were probably young females who, but for the factory, would have been without employment, and spending their time perniciously — a burden to their parents and society — trained up to vicious courses — but thus happily preserved from idleness and its attendant vices and crimes — and whose wages probably average $1.50 a week."[1]

A committee that investigated the manufactures of Philadelphia prepared a table showing the wages paid for various classes of work. These varied from $11.54 a week for the highest paid workers, who were engaged in making iron castings, to those who received but $2.70 a week for paper hanging and the making of playing cards.[2]

There is perhaps no better summary of the general conditions of the workers of this period than that given by Matthew Carey in his essay on "The Public Charities of Philadelphia," in which he says: —

"Thousands of our laboring people travel hundreds of miles in quest of employment on canals at $62\frac{1}{2}$, 75, and $87\frac{1}{2}$ cents per day, paying $1.50 to $2 a week for board, leaving families behind, depending upon them for support. They labor frequently in marshy grounds, where they inhale pestiferous miasmata, which destroy their health, often irrecoverably. They return to their poor families broken-hearted, and with ruined constitu-

[1] Matthew Carey, "Essays on Political Economy," Address to the Farmers of the United States, pp. 458–459.
[2] *Niles' Register*, Oct. 23, 1819, p. 117.

tions, with a sorry pittance, most laboriously earned, and take to their beds sick and unable to work. Hundreds are swept off annually, many of them leaving numerous and helpless families. Notwithstanding their wretched fate, their places are quickly supplied by others, although death stares them in the face. Hundreds are most laboriously employed on turnpikes, working from morning to night at from half a dollar to three-quarters a day, exposed to the broiling sun in summer, and all the inclemency of our severe winters. There is always a redundancy of wood-pilers in our cities, whose wages are so low that their utmost efforts do not enable them to earn more than thirty-five to fifty cents per day. . . . Finally, there is no employment whatever, how disagreeable or loathsome or deleterious soever it may be, or however reduced the wages, that does not find persons willing to follow it rather than beg or steal."

As is always the case, the minimum of wages was accompanied by the maximum of hours. From the regulations of a Paterson, New Jersey, mill we learn that their rules required "the women and children to be at their work at half-past four in the morning. They are allowed half an hour for breakfast and three-quarters of an hour for dinner, and then work as long as they can see." [1]

The spokesmen of the ruling class at this time were

[1] Seth Luther, "Address to the Workingmen of New England" (1836), pp. 42–43. Further information on the condition of labor at this time will be found in McMaster, "A Century of Social Betterment," in the *Atlantic Monthly*, Vol. LXXIX, p. 22; "History of the People of the United States," Vol. V, p. 121; Michael Chevalier, "The United States," pp. 137–144; *Niles' Register*, May 8, 1819, Oct. 5, 1816, Dec. 2, 1815.

CONDITION OF THE WORKERS 175

continually complaining that wages were "too high." The defenders of a protective tariff insisted that manufactures could not exist with such high wages without protection. The opponents of the tariff declared that these unreasonably high wages would always make manufacturing impossible, and that their existence was an insuperable obstacle to factories. Both sides agreed that wages were too high. President Monroe, in one of his annual messages, congratulated the manufacturers on the "fall in the price of labor, apparently so favorable to the success of domestic manufactures."

Perhaps public officials would not have been so frank to approve of low wages had the working class not been politically helpless. There was some sort of property qualification for voting in every state, and a still higher test for office holding. The governor of Massachusetts was required to be "a Christian worth £1000," while he who would aspire to the governorship of Georgia must be the possessor of 500 acres of land and £4000.

Indirect voting was the rule. Governors were commonly elected by the legislatures. Presidential candidates were selected by Congressional caucuses, composed of the members of Congress of each political party. The presidential electors were then chosen by the legislatures, and a property qualification was generally required of voters for members of the legislatures.

There was a nominal, universal, compulsory military service, with a farcical "training day" when every able-bodied man was required to report for drill under the direction of a petty popinjay with shoulder straps.

There is much complaint of class legislation and administration of justice to-day, but we have traveled a long way from the state of things in the early twenties. The laborer had no lien upon his product, and, in consequence, was frequently defrauded of his meager wages. On the other hand, he could be robbed of his utmost farthing by a creditor, as the principle of exemption of a certain minimum of wages and property from seizure for debts had not yet been established.

It was not alone that the debtor with too little property to secure the benefit of the newly enacted bankruptcy law could be stripped of every possession. If these failed to satisfy the debt, his person could be seized. The laborer who was thus unable either to discharge his debt or to secure relief through bankruptcy was subject to imprisonment. No matter how small the sum, he was sentenced to remain in jail until the debt was paid. Since the imprisonment effectually prevented the earning of any money with which to meet his obligations, it was no very infrequent thing for a man to be imprisoned for years or even for life because of a debt of a few shillings. Once in jail, the state made no provision for his food, clothing, or fuel.

The report of the Prison Discipline Society for 1829 estimated that more than 75,000 were imprisoned for debt annually in the United States, and that of these more than one half owed less than twenty dollars. Owing to the lack of any public provision for the most essential needs, the debtors' prisons became veritable chambers of horrors. There was no distinction made as to sex, age, or character. All were driven together into a common room. Even as far north as New York there was not always a shelter from the elements. With what appears to us now as grim irony, charitable societies were formed, not to abolish imprisonment for debt, or to pay the debts and secure the liberty of the victims, but to furnish sufficient food, clothing, and fuel to prolong the agony of the suffering prisoners.

The educational facilities of the United States were at their very lowest ebb in the years from 1814 to 1828.[1] The old social order had lost its strength. The new one had not had the time to develop an educational expression. The most efficient schools were the private academies of New England. The public schools, the only ones accessible to the wageworkers, were less efficient than at any period before or since. The management of the schools had been subdivided in response to the individualistic, competitive, separatist spirit of early capitalism until the little school districts were almost autonomous.[2] Religious education had declined with the overthrow of the theocracy, and the multitude of seceding sects had not yet built up educational institutions. Massachusetts, then, as throughout American history, at the head in educational matters, was expending but $2.75 per pupil annually in education. She spends more than ten times as much to-day, and the poorest equipped Southern state, where educational facilities are least, does more than did the Old Bay State at the close of the first quarter of the last century.[3]

The great outlet for such of the workers as were crushed beyond endurance as wage earners was the pioneer life in the Ohio Valley. Without the existence

---

[1] Edwin G. Dexter, "History of Education in the United States," pp. 97–98; Frank T. Carlton, "Economic Influences upon Educational Progress in the United States," Bulletin Univ. of Wisconsin, pp. 22–28.

[2] Carlton, *loc. cit.*, p. 20.   [3] Dexter, *loc. cit.*, p. 98.

of this "free land," the condition of labor would have been far worse. This fact was noted by all European observers. Michael Chevalier, who was sent to this country in 1834 by Thiers, then Minister of the Interior of France, makes this comparison between America and Europe:[1] —

"While the Americans have the vast domain of the West, a common fund from which, by industry, each may draw for himself and by himself an ample heritage, an extreme fall of wages is not to be apprehended. . . . In Europe a coalition of workmen can only signify one of these two things: raise our wages or we shall die of hunger with our wives and children, which is an absurdity; or raise our wages, if you do not, we shall take up arms, which is civil war. In Europe there is no other possible construction to be placed upon it. But in America, on the contrary, such a coalition means, raise our wages or we go to the West."

Out of this West a democratic breeze was blowing, that was to grow into a small storm before the end of the thirties. The equality of the pioneer struggle against the wilderness was finding expression in political democracy. The new states were coming into the Union on a basis of universal manhood suffrage. But not all of the workers who felt the goad of oppression were being driven to the West. Some were inclined to turn and fight that oppression. That fight was to introduce a new force into those that formulate American institutions. It was to give rise to the first real American labor movement.

[1] Michael Chevalier, "The United States," p. 144.

CHAPTER XVII

THE FIRST LABOR MOVEMENT — 1824-1836

THE introduction of even the beginnings of the factory system, displacing craftsmen and tools by the wage-worker and the machine, and the consequent gathering of large bodies of workers dealing with a single employer — in short, the rise of an exploited proletariat — was certain to create organized resistance to exploitation by that proletariat. There had been loose associations of workingmen for many years who sometimes "walked out" to secure better conditions. Such a "walk-out" had taken place among journeymen bakers in New York in 1741. It was not until 1825, however, that labor unions were generally established throughout the northeastern portion of the United States. By 1833 we find the following trades participating in a parade organized by the "Central Trade Union" of New York City: "Typographical Union, Journeymen House Carpenters, Book Binders, Leather Dressers, Coopers, Carvers and Gilders, Bakers, Cabinet Makers, Cordwainers (men), Cordwainers (women), Tailors, Silk Hatters, Stone Cutters, Tin-Plate and Sheet Iron Workers, Type Founders, Hat Finishers, Willow-Basket Makers, Chair Makers and Gilders, Sail Makers, and Block and Pump Makers."

Sixteen unions joined to found the "General Trade Union" of Boston in 1834. In this same year a writer in *The Workingman's Advocate* of New York estimated the number of members in the labor unions of New York, Brooklyn, Boston, Baltimore, Washington, and Newark at 26,250, an exceedingly high proportion of the number of wage-earners in those cities.

The first trade union journal in the world was the *Mechanics' Free Press*, published in Philadelphia from 1828 to 1831, antedating by two years any similar English periodical. There is also a dispute as to whether the first genuine trade union existed in this country or in England.[1] It is certain that the movement under discussion was taking place at the same time as the first important union movement in Great Britain, and that it is impossible for either country to claim either the blame or the credit for having originated this inevitable spontaneous resistance of Labor.

Between seventy-five and one hundred periodicals devoted to Labor appeared in the northeastern states about this time, a number scarcely exceeded in the same territory three quarters of a century later. Two daily papers, *The Man* and *The Daily Sentinel*, were maintained during a part of this period to present the cause of the workers. Considering the restricted numbers of the wageworkers, the undeveloped stage of printing and paper manufacture, and consequent difficulties in the road of periodical publication, this record is seen to be little short of marvelous.

These unions had benefit funds for the sick and out of work and those on strike. They had their union scales, and conducted strikes and declared boycotts to maintain them, and signed contracts with the employers when

[1] "Documentary History of American Industrial Society," Vol. V, pp. 21-22.

victorious. They had their pickets who were accused of "slugging scabs"; and in some cases at least the "union shop" was demanded and secured. Wages were increased in many trades, and the condition of Labor was bettered in many ways. Their most general demand on the economic field was for the ten-hour day, to secure which many strikes were conducted. They succeeded in securing this standard in a large number of trades; and finally, as a result of their agitation, President Van Buren announced the introduction of the ten-hour day in all government work.

Every economic movement has some sort of a political expression. This early labor movement was no exception. Workingmen's tickets were placed in nomination in New York, Rochester, Philadelphia, and several smaller cities, and a number of minor offices were captured. Legislative nominations were made in New York and Pennsylvania. In the former state Ebenezer Ford was elected to the Assembly upon the Workingman's ticket in 1829, polling a vote of 6166.

It is when we study the programs, platforms, and principles of this early labor movement and its political expression that its real importance as a factor in the evolution of American society appears. The things for which it fought, and many of which it secured directly, are just the features of our society of which Americans are most inclined to boast.

The one dominant feature of every section of this labor movement was the almost fanatical insistence upon the paramount importance of education. In political platforms, in resolutions of public meetings, and in the labor press the statement is repeated over and over, that the fundamental demand of Labor is for an adequate system of education.

A workingmen's meeting held in New York, March 20, 1830, adopted this resolution: —

"Resolved, that next to life and liberty we consider education the greatest blessing bestowed upon mankind.

"Resolved, that the public funds should be appropriated to the purpose of education, upon a regular system, that shall ensure the opportunity to every individual of obtaining a competent education before he shall have arrived at the age of maturity."[1]

A writer in the *Mechanics' Free Press* of Philadelphia, August 12, 1829, in reply to the question, "What do the workingmen expect? what do they wish?" said: "I have attended their late meetings in the city generally, and obtained the sentiments of a number of such as take an active part in their business, and find the great and primary object to be, a general system of education on an independent principle." The Pennsylvania system of education was particularly pernicious. It provided free schools only for those who were willing to declare themselves paupers. The rich sent their children to private institutions. There was no provision whatever for the children of those who were neither paupers nor wealthy.[2]

Again and again this cry for education is reiterated.[3] Nor were the workers content with merely protesting and

[1] *Free Enquirer*, Mar. 20, 1830.

[2] McMaster, "History of the People of the United States," Vol. V, pp. 360–362.

[3] *Free Enquirer*, Feb. 4, 1829; Aug. 12, 1829; Sept. 30, 1829; *Farmers', Mechanics' and Workingmen's Advocate*, Apr. 3, 1830; *Mechanics' Free Press*, Sept. 19, 1829.

resoluting. They were far in advance of their age in their knowledge of educational methods. One of the most remarkable documents of this time is a report prepared by a committee of Philadelphia workingmen who were appointed to study the educational situation.[1] This report is not only an extremely keen and scholarly criticism of the existing system, but outlines a scheme of education, embracing kindergartens, and a combination of manual training with education. They support their arguments for such a system by illustrations drawn from similar educational establishments in Switzerland, France, Prussia, and Great Britain.

There were undoubtedly other influences making for education at this time. The factory system requires a certain amount of trained intelligence for its operatives, and has always been accompanied by some form of popular education. Yet when this period is examined in detail there is no other single force making for education that can be compared with the working-class movement, and there is no escape from the conclusion that to this movement, more than to any other single cause, if not more than to all other causes combined, is due the common school system of the United States.

In all directions this movement was laying the foundation of democratic institutions. The far-sightedness and comprehensively progressive character of its program is remarkable. The chairman of a convention of workingmen held in Boston in 1833 gives the following summary of the measures advocated: —

"The operatives and producers are generally agreed that the abolition of all licensed monopolies and im-

[1] Published in *The Workingman's Advocate*, Mar. 6, 1830.

prisonment for debt, a revision of our present militia and law systems, equal taxation of property, an effective lien law, a district system of elections, the number of legislators reduced to the proportion of territory and population, a transfer of a greater part of the appointing power from the executive to the people, the credit and banking systems, mortgages, salaries, rotation in office, small districts for the recording of land titles, and the settlement of estates, the third article, the poll-tax, and, above all, an universal and useful education, afford subjects for their vigilant enquiry and severe investigation."

Measured by success in the attainment of its objects, this first American labor movement has but few equals in the history of the world. A study of the list of the things for which it worked is a study of the establishment of what is best in present society.[1] The platforms of the

[1] The platform upon which Ebenezer Ford was elected to the New York legislature read as follows:—

"Resolved, In the opinion of this meeting, the first appropriation of the soil of this state to private and exclusive possession was eminently and barbarously unjust.

"Resolved, That it was substantially feudal in its character, inasmuch as those who received enormous and unequal possessions were lords, and those who received little or nothing, were vassals.

"Resolved, That hereditary transmission of wealth on the one hand, and poverty on the other, has brought down to the present generation all the evils of the feudal system, — and this, in our opinion, is the prime cause of all our calamities.

"Resolved, In this view of the matter, the greatest knaves, impostors and paupers of the age are our bankers, who swear they have promised to pay their creditors thirty or thirty-five millions of dollars on demand, at the same time that they have, as they also swear, only three or four millions to do it with.

"Resolved, That more than one hundred broken banks within a few years past admonish the community to destroy banks altogether.

"Resolved, That exemption is a privilege; and as such the exemption

labor parties of this time are new Declarations of Independence, throwing off old shackles and drafting the lines

from taxation of churches and church property, and the property of priests to an amount not exceeding $1500 is a direct and positive robbery of the people."

A far more typical platform than this is the one submitted by a committee of fifty to a great workingmen's meeting held in Military Hall, New York, Dec. 29, 1829, and reported in the *Free Enquirer* for March 20, 1830. The following extracts are taken from this report:—

"We take the opportunity solemnly to aver . . . that we have no desire or intention of disturbing the rights of property in individuals or the public. . . .

"One principle that we contend for is the abolition of imprisonment for debt. . . .

"Resolved that we explicitly disavow all intention to intermeddle with rights of individuals either as to property or religion. . . .

"Resolved that we are in favor of searching laws for the detection of concealed or fraudulently conveyed property; and emphatically in favor of the entire abolition of imprisonment for debt.

. . . .

"Resolved that next to life and liberty, we consider education the greatest blessing bestowed upon mankind.

. . . .

"Resolved that our sentiments in relation to a well constructed lien law, which would secure to thousands of our fellow citizens that just recompense their services entitle them to, and prevent innumerable frauds on the producing classes, are well known to our representatives, and that we expect their efficient support for this measure.

"Resolved that our present militia system is highly oppressive to the producing classes of the community, without any beneficial result to individuals or the state.

"Resolved that the present auction system, which operates as a means of oppressing the producing classes, by introducing quantities of the products and labor of foreign countries, which otherwise would be furnished by our own mechanics, is fraught with alarming evils, and should be immediately restricted.

. . . .

"Resolved that the credit system on duties at our custom house, which furnishes the auctioneers and foreign importers with an additional capital of $15,000,000 at all times in this city, the greater part of which

along which progress was to be made for the next generation and more. There was little that was fantastic in their program. There was little of the populistic reaction that has so generally characterized the pioneers in their attacks upon a creditor class.

When the movement died out in 1835 to 1837, the face of society had been largely transformed. Imprisonment for debt was no more. A mechanics' lien law was in existence in nearly every state in the Union, and the principle that the producer has the first claim upon his product had become a fundamental principle in American jurisprudence. The credit system, as applied to the tariff, which, as was pointed out by the laborers,

is drawn from the producing classes, they being the consumers, is an evil of immense magnitude, and demands our immediate attention.

"Resolved that the banks under the administration of their present directors and officers, and by the concert of auctioneers and foreigners, aided by custom house credits, form a monopoly that is hostile to the equal rights of the American merchant, manufacturer, mechanic, and laboring-man; and that the renewal by the legislature of the charters prayed for will confirm and perpetuate an aristocracy which eventually may shake the foundations of our liberties and entail slavery upon our posterity.

"Resolved that our courts of justice should be so reformed that the producing classes may be placed upon an equality with the wealthy.

"Resolved that the present laws that compel the attendance of jurors and witnesses for days and weeks at our courts, without a fair compensation, are unjust, and require immediate attention.

. . . .

"Resolved, that with many of our past and present rulers the great qualification to obtain office is an ability, supposed or real, to render them or their party some political service.

"Resolved that there should be no intermediate body of men between the electors and the candidates. . . .

"Resolved that the State of New York ought to be divided into as many districts as there are members of the Assembly to represent it."

THE FIRST LABOR MOVEMENT — 1824-1836

granted immense loans to a few favored shippers, and was the means of building up some of the greatest fortunes in America,[1] was abolished. Horace Mann was leading the "educational revival," and the common school was an established institution in nearly every state.[2] The grotesque militia system had been abolished. Important reforms in land tenure were under way in New York State that were to wipe out the last of the feudal privileges of the land barons. The war upon the Bank had been taken up by Jackson and his frontier followers, and the present subtreasury system was being prepared to take its place. Payment for jurors and witnesses had become a part of American court practice, and other important reforms tending to democratize the courts had taken place. The first blow had been struck at the spoils system in office, and while little effect was produced at this time, because of the presence of forces that will be discussed in the next chapter, these early achievements stand as guideposts pointing the road that would be traveled many years later. Presidential electors were being elected by popular vote, and members of the legislature chosen by districts. Property qualifications for voting and for office had almost completely disappeared, and American politics took on the form of democracy for the first time.

It would be foolish to say that all of these changes were brought about directly by the working-class movement. But the organized workers were the only ones that were publicly and energetically demanding these

[1] Gustavus Myers, "Great American Fortunes," Vol. I, pp. 79–80.
[2] Edwin G. Dexter, "History of Education in the United States," pp. 98–100.

steps. They were strong enough to exert a great influence. No other force can begin to compete with the labor movement as a direct cause of these important steps. Is it, then, too much to say that this movement of the workers, measured by the impress it left, was the most important event in American history?

This labor movement had its philosophical as well as its political expression. Three writers at this time sought to express Labor's attitude toward the economic problems with which it was confronted. Thomas Skidmore wrote "Rights of Man to Property" in 1829. He was an active organizer of the New York Labor Party in the beginning, but was finally forced out of the organization in an internal dissension, and afterwards ran for office on an independent ticket. L. Byllesby wrote "Sources and Effects of Unequal Wealth" in 1826, and Stephen Simpson published his "Workingman's Manual" in 1831. It was to be nearly thirty years before another volume worthy of notice should be added to the literature of labor in the United States.

In these works we find attempts to construct a political economy based upon social relations as seen through the eyes of workers. It cannot be said that the attempt was a success, although the work of these writers compares fairly well with contemporaneous works on the same subject in other countries.

All three are based upon a more or less clear presentation of the labor value theory, and it is easy to find germs of a theory of exploitation based upon the principle of ownership. But an economic philosophy is not developed in so short a period as the life of this movement.

THE FIRST LABOR MOVEMENT—1824-1836 189

In the discussion of practical tactics much more was accomplished. The doctrine of the "class struggle," based upon contending economic interests, was clearly expressed. When Karl Marx was a boy of thirteen, Simpson was writing a paragraph that contains much of the germ of the Communist Manifesto. Simpson says, after a discussion of what he calls "personal parties": [1]

"Parties of interest . . . are less noxious, because one party may be brought to check or control another, as the party of stockholders and capitalists may be met and counteracted by the *party of the producers;* which is a real party of *general interest*, whose ascendency could not fail to shed a genial and prosperous beam upon the whole society. Such a party would merely exhibit the *interests of society*, concentrating for the true fulfillment of the original terms of the social compact, the happiness and the comfort of the whole. This we now behold in those parties of the workingmen, who . . . steadily follow in the path of science and justice, under the banner of — *labor the source of all wealth*, and *industry* the arbiter of its distribution" (italics in original).

The question of "pure and simple" trade unionism *vs.* political activity was debated at this period, with much the same arguments that are used to-day.

We search this period in vain, however, to find any general acceptance of the principles of collectivism. Not even when Robert Owen addressed great meetings

---

[1] "The Workingman's Manual" (1831), p. 23. See also *The Man*, May 30, 1834, communication by "Boston Mechanic"; Resolution in *Mechanics' Free Press*, Aug. 16, 1828; *ibid.*, Sept. 20, 1828; *Free Enquirer*, Feb. 4, 1829, for expressions on class struggle, and *The National Laborer*, June 24 and July 6, 1836, on political action.

of the workers and took a part in formulating their resolutions [1] was he able to impress his ideas upon this early labor movement. The factory system was not sufficiently ripe for a collectivist labor movement. Collectivism in all its forms was still a utopian scheme of dreamers in other classes of society. The rampant individualism of young competitive capitalism determined the *Zeitgeist* of the period, and that spirit made its influence felt even upon the labor movement that fought that capitalism.

[1] Meeting reported in *Workingman's Advocate*, Oct. 31, 1829.

CHAPTER XVIII

THE YOUTH OF CAPITALISM — 1830–1850

THE forces and interest whose germination took place about 1814 to 1819, came into full view during this period. It was a time in which economic interests were maneuvering to strengthen their position and prepare for coming struggles. Population was shifting rapidly, and the direction of that shifting was perhaps the most important feature of the period. Until this time settlement west of the Alleghenies had been confined almost exclusively to the neighborhood of the Ohio River. Michigan, Wisconsin, northern Ohio, Illinois, and Indiana were still almost as completely in the possession of the Indians as when the continent was discovered. Chicago was only a trading post in the midst of a swamp. The whole line of lake ports that have become such a prominent, and indeed almost dominant feature of the social and industrial life of this nation were largely but meeting places for fur traders and Indians.

Immigration had flowed down the Ohio River and up through Cumberland Gap from the slave states of Tennessee, Kentucky, and Virginia. Stephen A. Douglas, discussing the admission of Kansas in the United States Senate, February 29, 1860, spoke as follows of the immigration into Illinois prior to 1830: —

"The fact is that the people of the territory of Illinois, when it was a territory, were about all from the southern states, particularly from Kentucky and Tennessee. The southern end of the state was the only part at first settled. ... The northern part ... was then in the possession of the Indians, and so were northern Indiana and northern Ohio; and a Yankee could not get to Illinois at all, unless he passed down through Virginia and over into Tennessee and Kentucky. The consequence was that 99 out of 100 of the settlers were from the slave states. They carried the old family servants with them and kept them. ... When they assembled to make the constitution of Illinois in 1818 ... nearly every delegate to the convention brought his negro along with him to black his boots, play the fiddle, wait upon him and take care of his room. ...

"But they said, 'Experience proves that it is not going to be profitable in this climate.' They had no scruples about its being right, but they said, 'We cannot make any money by it, and as our state runs away up north, up to those eternal snows, perhaps we shall gain population faster if we stop slavery and invite in the northern population.'"

This attitude of indifference on the slavery question was soon to pass away. Upland cotton was carrying the slaveholding planters in great numbers into Alabama, Georgia, and Mississippi. Here slavery was immensely profitable. The slave owners therefore wished to control the national government, to defend and advance slavery.

By 1830 a new and northern gateway to this region had been opened up, and through this a throng of settlers from New England, New York, and later from Europe

THE YOUTH OF CAPITALISM — 1830-1850

were pouring into the lake states. These were founding a society in which another form of labor was more profitable than chattel slavery. They also were to demand the use of the national government to further the system from which they derived a profit. Out of the clash of these two systems was to come the Civil War.

Agriculture was still the occupation of far more than a majority of the population. The upper Mississippi Valley, henceforth the agricultural center of the United States, was being developed by 1830. Great quantities of grain were raised in these states, but the difficulty of marketing made such crops of little profit.[1]

Whenever corn is cheap and too plenty to be transformed into whisky, it is always made into pork. The hog has been the "walking corncrib" that has marketed the maize of the American farmer. Illinois, Indiana, Ohio, Kentucky, and Tennessee raised vast numbers of hogs.[2] In the beginning these were driven in great droves over the mountains to the seaport markets.

By 1820 a new and important step had been taken in this industry. Instead of driving the hogs to market while alive, packing plants were established along the Ohio River, where, during the winter, the animals were slaughtered and salted down for shipment.[3] These slaughtering establishments were little like the great packing houses of to-day. They were rented to the butchers for killing and dressing, and the dressed meat

---

[1] T. Flint, "Condensed Geography and History of the Western States," p. 227.

[2] J. N. Peck, "A Gazetteer of Illinois" (1834), p. 41.

[3] John Macgregor, "Progress of America" (1847); Semple, "American History and its Geographic Conditions," p. 358.

was then bought by the packers, who maintained establishments in close proximity to the slaughter houses.[1]

Illinois was in the "ranch stage" of cattle raising until about 1840. Great herds of cattle were fed on the prairies and then rounded up and driven into Ohio to receive further feeding prior to the final drive to the stall feeders of Pennsylvania.[2] This is the same combination of ranch, pasture, and feeders that existed on the eastern slope of the Alleghenies prior to the Revolution. These stages were continually moving west, and the ranch stage had already entered Missouri[3] by 1830, and reached Texas a few years later.[4] In Tennessee, Ohio, and Kentucky another stage had been reached. Here the first steps were being taken in the introduction of improved breeds of cattle.[5]

The products of these states were all pressing for a market, and competition marked out lines of communication and influence along which were to be waged industrial and political struggles.

While agriculture was still the oldest and largest of the industrial family, manufacturing had already grown to a lusty, clamoring young giant, boastful of achievement, lustful of power, and eager for government influence. Iron and the textiles had grasped the leading position and were directing tariff policies. Each of these

[1] Macgregor, *loc. cit.*

[2] J. N. Peck, "A Gazetteer of Illinois" (1834), p. 40; Flint, "Condensed Geography and History of the Western States," p. 128.

[3] Flint, *loc. cit.*, Vol. II, p. 73.

[4] *Census*, 1880, Vol. III. Special article by Charles Gordon, "The Production of Meat," p. 11.

[5] Census 1860, volume on "Agriculture," "Cattle and the Cattle Trade," p. cxxxiii.

THE YOUTH OF CAPITALISM — 1830-1850

had settled in the localities that they now occupy. By 1830 the United States was second only to England in the cotton industry. In 1840 three fourths of all American cotton goods were produced in New England.[1]

Two great inventions revolutionized the iron industry and gave it a tremendous impetus. The hot blast process was first applied in 1834, and at once increased the production of each furnace 40 per cent, with a saving of the same percentage in fuel.[2] In 1840 anthracite coal began to be used in the smelting of iron, and within ten years had almost supplanted the more expensive charcoal method.[3]

In 1831 iron was first used for pillars, window casings, and other general building purposes.[4] Wrought iron pipes were first manufactured in 1846, and one year later the first firm for the production of machinist tools was established in Nashua, New Hampshire.[5] The manufacture of power looms reached such a state of perfection that in 1831 they began to be exported to England.[6]

The close proximity of iron ore, limestone, and coal, the three essentials to the production of iron, had already determined that Pittsburg should be the center of the production of this metal.[7]

At first the entire upper Mississippi Valley expected to be the seat of manufacturing, a destiny which it was

---

[1] E. L. Bogart, "Economic History of the United States," p. 149.

[2] M. D. Swank, "History of the Manufacture of Iron in all Ages," p. 453.

[3] *Ibid.*, pp. 178, 354-362.

[4] L. Bishop, "History of American Manufactures," Vol. II, p. 402.

[5] *Ibid.*, p. 411.   [6] *Ibid.*, p. 363.

[7] M. D. Swank, "History of Iron in All Ages," pp. 176-178.

to attain in another generation. Travelers filled their notebooks with lists of the factories they met in this locality.[1] The temporary disappointment in this regard had important political consequences.

It was in transportation, however, that the great industrial revolution of this time was wrought. The canal craze that had been raging for several years reached its climax and scored its greatest triumph in the opening of the Erie Canal in 1825. The effect of this engineering work upon the next thirty years of American history can scarcely be exaggerated.

The next season after its opening 19,000 boats were counted as passing West Troy on the road to New York, most of which came from the West, over the Erie Canal.[2] These bore the products of the West to market. An equal number of boats carried a human cargo in the other direction. This new flood of immigration changed the current of history in the West, and later of the whole country. The Erie Canal "shifted the great trans-Allegheny route away from the Potomac, out of the belt of the slaveholding, agricultural South, to the free, industrial North, and placed it at the back door of New England, whence poured westward a tide of Puritan immigrants, infusing elements of vigorous conscience and energy into all the northern zone of states from the Genesee River to the Missouri and Minnesota."[3]

The whole district around the Great Lakes that had lain so long almost untouched by settlement was filled

---

[1] T. Flint, "Condensed Geography and History of the Western States," Vol. I, p. 224.

[2] Ellen C. Semple, "American History and its Geographic Conditions," pp. 268–269.   [3] *Ibid.*

with eager immigrants. From 1830 to 1840 the population of Michigan increased from 31,639 to 212,267, nearly all coming through the Erie Canal. Wisconsin and northern Illinois grew with almost equal rapidity, and received their increase by the same route.[1] Many of these immigrants came direct from Europe, thus introducing a new element into the population of this region.

The general application of steam to boats upon the Great Lakes which was taking place at this time served to accentuate nearly all the movements just described. It brought population to the lake ports, added to the importance of the Erie Canal, and built up the small farmer and trader and manufacturing class in the upper Mississippi Valley.

Then came the most revolutionary of all the inventions of a century of invention. Steam was applied to the hauling of cars upon rails.

At once the "circle of the market" — the space within which an article can be profitably sold — was multiplied several fold.[2] A factory could now deliver its product at much more distant points. It could reach more customers. It could grow to an hitherto inconceivable size.

The first railroads reflected all the crude anarchy that is characteristic of the effect of inventions under competition. It was not simply that the roads were mechanically crude, although the defects in that line were innumerable. All the problems of track, and rolling

[1] "History of the Great Lakes" (no author given), pp. 183–189.
[2] I. L. Ringwalt, "Development of Transportation Systems in the United States," p. 129.

stock and engine construction had to be solved with a lack of engineering skill and mechanical facilities almost inconceivable in these days.[1] There was an equal crudity and confusion in the relations of the various roads. Owned by a multitude of companies, laid out upon no definite plan, with no conception of future development, they reflected the anarchy of small capitalist individualism.[2] With or without system or order, railroads filled a most pressing need in a country of such magnificent distances as the United States, and they were built with remarkable rapidity.[3] The enthusiasm that had been devoted to canals was turned directly toward the new method of transportation. Since the canals had been built largely by governments, it was

[1] John Macgregor, "The Progress of America" (1847), Vol. II, p. 699: "No two railroads are constructed alike. The fish-bellied rails of some, weighing forty pounds per lineal yard, rest upon cast-iron chains, weighing sixteen pounds each; in others plate rails and malleable iron, 2½ inches broad and ½ inch thick, are fixed by iron spikes to wooden sleepers; in others a plate rail is spiked down to tree-nails of oak or locust wood, driven into jumper holes bored in the stone curb; in others longitudinal wooden runners, one foot in breadth, and from three to four inches in thickness, are imbedded in broken stone or gravel, on these runners are placed transverse sleepers, formed of round timbers with the bark left on, and wrought iron rails are affixed to the sleepers by long spikes, the heads of which are countersunk in the rail; in others round piles of timber, about 12 inches in diameter, are driven into the ground as far as they will go, about three feet apart; the tops are then crosscut, and the rails spiked to them."

[2] N. S. Shaler, "The United States of America," Vol. II, p. 72; *American Railroad Journal*, Vol. I, No. 1, Jan. 2, 1832.

[3] I. L. Ringwalt, *loc. cit.*, p. 75, gives following table of railroads constructed annually: —

Year	1830	1831	1832	1833	1834	1835	1836	1837	1838	1839
Miles	39.8	98.7	191.3	115.9	213.9	137.8	280	348.3	452.8	385.8

Total mileage built in decade, 2264.67.

but natural that railroads should be constructed in the same manner. Many of the state governments went heavily into debt to secure funds for railroad construction. Cities vied with one another in the same way.[1]

The panic of 1837 brought many of these projects, and with them the states that had financed them, to the verge of bankruptcy.[2] Indeed, in some instances the bankruptcy came before the railroads were even started. So it was that there came a strong reaction against government enterprise in railroad building. It could not have been different, in a society that was filled with the narrow individualism of youthful capitalism.

While the railroads constructed directly under municipal or state governments were insignificant, the struggle of various cities for commercial advantage had a far-reaching influence upon all forms of communication. The three great gateways through the Allegheny barrier had each a seaport at the eastern end. At first Baltimore, with the Cumberland Gap and the National Turnpike, had the advantage. Then Philadelphia, with her system of canals and inclined planes connecting her with the mouth of the Ohio, seemed destined to control the trade of the great trans-Allegheny region.[3] The completion of the Erie Canal had a revolutionary effect upon this struggle of cities on the Atlantic seaboard, as it had upon the forces struggling for supremacy at its

[1] McMaster, "History of the People of the United States," Vol. VI, pp. 347–350.
[2] McMaster, *loc. cit.*, Vol. VI, pp. 527, 530.
[3] H. S. Tanner, "General Outline of the United States" (1825), p. 67.

western end. New York leaped forward in wealth and population as if by magic.[1] The whole route of the canal through New York State was transformed. New cities sprang up. Real estate values multiplied at a rate that brought a golden harvest to dealers in that commodity. Not only in New York, but in Pennsylvania, the local politics of the time hinged on questions of canal building and maintenance.[2]

The coming of railways strengthened the tendencies set in motion by the Erie Canal. Although Baltimore was the first to make use of the new means of transportation to connect her with the West by means of the Baltimore and Ohio Railroad, and Philadelphia hastened to construct the Philadelphia and Columbia, connecting her with Pittsburg, yet when New York had once laid the rails that followed the route of the Erie Canal, low grades, and connection with the Great Lakes, whose

[1] The following table from Hunt's *Merchant Magazine*, Aug., 1868, p. 113, shows effect upon Philadelphia and New York:—

Year	Value of Imports		Value of Exports		Population	
	New York	Philadelphia	New York	Philadelphia	New York	Philadelphia
1820			$11,769,511	$5,743,549	123,706	137,097
1830	$38,556,064	$9,525,893	17,666,624	4,291,793	203,007	188,961
1840	60,064,942	8,464,882	32,408,689	6,820,145	312,712	258,832
1850	116,667,558	12,065,834	47,580,357	4,501,606	515,394	409,353

[2] Julius Winden, "The Influence of the Erie Canal upon the Population along its Course"; quoted in A. B. Hulbert, "Great American Canals," Vol. II, Chap. V. See also Charles McCarthy, "The Anti-Masonic Party," in *American Historical Association Reports*, 1902, *passim;* Wm. Grant, in Hudson River Railroad Reports, pp. 9–10.

THE YOUTH OF CAPITALISM — 1830-1850

influence as avenues of commerce was now being felt, renewed the advantage given by the canal and which she has retained to the present day.[1]

New Orleans was another competitor for this western trade. Already she was losing the advantage which a favorable river current had given her, and this change in trade routes was building up forces that were determining the outcome of the great conflict between the North and the South.

In the midst of this industrial struggle, certain fairly well defined interests can be traced. New England, while still possessing powerful commercial interests, was dominated by the new manufacturing and financial class. The Middle states were more closely affiliated with her than with any other section, but the strong manufacturing influence of Pennsylvania was already making her the leader in all demands for high tariff. The South, fairly prosperous and contented with the rapid extension of the cultivation of upland cotton, was united, but by no means aggressive in defending its interests save in regard to the tariff. The most striking interest was undoubtedly the young, virile, belligerent West. It played so prominent a part that most historians speak of this time as the "Rule of the Frontier." The frontier that ruled, however, was not that of the pioneer settler of the land, but the little-capitalist, petty trading, social frontier. How this outlook came to dominate is the real story of this period.

In the decade preceding 1830 New England had be-

[1] Chauncey M. Depew (editor), "One Hundred Years of American Commerce"; chapter on "Interstate Commerce," by Edward A. Moseley, p. 27.

come manufacturing and high tariff.[1] The South had become agricultural and free trade.

In the beginning the West sided with the North Atlantic states for the tariff, and Henry Clay was "the Father of the American System." But by 1832, when Calhoun had evolved from a protectionist to a "Nullifier," ready to urge his native state to leave the Union rather than endure a high tariff, and Webster had undergone an identical evolution in the opposite direction from free trader to protectionist, Henry Clay had also undergone a change. He now appeared as "the Great Compromiser," with the Compromise of 1832 providing for a gradual reduction of the tariff, much more in accord with the ideas of the South than of New England.

The evolution of Clay, like that of Webster and Calhoun, was due to economic changes in the district from which he came. Until about 1830 the West thought itself destined to become quickly a great manufacturing district. The crying need for the upper Mississippi Valley was a market for its crops This market was to be furnished by the great manufacturing centers soon to be established. So it was that the "home market" argument made the West protectionist. But as time passed the manufactures of the West grew slowly. At the same time it became possible to export the agricultural products over the improved transportation routes. The West grew indifferent to protection. Other interests tended to alienate it still further from its former ally.

New England and the Middle Atlantic states, where manufacturing was increasing by stupendous leaps, wanted cheap wage labor. The West wanted settlers;

[1] F. J. Turner, "Rise of the New West," pp. 314-317.

and every western pioneer who left the manufacturing centers reduced the supply of labor power and raised its price. Therefore the manufacturing states opposed the development of the West. They sought to restrict settlement, and opposed all measures looking to a liberal land policy. At the time when the West was quivering in the balance in its allegiance to the protective policy and the northeastern states, there came a dramatic incident whose significance has been almost completely overlooked by those who are familiar with some of its phases. Tens of thousands of American schoolboys have declaimed Daniel Webster's great peroration, with its conclusion of "Liberty and the Union, now and forever, one and inseparable"; but how many of these know that this speech was delivered in support of a resolution offered by Senator Foote of Connecticut, proposing to stop the survey of public lands, limit the sales to those already in the market, and abolish the office of surveyor-general?

When this resolution was presented in the Senate, Benton of Missouri, long the spokesman of western interests, attacked it bitterly. Hayne of South Carolina, seeing an opportunity to draw the West from its alliance with the Northeast, came to Benton's support, and pointed out that the object of this resolution was to restrict the expansion of population until a servile and helpless wageworking class should develop to supply cheap labor for manufactures. Webster accepted the challenge, and, ignoring Benton, whose support he wished to retain, attacked Hayne in the orations that have become so famous. Although generations of elocutionists have sung the praises of Webster and celebrated his victory in forensic fireworks, yet he temporarily lost the cause for which he fought. The West was the ally of the South for the next generation.[1]

There were other causes of hostility between the West and the Northeast. The fish of New England and the flesh of the Mississippi Valley came into competition in the markets of the world, and competitors never love one another. The temper of the West was not improved on this question by the fact that the salt which was so necessary to the packing of western meat was subject to a high tariff, which was rebated to the fishers of New England. This rebate, in the form of a bounty, was a dearly loved privilege of the fishermen, which gave them a great advantage in the markets of the world and was another illustration of the value of class influence upon government.[2]

The whole Indian question caused further friction. The traders who exchanged the cheap trinkets, flimsy fabrics, and poor whisky for the rich furs of the Indians, objected to the advance of settlement that interfered with

[1] McMaster, "History of the People of the United States," Vol. VI, pp. 11-29; Thomas H. Benton, "Thirty Years' View," Vol. I, pp. 130-143. Woodrow Wilson, "A History of the American People," Vol. IV, p. 22: "The New England men wanted the settlement of the West held back as much as possible. So long as land was to be had there almost for the mere asking, at no cost except that of a journey and of a few farmers' tools and a beast or two for the plough, the active men of their own section, whom they counted on as skilled workmen in building up their manufactures, must be constantly enticed away by the score and hundred to seek an independent life and livelihood in the West; high wages, very high wages, must be paid to keep them, if indeed they could be kept at all; and the maintenance of manufactures must cost more than mere protective tariffs could make good." See also Thomas Donaldson, "The Public Domain," p. 205; and Charles H. Peck, "The Jacksonian Epoch," p. 162.

[2] Benton, *loc. cit.*, pp. 143-148, 154-157.

THE YOUTH OF CAPITALISM — 1830-1850   205

their trade. This trade was now at its most profitable stage. The American Fur Company of John Jacob Astor was making enormous profits, and had become a power in politics.[1] It was especially active in Michigan and Wisconsin, although its representatives had now reached the Pacific coast.

An elaborate commercial system had developed with the far western tribes of Indians and with the Mexicans over the famous Santa Fé Trail, that was at its height from 1820 to 1840.[2]

There was in addition the long-standing antagonism between debtors and creditors that had always been a source of friction between the frontier and the coast. This antagonism found a convenient and conspicuous target in the second Bank of the United States that had been chartered in 1816.

Daniel Webster had opposed the granting of the charter. At that time New England was still commercial, and, being opposed to the war and the policy of the national government, which was controlled by the South, was also opposed to all measures strengthening the power of the national government. At this time the overwhelming majority of the shares were owned in the South.[3] By 1831 the general shifting of industrial conditions had reversed attitudes on the bank question, as well as on the tariff, and many other questions. In this year a meeting of the stockholders was held in

[1] Gustavus Myers, "History of Great American Fortunes," Vol. I, pp. 124-125, *et passim*; F. J. Turner, "Rise of the New West," p. 113.
[2] H. M. Chittenden, "The American Fur Trade of the Far West," Vol. II, p. 518.
[3] McMaster, "History of the People of the United States."

Philadelphia, with Stephen Girard as president. It was then officially reported that of the 350,000 shares of $100 each the United States held 70,000, that 79,000 were held abroad, and that the remainder were owned in the following states in the order given: Pennsylvania, South Carolina, Maryland, New York, and Massachusetts, while scarcely a share was owned west of the Appalachians.[1]

Webster was now the champion of the Bank, the South was indifferent and becoming hostile to it, while to the West it typified all that the words "Wall Street" conveyed to the mind of the Populist of 1890. The West was young, vigorous, militant, and took the lead in the fight. Therefore the Bank became the principal issue of the period.

It was not difficult for the opponents of the Bank to show that it had been conducted in a fraudulent manner in its very beginning.[2] It had entered politics secretly from the first, and when attacked, threw off the mask and fought with the weapons that powerful financial interests have always used in a country of universal suffrage.

The Bank, in the eyes of the debtor West, stood for the whole hated creditor class. It had loaned heavily on western mortages, and had foreclosed many of these mortgages, until it was alleged that it owned great tracts of farm and city property.[3] It had favored the Eastern land speculator rather than the actual settler

[1] J. Schouler, "History of the United States," Vol. VI, p. 48.

[2] William M. Gouge, "Short History of Paper Money and Banking," pp. 31–32; Horace White, "Money and Banking"; Gustavus Myers, "History of Great American Fortunes," Vol. I, pp. 89–90.

[3] T. Benton, "Thirty Years' View," Vol. I, p. 198.

in the matter of loans, and had refused to extend credit to the residents of the West as freely as the state banks. Thus the state banks, to whom the United States Bank stood in the relation of a powerful competitor, were anxious to fan the antagonism of the frontier.

The South had favored western expansion, and was now ready to make an alliance with the West in the attack upon the Bank in return for support in reducing the tariff. In this alliance the West, being the more virile rising element, dominated, and Andrew Jackson, who was largely typical of the speculative, small farmer and trader frontier, became President. In 1834 he finished his fight upon the Bank by removing the funds deposited with it by the national government. This so crippled the Bank that it sank into obscurity, and failed within a few years.

The tremendous flood of immigration to the West had been accompanied, as such movements have always been, by a wild speculation in land. Starting immediately after the panic of 1819, this craze grew steadily, save for a brief setback following the withdrawal of the deposits from the Bank in 1833-1834, until it climaxed and collapsed in the panic of 1837. Shares in canals and the newly projected railroads added to the insanity, fanned still faster by the willingness of the "wildcat" banks to issue "scrip" which was accepted as payment for public lands, until at a time when every one was buying land, they were all too crazy to farm, and wheat was actually imported from Russia and sold to land speculators in the West for $2 a bushel.[1]

[1] J. B. McMaster, "History of the People of the United States," Vol. VI, pp. 323-389; Anon., "Eighty Years' Progress," pp. 147-152.

The income from the sale of public land leaped from less than four million dollars in 1833 to more than $24,000,000 in 1836.[1] The public income was so great that a surplus accumulated in the United States treasury, and was distributed to the several states. In short, there were all the phenomena of inflation that precede a competitive crisis. Just as the bubble was blown to the bursting point, President Jackson furnished the pin-prick that burst it by issuing his famous "Specie Circular." This simply stated that nothing but specie would be received in payment for land. All the vast quantities of bank notes, being no longer received by the government, lost much of their value, and the whole industrial structure came tumbling down.

Bad harvests in the wheat country and a simultaneous panic in England completed the prostration of industry. There were new investigations of the cause of distress. More charity societies were organized. The unemployed filled the streets. Mobs in New York City stormed the shops of those who were alleged to have monopolized breadstuffs, and destroyed great quantities of wheat and flour. The new corporation stocks set the example that has been followed by generation after generation of similar stocks, and promptly lost all value. Failure after failure of banks, merchants, and manufacturers were heralded in the journals. Prices of all goods fell rapidly, but no one had the means to purchase at any price. Specie payments were suspended by all the banks, these being the only establishments that, even at this early date, were allowed to refuse to pay their debts and still continue to do business. As money disappeared from

[1] Donaldson, "The Public Domain," pp. 201-203.

circulation, all sorts of expedients were resorted to. Individuals issued scrip, and checks for subsidiary coins; and the larger portion of the population, especially in rural districts, relapsed once more to the stage of barter.[1]

Then came the slow process of recovery. There was a great western movement of actual settlers, a slow readjustment of industry, a growing discontent which found expression, as it has so often done since, by changing political rulers; and then industry started upon another upward climb toward another plunge into the depths.

On the basis of the industrial stage just described there developed a peculiar mental attitude, and a set of social and political principles and institutions that set their stamp upon all subsequent history.

The common interpretation of this period is that it was the rule of the frontier, and that it was an example of perfect democracy. There is more than a semblance of truth in these statements.

The two largest elements of the population that possessed that sense of coming social power which alone gives the class consciousness necessary to effective action were the frontiersmen and the wageworkers of the cities. The latter fired into brief activity, and were then swallowed up in other classes, largely in that of the pioneers of the Northwest. Those who remained at home accepted the mental attitude of the small manufacturers, — the rising bourgeoisie. Those who went west developed much the same psychology.

Out of this industrial condition sprang that peculiar thing that has been called "Jacksonian Democracy."

[1] J. B. McMaster, *loc. cit.*, Vol. VI, Chap. LXV.

It was neither frontier, nor wageworking, nor even purely capitalist in its mental make-up. It can be better characterized as the "democracy of expectant capitalists." It borrowed something from the frontier. Its brutality, crudeness, coarseness, admiration for boorishness and ignorance, have been especially ascribed to the frontier, but they belong equally well to crude, competitive capitalism. These were the features that impressed such foreign visitors as Charles Dickens,[1] Harriet Martineau,[2] and Alexander De Tocqueville.[3]

It was a society made up of units each of which believed that it was destined to become rich and powerful. Its democracy was based upon the idea of equality in the struggle for office. Office was considered as a goal to be fought for. Public office was a private snap. Therefore it should be passed around. Hence the pernicious idea of rotation in office that has cursed American politics until the present time.

The only way to secure office was to deceive a majority of the voters. Hence the deification of majorities. The one idea which is met with over and over again in all the literature of the period is that the majority is always right. Whoever could get a majority of the votes was therefore right. The hardest way to get majorities being through appeals to reason, that method was neglected.

Political machines, whose origin in Tammany Hall we have already traced, now spread from this germ until they controlled the whole national political field. The

[1] Charles Dickens, "American Notes."
[2] Harriet Martineau, "Society in America" (1837).
[3] Alexander De Tocqueville, "Democracy in America" (1833).

mad rush for wealth, the deification of success, the fierce competition of the early days of capitalism, combined to make politics a trade.[1] The workers could not, the madly competing little capitalists had no time to, enter politics directly. Besides, the whole end and aim of life being to make money, why should not politics be left to individual initiative in the pursuit of profit?

The national political convention, originating nominally in a gathering of the "Anti-Masonic" party in 1820, first became a national force when Jackson was nominated in 1828. By this time Van Buren, pupil of Aaron Burr and Tammany, had extended the system he had helped create in New York City first to the state and now to the nation.

This machine existed for the purpose of getting majorities, and through these the spoils of office. It did not try to teach the voters. The more ignorant they were, the easier to manage. Hence the exaltation of ignorance, the glorification of the "horny hand," that has been a part of the stock in trade of every demagogue to the present day.

Principles are a distinct handicap to a political party working on these lines. Hence they are avoided as much as possible. Personalities are emphasized. Trickery, cabals, bribery, and intrigue are used within the party to determine nominations. After the nominations are made, the majority are to be swayed by phrases, shibboleths, "blessed words," appeals to party solidarity, and principally by infusing the multitude with a sort of hypnotic enthusiasm and the mob spirit.[2]

[1] M. Ostrogorski, "Democracy and the Organization of Political Parties," Vol. II, p. 78.   [2] Ostrogorski, *loc. cit.*, Chap. II.

These methods were first seized upon by the Democratic party. By their use Jackson and Van Buren were elected. Then others learned the lesson. Webster and New England, shut out of the Van Buren-Jackson political combination, proceeded to manufacture a machine of their own, — the Whig party. It never had any principles.[1] The whole country was so uniformly small-capitalist, save in the chattel-slave-owning localities, whose interests were as yet not challenged, that there was little on which politicians disagreed.

But the Whigs had, from the start, greater resources than the Jackson and Van Buren combination. Henry Clay had quarreled with Jackson and gone over to the new party, and was its logical candidate. He was cast aside on the ground that, having a public record, he had enemies, and might not be the most available vote-getter. William H. Harrison was nominated instead. His only claim to fame was that he had been a general in a successful battle against the Indians some thirty years before. The machine then proceeded to make full use of the new methods of arousing enthusiasm. Enormous meetings were worked up, whose size was measured by acres, and not by the arguments presented. Monster processions passed through the streets of the cities, led by members of Congress who came from all parts of the Union for this purpose. An excellent phrase for the purpose of arousing the ignorant, unthinking vote was created for the Whigs when some opponent

---

[1] Charles H. Peck, "The Jacksonian System," p. 420: "John Randolph once remarked that the principles of the Whig party were seven — five loaves and two fishes. This sarcasm contained much truth. The party was a heterogeneous composition."

sneeringly declared that Harrison would be content if he could sit in the door of a log cabin and drink hard cider. Although there is no evidence that he had ever so sat, and while he was, for that time, a comparatively wealthy man, this phrase was seized upon, Harrison became the "log-cabin candidate," and was swept into the highest office in the nation.

Unfortunately for the Whigs, in their anxiety to secure a victory they had selected John Tyler for Vice-President. He was more nearly a Democrat than a Whig (another illustration of the disregard of principles for expediency); and when Harrison died after a few weeks in office, Tyler became President, and the Democrats were once more in places of power. Before Tyler's term had expired, the long-blurred class lines again became distinct in the field of politics. The new divisions were wholly different from the old ones, and were along the lines that were later to lead to Civil War.

It would be a mistake to conclude that the democracy of this period was all a sham and a cover for scheming demagogues. It did strike heavy blows at all forms of privilege. It extended the suffrage and the public school system, and developed many things that had been set in motion by the labor movement of the preceding period.

It was a time of strange, erratic, hysterical, and violent social movements. Antirent riots in New York secured the abolition of the remnants of the old patroon privileges that had remained from the days of Dutch control. The anarchistic competitive industrial atmosphere produced extreme individualism in religion, resulting in hysterical revivals, and the growth of strange sects that were fiercely persecuted, as in the case of the Mormons. Political parties fought violently over strange issues. An anti-Masonic party threatened to capture several of the Northern states, and was a deciding influence in the local politics for several years.

New England stood a little apart from this confusion. The old commercial class had lost its industrial and political power. It was dying out in a blaze of intellectual fireworks, commonly known as the "Transcendental movement," because of its metaphysical base. To this movement belonged Emerson and Channing and Ripley and Thoreau, and several other of the brightest names in American literature.

As in Europe, so here, this small competitive stage of capitalism was accompanied by a wave of communistic Utopian Socialism. It was during this period that Brook Farm was established, Brisbane was preaching the gospel of Fourier, and the followers of Cabet were preparing to build "Icarias" in the new world, with the assistance of local sympathizers.

This communistic movement was a natural outgrowth of the combination of bourgeois democracy, New England liberalism in theology, metaphysical transcendentalism, and the small-capitalist ideal of equality transmuted into transcendental phraseology. All of these things were most pronounced in their development in New England. Elsewhere there were disturbing currents that prevented the appearance of this intellectual and social efflorescence of the industrial trunk of American society.

The whole tendency of bourgeois democracy and primitive communism is to level down, not up; to praise what is common to all, though it be base and degrading, rather than to aim at building up in the many what at first was the property of the few.

This political power of the small bourgeoisie was now to be momentarily submerged in national affairs by the chattel-slave interests, then, after a period of development and growth and change, to seize the reins of social control, and wield them until it handed them over to its legitimate heirs in the line of social succession.

CHAPTER XIX

WHY THE CIVIL WAR CAME

THERE are very definite reasons why the Civil War came at the exact time it did, and not a century earlier or a decade later. These reasons are not found either in the wickedness of chattel slavery, nor the growing moral consciousness of the North. It is probable that the slaves were as well, if not better, treated in 1860 than at any time in the history of slavery. They were more valuable, and masters were more interested in their welfare. It is certain that the general moral conscience of the North had seldom been lower than in the years when competitive capitalism was gaining the mastery in American industrial life.

Sectional antagonism has always existed in the United States, and has many times led to threats of secession. New England proposed to secede because of opposition to the War of 1812. South Carolina was ready to leave the Union to escape the tariff in 1830, although she had favored a tariff little more than ten years before. The West had repeatedly threatened secession and intrigued for an alliance with Spain, and had even taken steps to organize a trans-Allegheny empire when it felt itself oppressed by the Eastern states. It would be hard to find a state a majority of whose inhabitants had not at some time prior to 1860 favored secession. Finally, the Abolitionists were, in the beginning, the most rabid secessionists. This fact should be ample proof that the Civil War was not caused by a fervent love for the abstract idea of union and a corresponding hatred of the principle of secession.[1]

A series of questions present themselves to any student of this period that are not answered by any of the conventional explanations of the cause of the war between the North and the South. The explanation that it was caused by hostility to slavery fails to explain why Wendell Phillips and William Lloyd Garrison were mobbed in Boston, and why Lovejoy was lynched and Stephen A. Douglas sent to the United States Senate by the State that furnished Lincoln. Neither does it

---

[1] Pollard, "The Lost Cause," p. 52: "In the North there was never any lack of rhetorical fervor for the Union; its praises were sung in every note of turgid literature, and it was familiarly entitled 'the glorious.' But the North worshipped the union in a very low commercial sense, it was a source of boundless profits; it was productive of tariffs and bounties, and it had been used for years as a means of sectional aggrandizement." The attitude of the Abolitionists is shown freely in their literature. No. 11 of the Anti-Slavery Tracts is "Disunion our Wisdom and Duty," by Rev. Charles E. Hodges. It is published by the American Anti-Slavery Society, and is an argument for dissolving the Union. Wendell Phillips' "Speeches, Lectures and Letters," Vol. I, p. 343 et seq., containing his speech on "Disunion," delivered January, 1861, after secession had already taken place, contains these sentences: "'The Lord reigneth; let the earth rejoice.' 'The covenant with death' is annulled; 'the agreement with hell' is broken to pieces. The chain which has held the slave system since 1787 is parted. Thirty years ago northern abolitionists announced their purpose to seek the dissolution of the American union. Who dreamed that success would come so soon?" Later, in August, 1862, Phillips wrote a letter to the *New York Tribune* in which he said: "From 1843 to 1861 I was a disunionist ... Sumter changed the whole question. After that peace and justice both forbade disunion."

help us to understand why slavery was not a political issue until it suddenly blazed into such a fierce fire, nor why the victory of the Republican party in the nation necessarily led to civil war when that party had never suggested abolition, and finally, why that war should have come in spite of the most earnest pledges of the government of Lincoln that slavery would not be disturbed.

There is always a tendency to read the present into the past, until historians write as if the people of 1840 acted with a full foreknowledge of the coming secession, Civil War, and emancipation, if not of negro enfranchisement and reconstruction.

The attitude of the various sections of the country toward chattel slavery has always been determined directly by the dominant economic interests of the section in question. Massachusetts abolished slavery at an early date, and we have it on the authority of John Adams that: —

"Argument might have had some weight in the abolition of slavery in Massachusetts, but the real cause was the multiplication of laboring white people, who would not longer suffer the rich to employ these sable rivals so much to their injury."[1]

[1] A work by a writer using the name of "Barbarossa," entitled "The Lost Principles of Sectional Equilibrium," published in 1860, has this statement (p. 39, note): "In the Congress of 1776 John Adams observed that the number of persons were taken by this article (on taxation) as the index of the wealth of the state, and not as subjects of taxation. That as to this matter, it was of no consequence by what name you called your people, whether by that of freemen or of slaves. That in some countries the laboring poor were called freemen; in others they were called slaves: but that the difference was imaginary only. What matters it whether a landlord employing ten laborers on his farm gives them annually as much as will buy the necessaries of life, or gives them

At the time when Jackson was President there were a number of Abolitionist societies, but these were nearly all in the northern tier of slave-holding states, although one or more such societies could be found in every state in the Union except a few extreme Southern states, Indiana, and those of New England.[1]

About this time sentiment began to change, and a fierce hostility to Abolitionism arose, not only in the South, but through almost the entire North, with the exception of the Middle Atlantic states.[2] We find the cause of this in the fact that the value of the cotton crop raised by slave labor was increasing as perhaps few crops have ever increased.[3] New England was weaving this cotton, or carrying it to foreign ports, and the Middle West was supplying the food for the slaves and farm animals for the plantations upon which the cotton was raised. Only in the iron and steel manufacturing region and in the district dependent upon the Great Lakes was there developing a population deriving no material benefit from chattel slavery.

So long as the various sections of the country were mutually complementary and not competitive, there was no deep-seated antagonism. "King Cotton" and "King Cotton Goods" had no quarrel until their interests began to move in opposite directions.

---

those necessaries at first hand?" Williams, "History of the Negro Race in America," p. 209, quotes from a report of a committee appointed by the Massachusetts Council in 1706, stating that negro slavery should be abolished because "white servants" were cheaper and more profitable to the colony.

[1] Albert Bushnell Hart, "Slavery and Abolition," p. 161.
[2] *Ibid.*, pp. 245–246.
[3] Charles H. Peck, "The Jacksonian Epoch," p. 268.

There was a series of these antagonistic interests that culminated about 1860, any one of which might have produced a civil war, all of which could scarcely avoid causing an armed conflict.

There was a conflict of territory. Both the wage system and chattel slavery require constant expansion. When the wave of population crossed the Mississippi and began to climb the eastern slope of the Rockies, a struggle arose over the question of which system should possess the level plains that lay on the border between the two social systems. Then came the "Nebraska War," the "Missouri Compromise," and "Bloody Kansas." The system of small capitalism required that land should be divided into small freeholds and distributed to settlers in the form of homesteads. Chattel slavery demanded auction sales of great strips for plantations.

The rise of the factory system and the coming of foreign immigration, with the development of cities, all a part of the society based upon the wage system, created a social and individual psychology so wholly different from that based upon chattel slavery as to be sure to give rise to mutual distrust and hostility. This social system could not arise in the North until factory production and railroad transportation had given a unity to its social life.

The South had to learn that chattel slavery was largely confined to the cotton belt, and that therefore it could never hope to rival in size and power the wage-slave territory, which had no narrow geographical bonds. It was to try to force itself and its system into new territories until further expansion was almost impossible before it realized the existence of an "inevitable conflict."

WHY THE CIVIL WAR CAME

Even more significant than any of these, although to a large extent growing out of them, was the antagonism arising from the attempt of the two social systems to use the national government in opposite ways for the furtherance of their respective interests. During the period prior to 1850 this need was not sharply felt by either section. This largely accounts for the political chaos, and utter lack of even a semblance of principles in national elections. Both the Whig and the Democrat parties, in the generation prior to the above date, had sought only to win offices, and had represented no clear class interests of national scope.

As Northern capitalism grew stronger, wider in its scope, more definite in its objects, more united in its interests, more in need of national action to protect these interests both at home and abroad, it developed a political party to express those interests. That party found itself in sharp opposition to the interests of the system based upon chattel slavery.

When that party obtained control of the national government, the chattel slave interests, realizing that no social system can hope to prosper within a government which it does not control, felt that secession was necessary.

The growth of these divergent and antagonistic interests and their clash for power will be the subject of the next three chapters.

CHAPTER XX

THE CRISIS IN THE CHATTEL SLAVE SYSTEM

INTERNALLY the industrial society based upon the plantation system and chattel slavery was near to a crisis by 1860. This society, first established on the seaboard for the production of tobacco, indigo, and rice, maintained its general form as it moved across the country. In each successive stage of the westward march it followed the hunter and small farmer stage, and there was a brief struggle between these two systems for supremacy.[1]

Soil and climate determined the outcome of this conflict. There was a definite belt of land where upland cotton could be raised.[2] Where this belt broke against the foot of the mountains, cotton and slavery stopped, and the whole character of the population changed.[3] Because those engaged in the production of cotton in this comparatively small portion of the soil were the industrial, political, and social rulers of the South, it is the portion which is commonly referred to when the antebellum South is named.

---

[1] U. B. Phillips, "Origin and Growth of the Southern Black Belts," in *American Historical Review*, July, 1906.

[2] Wm. G. Brown, "The Lower South in American History," pp. 25–26.

[3] W. A. Schaper, "Sectionalism and Representation in South Carolina," *Am. Hist. Ass'n Rept.*, 1900. Vol. I, p. 253. *et passim*.

Although the statement is frequently made that the plantation system had remained unchanged for more than a century,[1] there were some important alterations in the generation preceding the Civil War.

Chattel slavery and the plantation system could be maintained only in connection with an industry having certain characteristics. Such an industry must be extremely simple in its operation, requiring few processes and no complex machinery. Because slavery is applicable only to a "one-crop" system of agriculture, it demands an exhaustless supply of new and fertile lands that can be brought into cultivation as the old ones are exhausted. Because the slave represents a permanent investment on the part of the master, and must be supported continuously, without regard to the continuity of industry, it is essential that employment be steady. Cotton cultivation with ginning occupied the slaves for nearly nine months in the year — longer than almost any other crop.

The supplies in which the slave receives his wages should not be costly. Otherwise wage labor would be cheaper. The warm climate of the South relieved the master of the necessity of providing anything but the cheapest, coarsest clothing and food, and a miserable shelter.

Slaves must be worked in large gangs under a common overseer. The cultivation and picking of cotton again made this possible.[2]

The same internal compulsion that leads to concentra-

[1] E. L. Bogart, "Economic History of the United States," p. 251.
[2] M. B. Hammond, "The Cotton Industry," *Pub. Am. Econ. Ass'n*, Vol. I, No. 1, pp. 34–66.

tion in modern industry operated with the production of cotton. To this compulsion was added the fact that the extension of land ownership for the great plantations literally drove the defeated competitors off the earth. As the system approached its conclusion, the number of its beneficiaries grew fewer and fewer, more and more powerful, more defiant and arrogant, more greedy for rulership.

By 1860, not more than half a million of the nine million Southern whites made an actual profit from chattel slavery. Out of this half million was further selected not more than ten thousand, who were the economic, social, and political rulers of the South.[1] The problem that confronted these few rulers was to maintain their dominant position under universal white suffrage. They were aided by the fact that the clergy and the professional men were with them. This was due partly to the fact that the more successful members of this class usually owned one or two slaves for personal service. This

[1] A. B. Hart, "Slavery and Abolition," p. 68; Edward Ingle, "Southern Side Lights," p. 263; Brown, "The Lower South in American History," p. 34. Hinton Rowan Helper, "The Impending Crisis," p. 146, gives this table for 1850: —

Holders of	1 slave	68,820
Holders of	1 and under 5	105,683
Holders of	5 and under 10	80,765
Holders of	10 and under 20	54,595
Holders of	20 and under 50	29,733
Holders of	50 and under 100	6,196
Holders of	100 and under 200	1,479
Holders of	200 and under 300	187
Holders of	300 and under 500	56
Holders of	500 and under 1000	9
Holders of	1000 and over	2
Aggregate number of slaveholders in United States		347,525

THE CRISIS IN THE CHATTEL SLAVE SYSTEM 225

created a class of social retainers who defended the interest of the ruling class. Always there is a large section of society that follows the leaders and defends the interests of those leaders more energetically than its own.

The slave oligarchy in the South was well aware of the uncertainty of social rule by a minority, and comforted themselves with the conclusion that "The proportion which the slaveholders of the South bear to the entire population is greater than that of the owners of land or houses, agricultural stock, state, bank, or other corporation securities elsewhere."[1] Until the verge of the Civil War the majority of the non-slave-owning whites were firm in their allegiance to their slave-owning rulers. Indeed, Von Holst claims that "It was precisely the poorest and most abject whites who found the greatest satisfaction for their self-love in the thought that they were members of the privileged class. He who wished to span the broad gulf that separated them from the slaves, or was suspected of entertaining this wish, was their deadly enemy, for he threatened to expose them in all their neediness, defenseless and naked; he disputed their 'right' to the beggarly pomp that was due only to the deeper degradation of others; and he therefore trespassed upon their 'freedom.' "[2]

Representatives of the Southern ruling class were fond of taunting those who lived under the wage system with the security of a society based on chattel slavery

[1] J. D. B. DeBow, "The Non-Slave-Holders of the South," in *DeBow's Review*, 1861, p. 68.

[2] Von Holst, "Constitutional History of the United States," Vol. I, pp. 349–350.

as compared with one depending upon hired laborers. They were continually boasting of the fact that chattel slavery made any uprising of the workers impossible. As one writer put it, "There is perhaps no solution of the great problem of reconciling the interests of labor and capital, so as to protect each from the encroachments and oppression of the other, so simple and effective as negro slavery. By making the laborer himself capital, the conflict ceases, and the interests become identical."[1]

But no such simple solution of class struggles is possible. The negro refused to be entirely contented in his slavery, and the imagination of the white owners, reading into the slave's mind an even greater unrest than existed, painted horrible pictures of impending slave insurrections, until these became the social nightmare of the South. This fear, which kept the entire South in a state of hysterical apprehension, was a strong factor in creating the sentiment for secession. Only under a national government controlled by slave owners could the South sleep secure in the feeling that all efforts to incite such

[1] Thomas R. R. Cobb, "Historical Sketch of Slavery" (1858), p. 214; Frank E. Chadwick, "Causes of the Civil War" (Am. Nation Series), pp. 41–42. E. Von Holst, "Life of J. C. Calhoun," p. 175, quotes as follows from a speech of Calhoun's: "I fearlessly assert that the existing relations between the two races in the South . . . forms the most solid and desirable foundation on which to rear free and stable political institutions. It is useless to disguise the fact. There is, and always has been, in an advanced stage of wealth and civilization, a conflict between labor and capital. The condition of society in the South exempts us from the disorders and dangers resulting from this conflict; and explains why it is that the condition of the slaveholding states has been so much more stable and quiet than that of the North. The advantages of the former in this respect will become more and more manifest if left undisturbed by interference from without, as the country advances in wealth and numbers."

insurrections would be sternly suppressed. We now know that this terror was largely self-inspired. The negroes did not rise when opportunity offered.

On the other hand, the poor whites were showing unmistakable signs of dissatisfaction with the rule of the plantation barons. The propertyless whites were in a most helpless and abject state of industrial, social, and political dependence. They were permitted no share in the government, were shut out from the industrial life of the South, and were the despised hangers-on in the social world. To the north they saw the members of their class attaining to social and political rulership, and they began to move beneath the foundations of Southern society.

By 1850 DeBow, the great literary spokesman of Southern sentiment, was beginning to urge upon the plantation owners the necessity of finding some employment for the poor whites. "The great mass of our poor white population," he says, "begin to understand that they have rights, and that they, too, are entitled to some of the sympathy which falls upon the suffering. They are fast learning that there is an almost infinite world of industry opening before them, by which they can elevate themselves and their families from wretchedness and ignorance to competence and intelligence. *It is this great upbearing of our masses that we are to fear, so far as our institutions are concerned.*" [1]

In 1856 George M. Weston published a book entitled "The Poor Whites of the South." He described the industrial and physical and mental degradation of this

[1] Editorial in *DeBow's Review* (1850), Vol. VIII, p. 25. Italics in original.

class, as well as their political insignificance. "I have been for twenty years a reader of southern newspapers, and a hearer of Congressional debates," he says, "but in all that time, I do not recollect ever to have seen or heard these non-slave-holding whites referred to by southern gentlemen as constituting any part of what they call 'The South.'"[1]

Finally, in 1856, there came a book which voiced the interests and the demands of this class in such thunderous tones that it shook the weakening pillars of Southern society like reeds, and had very much more to do with bringing on the Civil War than did the much talked-about "Uncle Tom's Cabin." This book was Hinton Rowan Helper's "The Impending Crisis."

Reading this book to-day, it is difficult to understand its effect when published. It is composed largely of cold statistical proof that chattel slavery was hindering the progress of Southern society. Page after page of comparisons between the North and the South are given. In every instance the North has far outstripped the South in wealth. This tempting vision of the flesh-pots of profits from wage labor was dangled before the eyes of the non-slaveholding whites of the South; and the burden of the book, though never expressed directly, is: "But for chattel slavery you might be enjoying the things upon which your fellow little bourgeoisie in the North are fattening." Helper shows how much faster Northern cities have grown, how much more valuable is Northern land, both agricultural and urban, how in the North more railroads are built, more patents obtained, more ships are sailed; how, in short, there were more

[1] George M. Weston, "The Poor Whites of the South" (1856).

THE CRISIS IN THE CHATTEL SLAVE SYSTEM 229

of all the things that are the gods of the class of little capitalists to which the poor whites longed to belong, and to which, by the laws of social evolution, they should have been tending.

Helper taunts the non-slaveholders with the contempt in which they are held by the slave owners.[1] He says of the poor whites: "They have never yet had any part or lot in framing the laws under which they live. There is no legislation except for the benefit of slavery and slaveholders. . . . To all intents and purposes, they are disfranchised, and outlawed, and the only privilege extended to them is a shallow and circumscribed participation in the political movements that usher slaveholders into office." [2] He shows them how mercilessly the great plantations are devouring the small farms and leaving the country a wilderness when the soil has been exhausted.[3] He tabulates the offices controlled by the slavocracy since the foundation of the government, and shows that during nearly all of that time the presidency, vice-presidency, speakership of the House, Supreme Court, and the Cabinet have been filled with representatives of this small class of slave owners.[4]

From first to last he bases his case upon the material interest of the class he is seeking to arouse, and points that the way out is to use political power in the furtherance of class interests, exactly as the slaveholders have been doing.

The publication of this book exposed the Achilles' heel of the South. It was greeted with a perfect explosion of denunciation. Southern postmasters refused to

[1] Hinton Rowan Helper, "The Impending Crisis," p. 41.
[2] *Ibid.*, p. 42.   [3] *Ibid.*, pp. 57–58.   [4] *Ibid.*, pp. 307–317.

deliver it. Great bonfires were made of such copies as could be found in the South. Ownership of a copy in a Southern state was to invite mob violence.[1] Because John Sherman was reported to have contributed to a fund for its circulation, he was defeated for the speakership of the House of Representatives.[2]

There was but one way to meet this situation, and retain the allegiance of the poor whites for slavery. That was to introduce capitalism into the South alongside of the plantation system. This sounds almost grotesque. It was the only hope of escape, and was so recognized by the class-conscious slave owners.

The most strenuous efforts were made to introduce manufacturing. "In Alabama . . . there was a sort of frenzy over railroads in the early fifties."[3] State and local societies and "Institutes for the Promotion of Art, Mechanical Ingenuity, Industry, and Manufactures in the South" were formed. Before the South Carolina society of this name one William Gregg made an impassioned plea to the South not to content itself "to stand in the same relation to the Northern States and the balance of the manufacturing world, that Ireland, poor Ireland, does to England — hewers of

---

[1] John Spencer Bassett, "Anti-Slave Leaders of North Carolina," in *Johns Hopkins University Studies in History and Political Science*, p. 15.

[2] *Ibid.*, pp. 17–18.

[3] Wm. G. Brown, "The Lower South in American History," pp. 95–96. A few years ago press reports stated that Hinton R. Helper was found dead on a bench in a Washington, D.C., park. There is a grim irony in the fact that the man who was largely responsible for the vast financial and political power of American capitalists should have died an outcast.

wood and drawers of water."[1] He proceeds to urge the establishment of manufactures for the especial benefit of a large portion of our "poor white people, who are wholly neglected, and are suffered to while away an existence but one step in advance of the Indian of the forest."[2] Yet while he is planning an opportunity for these poor whites to become wageworkers, he is not blind to the fact that the presence of chattel slavery will permit the plantation class to retain their social leadership, since "capital will be able to control labor, even in manufacture with whites, for blacks can always be resorted to in case of need."[3]

These efforts to establish manufactures were not wholly in vain. Numerous factories using either white wage or negro chattel slave labor were running in the years just prior to the Civil War, and were greatly boasted by the Southern spokesmen.[4] But the two systems of industry could not exist side by side. The demands which they made upon government were different. The social classes which they raised to power were antagonistic. The effort to create manufactures with wage labor alongside of plantation agriculture operated by chattel slaves was only a sign of the disintegration of the latter system.

[1] *DeBow's Review*, Vol. II (1851), Address of William Gregg before the South Carolina Institute for the Promotion of Art, Mechanical Ingenuity, Industry, and Manufactures in South Carolina and the South, p. 127.
[2] *Ibid.*, p. 135.   [3] *Ibid.*, p. 130.
[4] Ingle, "Southern Side Lights," pp. 75–83; DeBow, "Industrial Resources of the Southern and Western States," Supplement to *DeBow's Review*, Vol. II (1846), pp. 230–231; *ibid.*, p. 332; Thomas P. Kettel, "Southern Wealth and Northern Profits," pp. 53–62.

The germs of disintegration were within the very elements that seemed to indicate the greatest prosperity for the chattel slave system of production. The friends of this system rested their case upon the domination of cotton. As the demand for cotton increased, the slave system seemed more firmly entrenched.

The following table gives the principal statistical facts in the growth of the Southern industrial system:—

Year	Value of all Products	Value of Cotton	Number of Slaves	Value of all Products per Slave
1800	$14,385,000	$5,252,000	893,041	$16.10
1810	28,255,000	15,108,000	1,191,364	19.50
1820	37,934,111	26,309,000	1,543,688	24.63
1830	45,225,838	34,084,883	2,009,053	22.00
1840	92,292,260	74,640,307	2,487,355	37.11
1850	130,556,050	101,334,616	3,179,509	43.51
1851	165,084,517	137,315,317	3,200,000	51.90

At first sight this would seem to show swiftly rising prosperity for the slave owners. But there is an inherent contradiction in chattel slavery, as within the competitive system, and this was the first time in the history of society that chattel slavery, on a large scale, had entered into the competitive system. This is the peculiarity: the increased productivity of the slave, or the increased profits from his employment, are constantly capitalized and absorbed in the ever increasing value of the slave.[1]

---

[1] Daniel R. Goodloe, "Is it Expedient to Introduce Slavery into Kansas?" p. 50: "The cultivation of land by slave labor requires a five-fold greater outlay of capital than is necessary with the use of free labor. The employer of slave labor must not only have the land, houses,

Since the yearly earnings in the most profitable industry where slaves were employed were thus capitalized and applied to the price of all slaves, the price rose in a most astonishing manner. This tendency was still further aggravated by the restrictions upon the foreign slave trade, which prevented the importation of any save those that could be smuggled past the watchful revenue cruisers. Consequently the price rose from less than $150 in 1808 to between two and four thousand dollars for field hands in the years immediately preceding the war.[1]

At these prices only the largest plantations, working the slaves in the most effective manner upon the richest lands, raising the most profitable crops, could survive. It had become a common saying that the slave owner grew more cotton to get more money to buy more slaves, to raise more cotton, and so on in an endless and ever rising spiral.

This development, combined with the exhaustive one-crop system of farming, drove the slave owner on toward the extreme south and west. A moving picture

fences, cattle, provisions, etc., which, the employing of free labor requires, but in addition he must own a slave, worth from $800 to $1000, for every twenty acres of land which he proposes to cultivate."

[1] Kettel, "Southern Wealth and Northern Profits," p. 171. "The Documentary History of American Industrial Society," Vol. II, pp. 73-74, quotes from the Milledgeville, Ga., *Federal Union* of Jan. 17, 1860, as follows: "Men are borrowing money at exorbitant rates of interest to buy negroes at exorbitant prices. . . . The old rule of pricing a negro by the price of cotton by the pound — that is to say, if cotton is worth twelve cents, a negro man is worth $1200, if at fifteen cents, then $1500 — does not seem to be regarded. Negroes are 25 per cent higher now with cotton at ten and one-half cents than they were two or three years ago, when it was worth fifteen and sixteen cents. Men are demented upon the subject. A reverse will surely come." M. B. Hammond, "The Cotton Industry," pp. 50-51.

of the black population of the South and its white owners during the last ten years of chattel slavery would suggest some thick dark fluid flowing toward the Gulf of Mexico.[1] Thus the South became divided into the "slave-using" and the "slave-breeding" states. Virginia and Maryland were the two great sources of the slave supply, from whence the "coffles" of slaves were gathered by the buyers to be shipped to the sugar and cotton plantations further south.[2] It was not profitable to keep slaves in the border states except for breeding purposes, and there was somewhat of a sentiment against this. Therefore the number of slaves in the border states steadily decreased in numbers.

There were at least two elements of disintegration added by this movement to the already crumbling fabric of chattel slavery. The conflict of interest which always exists between buyers and sellers arose between these two sections of the South. This showed itself in the agitation for the reopening of the foreign slave trade on the part of the slave-using states. This was urged in the hope of lowering the price of slaves and thereby preventing the collapse of slavery by the absorption of all profits in the values of the laborers.[3] It was also urged that such a reduction in price would enable the chattel slave owners to compete with the wage system in the settlement of new territory to the west.[4]

[1] James Baker, essay on American Slavery in *North American Review*, October, 1851, p. 12; Hammond, "The Cotton Industry," pp. 50–51.

[2] James F. W. Johnson, "Notes on North America" (1851), Vol. II, pp. 354–355.

[3] George Fitzhugh, "The Wealth of the North and South," in *De-Bow's Review*, Vol. XXIII (1857), p. 592.

[4] *Ibid.*, p. 594: "The revival of the African slave trade, the reduction in the price of negroes, and the increase of their numbers, will enable us

THE CRISIS IN THE CHATTEL SLAVE SYSTEM

When this proposition to reopen the slave trade was brought up in one of the many trade conventions that were held in the South during the years from 1850 to 1860, the opposition of the slave-breeding states, who were profiting by the high price of slaves, was so great that the resolution on this point was finally dropped "because the resolution was impolitic as affecting the interests of such states as Virginia, Kentucky, Missouri, and North Carolina."[1]

Another great weakness of the chattel slave and plantation system is found in the fact that it was so completely dependent upon other societies. It was always a debtor society, unable to market its crop without the ships and mills of New and old England. It had but one crop to bring to market, and brought this in the raw stage. Then, as now, the greatest profits went to those who controlled the later stages of production. Whenever the interests of these two stages of society conflicted, the advantage was all with the one representing the later industrial epoch. One of the points where this clash came was on the tariff question, and the first and some of the sharpest conflicts between the capitalist North and the semi-feudal South were on this question.[2] Just why this

successfully to contend in the establishment of new territories with the vast emigration from the North."

[1] Ingle, "Southern Side Lights," p. 250.

[2] E. Von Holst, "Life of J. C. Calhoun," pp. 75–76; An American, "Cotton is King," pp. 64–81. On p. 67 of this work, which was one of the most commonly circulated books by the defenders of the South, the position of that section is summed up as follows: "If they [the Southern planters] could establish free trade, it would insure the American market to foreign manufacturers; secure foreign markets for their leading staple; repress home manufactures; force a larger number of the northern men into agriculture; multiply the growth and diminish the

clash was particularly sharp about 1860 will be pointed out in the next chapter.

The absolute need for territorial expansion by a one-crop society was bringing the South into another *cul de sac*. With the national government completely in its control, it was able to force the annexation of Texas and a large extent of other territory after an almost unprovoked war with Mexico.[1] At the same time a large amount of territory in the northwest to which the title of the United States was fairly clear was surrendered almost without a protest.[2]

The bounds of possible expansion were soon reached, so far as continental America was concerned. Much of the land which was obtained in the war with Mexico was closed to chattel slavery by the ever encroaching wage labor society to the north. The South in desperation turned to the tropical countries and islands further south. They talked in terms of a "manifest destiny" that was driving them on to the possession of Cuba and the valley of the Amazon.[3] Envious eyes

price of provisions; feed and clothe their slaves at lower rates; produce their cotton for a third or fourth of former prices; rival all other countries in its cultivation; monopolize the trade in the article throughout the whole of Europe; and build up a commerce and a navy that would make us the rulers of the seas."

[1] E. Von Holst, "Life of J. C. Calhoun," pp. 220–259, 237: "Because the slave-holding states thought their peculiar institution endangered by the existence of an independent free state, it was declared to be the 'imperative duty' and a 'sacred obligation' of the United States, imposed by their constitutional compact, to absorb that state into the Union in order to prevent the abolition of slavery in it."

[2] *Ibid.*, p. 267 *et seq.*

[3] *DeBow's Review*, Vol. XVII, p. 280. *Ibid.*, Vol. XV, p. 263, contains a report of a convention held at Memphis in 1853, where a long resolution on the opening of the Amazon, was adopted, beginning as follows:

were cast upon Cuba at this time, and the descriptions of the atrocities of Spanish rule in that island read very much like the writings which appeared upon that same subject almost fifty years later, when Northern capitalism was, in its turn, struggling for expansion.[1]

All its efforts in this direction were in vain. The hold of the South upon the national government was slipping away, and it was impossible to use that government for another war of conquest.

Internally the chattel slave system was devouring itself; externally it was being strangled for lack of room to expand. The inherent contradictions that arise within every industrial system based upon exploitation were rending it asunder, while a rival industrial system was proving superior in the great struggle for existence by which social systems are tried out in the laboratory of history.

At such a critical time possession of the national government was essential to even a temporary prolongation of existence. When that government passed into the hands of its rival in the battle for survival, the Southern slavocracy tried to secede and establish a government it could control.[2]

"Resolved, that the interests of commerce, the cause of civilization, and the mandates of high heaven, require the Atlantic slopes of South America to be subdued and replenished." Wilson, "History of the American People," Vol. IV, pp. 173-174.

[1] Henry Wilson, "History of the Rise and Fall of the Slave Power in America," Vol. II, pp. 608-614; *DeBow's Review*, Vol. XVIII, pp. 163-167 and 305-313.

[2] Brown, "The Lower South in American History," p. 83: "The struggle for ascendency was, in fact, a struggle for existence. . . . The lower South was from the beginning under a necessity either to control the national government or radically to change its own industrial and social system."

CHAPTER XXI

RISE OF NORTHERN CAPITALISM

WHILE Southern society was approaching the final stages of its development and displaying signs of inevitable disintegration, Northern society was leaping into the vigorous strength of adult power. The industrial revolution that brought the factory system, the growth of great cities, the annihilation of space, the piling up of vast profits, was in full swing.

The railroad had passed the experimental stage mechanically, financially, and politically. It was now ready to work the social transformation of which it was capable. Until about 1845 railroads were built simply to unite two neighboring cities, or as links in a canal system, or to bring some specific product to market. Each important city was a "terminal" of one or more roads connecting it with some comparatively near-by place. There was no idea of a general system binding a whole section or sections of the country together.[1]

The total mileage had been steadily increasing. There were 23 miles in 1830, 2818 in 1840, and 9021 in 1850. When these were welded into systems covering large sections and giving to these sections an industrial and social unity they had not and could not have known before, the mileage leaped to 30,635 by 1860.[2]

[1] Emory R. Johnson, "American Railway Transportation," p. 25.
[2] A. S. Bolles, "Industrial History of the United States," p. 635.

RISE OF NORTHERN CAPITALISM

The North had far outstripped the South in the extent of its railroad building. According to Helper the "free" states had 17,855 miles of railroad in 1857, while the "slave" states contained but 6859 miles.[1] Yet because the South controlled the national government, that section had been especially favored in the matter of land grants. The system of giving land from the public domain to corporations with which to build railroads that should remain in private hands was begun with the grant to the Illinois Central in 1850. Although this road was located in a wage labor state, it was intended to benefit the South by linking the upper Mississippi Valley with the Gulf of Mexico.[2]

This use of the national government for internal improvements was one of the points where the interests of the North and the South clashed. The South did not favor internal improvements in any whole-hearted manner, and when it did favor any specific improvement it demanded that it be located in the South.[3] The Pacific railway could not be built while the South controlled the national government.[4] There was a feature of the discussion of the Pacific Railway that showed how the North was beginning to shape the national mind. Until about 1850, in all discussions of a railway across the continent, it was taken for granted that it was to be built by the national government, and be owned by that government. By 1855 the idea of individual or corporate ownership

---

[1] H. R. Helper, "The Impending Crisis," p. 285.

[2] A. S. Bolles, *loc. cit.*, p. 643.

[3] John P. Davis, "The Union Pacific Railway," Chap. III; Brown, "The Lower South in American History," p. 68.

[4] Davis, *loc. cit.*, pp. 66–67.

was accepted in Congressional discussions with almost equal unanimity.[1]

Along the railroad went the telegraph, completing the work of solidifying the life of the industrial sections. The first telegraph line was built from Washington to Baltimore in 1844. It was extended to New York the same year, and to Boston the next. By 1850 there were 22,000 miles of telegraph in operation, and by 1860 this had grown to 50,000, and the Western Union had laid the foundation of its monopoly.

It was the telegraph that really made possible an extensive railroad system. It is hard to-day to think of railroad operation without some method of communication independent of and faster than the trains themselves.

The telegraph annihilated space in the transmission of information, and made it possible for a whole section, and later for a whole nation and the whole world, to think together. It made bargaining and the carrying on of financial transactions between widely separated parties possible, and revolutionized systems of commercial procedure that had endured for centuries.[2] It created the

---

[1] Davis, *loc. cit.*, pp. 66–67.

[2] "Memorial History of New York," Vol. III, p. 414: "The telegraph, which had come fairly into use by 1847, revolutionized the methods of business. Heretofore it had been the custom of the merchants of Pittsburg, Buffalo, Cleveland, and Cincinnati, and all the larger interior towns, to visit New York once a year and select their stock of goods for the coming year. Now all this was changed. The development of the railroad and the telegraph made it possible for the merchants of the interior to order any particular goods wanted, and to receive them within a day or two, so that the great wholesale houses, instead of carrying a large and miscellaneous stock of goods, began to limit themselves to a single line, and their customers in ordering would divide their orders among perhaps a dozen houses."

daily newspaper as a medium for the reception and dissemination of the events of the world without delay. Here, again, it was the North whose solidarity was strengthened and social mentality unified and quickened by the telegraph.

One method of communication was still in an extremely imperfect state, and was showing little signs of improvement. This was the postal service. Mails were carried only in the daytime. Not until 1860 do we read in a report of the postmaster-general of an "experiment" with a night mail between New York and Boston.

The systematic and complicated schemes of distribution, which are the foundation of present postal systems, were as yet unthought of. All distributing was done in the post-offices. No one had suggested a railway mail car for distribution en route. If the reader will try to work out a system of mail distribution on this plan to include 18,000 post-offices, the number that existed in 1850, he will gain some idea of the confusion and delay that prevailed. Separate pieces of mail would be received in each large city for nearly all of these post-offices. To sort this mail properly would require 18,000 mail sacks. This being impossible, all the mail going in one direction was sent in one sack. As this arrived at each office en route, it was opened, the contents taken out, sorted for the letters belonging to this particular office, and then the remainder of the mail returned to the sack to continue on its journey.

By the late fifties this plan had become absolutely unworkable, and it had been supplemented by another only a trifle less clumsy. Several larger cities were designated as "distributing centers" for all offices near by.

Each "distributing center" had its separate pouch containing the mail for all contiguous offices. The mail was re-sorted at the "center" for the smaller offices. Soon "subsidiary distributing offices" had to be selected, so that mail was often stopped at two or three places for distribution. Two towns but a few miles apart, but within different "distributing centers," were sometimes compelled to wait weeks for the mail to go from one to the other, although passengers were regularly making the trip in a few hours.

The cost was very high for this inefficient service. Until 1845 rates for the minimum weight of letters was as follows: under 30 miles, six cents; 30 to 80 miles, ten cents; 80 to 150 miles, $12\frac{1}{2}$ cents; 150 to 400 miles, $18\frac{3}{4}$ cents, and over 400 miles, 25 cents. While these rates lasted, many of the most important features of modern industry were impossible. They tended very strongly to the development of sectional as contrasted with national solidarity.

Population, transportation, and industry had now reached a stage where it was profitable for private enterprise to enter into competition with the post-office in the carrying of small parcels. Accordingly, William Harnden began what has since developed into the express business by carrying parcels between New York and Boston in 1839. The Adams Express Company grew out of this undertaking the next year, and the American Express Company came into existence one year later. The powerful Wells Fargo, that was to play so large a part in the control of Western trade, and especially of the traffic incident to the discovery of gold in California, was founded in 1852.[1] The United States Express Company started two years later. The express business is peculiarly American. In all other countries the functions performed by express companies are divided between the freight departments of the railroads and the post-office. This would undoubtedly have been the case in this country, had it not been for the fact that the demand for this service came at a time when the idea of *laissez faire* and individual initiative ruled industrial and political life.

At the very time when the mails were being changed from stagecoach to railroads, and when the government was beginning its policy of giving the land with which railroads were to be built, the express companies entered upon the scene and absorbed the most profitable portion of the mail business. Railroad charges prevented the post-office from entering into any effective competition with the express companies. Caught thus between the upper and the nether millstone, the post-office started upon that long career of deficits that have since served to hamper its operation.

The officials who had charge of the post-office at this time were not blind to the dangers that threatened the postal system through the invasion of its profitable business by the express companies. Postmaster-General Wickliffe, who was in office from 1841 to 1845, protested in almost every report that the express companies were violating the constitutional provision which gave the government a monopoly of the postal business, and that they were doing this only over the short hauls and in the

[1] A. L. Stimpson, "History of the Express Business," pp. 34–79.

most thickly settled districts, leaving the unprofitable business to the government.[1] His protests went unheeded, save in so far as they may have led Congress to the reduction of the rates of postage in 1845 to five cents per half ounce for less than 300 miles and ten cents for all distances over 500 miles.

By this time a movement had been started by Sir Rowland Hill in England for "penny postage." The essential point of this idea was not the penny unit, but the abolition of the distance charge; and in 1851 the rate for letters in the United States was reduced to three cents, without regard to distance.

We can hardly think of a letter and postal service apart from postage stamps, yet the adhesive stamp was first authorized in the United States in 1847, and made compulsory in 1856. In 1854 the system of registry for valuable letters was introduced.

The postal service still lacked railroad distribution, money orders, low newspaper postage, free delivery, and several other things prominent at the present time. It was too imperfect to build up national solidarity, but was eminently fitted to bring much closer together the people of considerable sections of the nation.

Since the need of communication was much more strongly felt, and brought much greater material benefits to an industrial than an agricultural nation, nearly all steps looking to the improvement of the post-office met with the indifference or active opposition of the chattel slave-owning cotton raisers of the agricultural South.

---

[1] Reports of Postmaster-General, 1841, 1845; and opinion of Attorney-General, Nov. 13, 1843; also report of Congressional Committee in February, 1844.

The factory system, now firmly established, was extending and developing in all directions. Inventions, always the index of mechanical progress, were multiplying. Up to 1840 there had been 11,908 patents issued. This was the result of half a century. 31,523 patents were issued during the next twenty years. In other words, man's control over nature, and the accompanying transformation in all social relations, was almost three times as great in these twenty as in the previous fifty years.

These inventions were largely basic and revolutionary in their character. Elias Howe made the first sewing machine for which a patent was granted in 1846. McCormick patented the reaper in 1831, but never was able to make as many as five hundred in one year until 1845. In 1844 Goodyear laid the foundation of the present rubber industry by his discovery of the process of vulcanizing rubber. Iron rails were first rolled in this country in 1844, but only as an experiment. Even in 1855, when the Cambria Iron Company of Johnstown, Pennsylvania, rolled the first thirty-foot rails, it found no market for them. But by 1860 more than 200,000 tons of iron rails were manufactured in the United States. The center of this industry was now definitely located in the Pittsburg district, and it was here that the growth was most rapid.

A revolutionary change had taken place in the production of iron. In 1839 anthracite coal was first successfully used in a blast furnace. By 1855 more iron was being produced with coal than with wood.[1] Hitherto iron had

[1] James M. Swank, "The Manufacture of Iron in All Ages," Chap. XXXV; A. S. Bolles, "Industrial History of the United States," pp. 202–204.

been made with charcoal, and the furnace must be kept close to the ever retreating forest. Now the elements in its manufacture were fixed as to location for long terms of years. Hereafter the location of the iron and steel industry was to depend upon the relation of four items: ore, coal, limestone, and the market for the finished product.

In commerce, too, this was a time of swift upward development. By 1846 the tremendous tonnage of the Napoleonic days was equaled, and for the next ten years it shot up at an unparalleled rate, until American ships had a tonnage of more than 2,300,000, or nearly three times as great as at any period prior to 1845.[1] These were the days of the famous "clipper" ships, the fastest sailing vessels ever launched.

Three inventions came in the years 1836 to 1838 that sounded the doom of American maritime supremacy. These were the use of iron in shipbuilding, the application of steam to ocean vessels, and the invention of the screw propeller.[2] The cheaper iron of England was soon to drive the wooden ships of America from the ocean. The shipbuilding trade declined on American soil. This fatal competition had not progressed far enough prior to the Civil War to produce any social effects of importance. In 1860 shipping was still in a stage of great prosperity.

The spread of railroads had not prevented a swift increase in the amount of traffic on the inland waterways. While the efforts to use steam in transatlantic travel

[1] Coman, "Industrial History of the United States," pp. 228–229.

[2] Bogart, "Economic History of the United States," pp. 206–207; Bolles, "Industrial History of the United States," pp. 591–595.

were unsatisfactory, because the imperfect machinery made it necessary to use nearly all the storage capacity of the ship for fuel, no such difficulty existed on the rivers and lakes of the Mississippi Valley, where fuel grew thick upon every bank. A type of steamer new to the history of shipbuilding was constructed for Mississippi River traffic. It was a broad, shallow craft, built low to the water's edge, but with two or more decks above, and great carrying capacity. So many of these were built that by 1856 the steam tonnage of the Mississippi River equaled that of the whole empire of Great Britain.[1]

The most important development of inland water transportation in this epoch was connected with the great system of inland lakes at the head of the Mississippi Valley, with their outlet to the East into the Atlantic. These Great Lakes were the highway that bound together a group of states with a common industrial and social structure. This group was to constitute the pivot upon which American politics were to make their greatest turn. The tonnage of vessels on this inland waterway, the greatest on the globe, grew from 75,000 in 1840 to 215,787 in 1850, and to nearly 500,000 in 1860.[2]

Yet it must not be forgotten that fast as all forms of inland water navigation were growing, railroad transportation was leaping forward at a far faster rate. By 1860 it was estimated that two thirds of the total internal trade moved over iron rails.[3]

The wave of progress that was working such changes in

[1] Bolles, "Industrial History of the United States," pp. 588–595.
[2] Bogart, "Economic History of the United States," pp. 209–210.
[3] *Ibid.*

manufacture and commerce was lifting the foundations of that greatest and oldest and most immovable of industries — agriculture. Had the Roman Cincinnatus been raised from his sleep of centuries and placed upon an American farm in 1830, he would have seen few implements whose use he would not have been able to understand. The greatest change would perhaps have been the addition of a long and crooked handle and a number of fingers to an elongated blade of a sickle, by which process the grain cradle had been evolved. But farm labor was still hand labor. Almost no use was made of animals save for hauling loads and pulling the plow. A new era was at hand.

"The decade 1850 to 1860 was a period when American inventors were earnestly endeavoring to improve all classes of farm implements and machinery. It witnessed the beginning of the practical use of horse-driven machinery for cutting and threshing grain, the first of a series of changes that subsequently revolutionized the methods of work on all farms in the United States outside of those devoted to cotton-growing."[1]

The reason for this is found largely in the fact that this was the period of the opening up of the first broad strip of prairie embracing Illinois, Iowa, and eastern Kansas and Nebraska. Here it was possible to use many tools which could not be employed upon the stony, stumpy farms of New England and the Ohio Valley.

Factory methods in the production of agricultural machinery were impossible before the railroad system of the country was sufficiently developed to place a large

[1] Census 1900, Vol. V, Pt. I, p. xxvi.

RISE OF NORTHERN CAPITALISM

number of farms within reach of a single central point.[1] The application of agricultural machinery also requires a market for a crop in the raising of which such machinery can be used. When the railroads and the Great Lakes and canals opened a highway for the grain trade, this third condition was fulfilled. The first shipment of grain ever made from Chicago was in 1838, and the total amount sent out that year was 78 bushels. By 1845 more than a million bushels passed through this same port on the way to the markets of the world. In 1860 a total of 31,109,059 bushels went through the same gateway.[2]

The most important population movement of this period was the filling up of the Great Lakes region. Hostile Indian tribes, imperfect transportation, and the fact that immigration had come largely from slave territory and could not bring its favorite institution into this locality with profit, all had contributed to keep this great stretch of territory unsettled. Now all these obstacles were removed at once. The Erie Canal and steam upon the lakes, followed by the railroad, threw wide the gates to the incoming hosts. And the hosts were ready to come. The manufacturing states of New England and New York and Pennsylvania were casting out the first battalions of workless workers displaced by

---

[1] Census 1900, Bulletin No. 200, on "Agricultural Implements," p. 18: "It was not until the western movement of the population had converted the rich alluvial plains of the western states into productive farms, and the railroad systems of the country had extended their lines for the distribution of farm products, that the progress and development of this industry (manufacture of agricultural machinery) found its full expression."

[2] Eighth Census.

the machine and the superabundance of their own product. This army was reënforced by shiploads of immigrants. Europe, in the throes of the Revolution of 1848, was outlawing her rebellious workers and driving them by tens of thousands to America.

Natural calamity added to political upheaval in driving the European workers to the New World. A potato famine in Ireland in 1848 started the tremendous flood of Irish toward America, adding one of the most important factors of the social life of this country.[1]

Within the Northern states there was a great drift of population cityward. In 1830 only 6.7 per cent of the population of the country lived in cities of more than 8000 inhabitants. Twenty years later this percentage was 16.1.[2] This was the time of the birth of the modern city proletariat, one of the most definite products of the capitalist system.

This great Northwest that was now being settled with such rapidity was quickly seen to hold the balance of power between the hitherto contending sections of the country. Whichever side could bind this section to it with bonds of economic interest could dominate in the national government. The South had the start in the race. The commercial artery of the section was the southward-flowing Mississippi. The South bought its mules and the hay with which they were fed, as well as

[1] Industrial Commission Report, Vol. XV, pp. 260–277. The total immigration by decades from 1821 was as follows: 1821 to 1830, 143,439; 1831 to 1840, 599,125; 1841 to 1850, 1,713,251; 1851 to 1860, 2,598,214. Of those who came between 1841 and 1860, 1,694,838 came from Ireland, and 1,386,293 from Germany.

[2] "Statistical Atlas of the United States," 1900, p. 40.

the corn meal and pork that formed the slave ration, from this section.[1]

The East and the West were competing in agriculture. There was no little complaint over the fact that the cheapness with which grain could be raised in the West was depreciating farm values in New York and New England.[2]

When manufacture and commerce dominated the East, it became a buyer of agricultural products. It then competed with the South as a market for the agricultural West, instead of competing with the West as a seller in the Southern and all other markets. Henceforth the fight for the favor of the West was a fight of transportation routes. While nature seemed to favor the South in the beginning of this struggle, each new invention gave more advantage to the East. Moreover, in this direction lies Europe, to which much of the products of the prairies of the West was destined to flow.

The cities of New York, Philadelphia, Boston, and Baltimore fought with each other in the effort to divert

[1] Brown, "The Lower South in American History," p. 35.

[2] Timothy Dwight, in the *New England Magazine* for April, 1848, says: "Soon after the completion of the Erie Canal, lands in New York began to increase in price, and rose steadily in value, until they were sold in many cases at from $60 to $100 an acre. But as soon as Ohio and Michigan began to produce wheat in quantities greatly exceeding their own consumption, and were able to deliver in Buffalo several million of bushels annually, the value of these lands began to decline. A year or two since we were informed that the depreciation was so great that lands which some years before had been mortgaged for two-thirds or three-fourths of their value would not at that time sell for the amount of the mortgage. The same thing is strikingly evinced by the fact that the aggregate population of twenty-four counties in the State of New York, comprising some of the most fertile in the central and western parts of the State, was less in 1845 than in 1840."

this trade through their gates.[1] When, in 1853, the first railroad united Chicago with the Atlantic coast, DeBow estimated that the state of New York alone had expended more than a hundred million dollars in improving the routes to the Northwest which ran through her boundaries.[2] In 1861 an English observer, quoted in the *New York Times*, estimated that $500,000,000 had been expended to "change the direction of the commerce of the Mississippi."[3]

This "reversing the mouths of the Mississippi" did not go on without protest from the South. At the numerous Southern conventions held in the years immediately preceding the war, one of the perennial subjects, along with the foreign slave trade, the conquest of new slave territory, and the encouragement of Southern manufactures, was the question of how this trade could be

[1] William Grant, "Observations on the Western Trade," in Hudson River R.R. Reports, pp. 12–16.

[2] *DeBow's Review*, September, 1853, p. 313.

[3] Fite, "Social and Industrial Conditions in the North during the Civil War," p. 14: "Still another piece of good fortune for the West was the trunk line railroads. These were bands of iron binding the farming sections to the East, helping to hold them in the Union by providing a market for their produce. In the ten years preceding, in the states of Indiana, Illinois, Wisconsin, and Iowa seven thousand miles of railroad were constructed, provision far in advance of the needs of the country, but, as it proved, a magnificent preparation for the unforeseen strain of war. The Mississippi formerly had been the outlet of these sections to a market, carrying the grain and other produce to New Orleans, where it was distributed in all directions. After the war closed the River, if the railroads had not been in existence, the West would have been isolated without a market, and it was believed by some that rather than lose this, the section would have followed its market into secession. According to this view, the Union was saved by the railroads. Others with less confidence in the roads, or perhaps even ignoring their existence, openly feared the western secession, and many in the South prophesied it."

retained by the South. DeBow never ceased to urge the South to enter into competition with the North in the building of railroads. In 1851 he exclaims, "New Orleans in every period of her history has been the emporium of the West, and New Orleans will only give up that distinction after the most unremitting and herculean struggles have exhausted her energy. The sceptre has *not yet* departed, and if her citizens are true to themselves, the sceptre shall not depart."

The scepter did depart, however. The industrial capitalist had too great an advantage in such a struggle. The surplus value taken from wageworkers is much larger than that obtained from chattel slaves, and it is more readily converted into the capital needed for internal improvements. Wage labor is much more adapted to the construction of such works. It was but natural, therefore, that a railroad map of the United States published by DeBow in 1851 shows that not only are the roads actually constructed in the North much greater in mileage, while our later knowledge tells us that most of those dotted lines in the South indicating "projected roads" were not constructed until long after chattel slavery had disappeared.

In 1848 came the discovery of gold in California, followed by the wild rush to the Pacific coast, the inflation of the money basis, the possibility of a gold standard, and a safer system of banking. All these things helped to unify and strengthen the growing power of capitalism.

All things had worked together to weld the North into a compact section with common interests. The railroad and telegraph had given it industrial and social unity. The progress of invention, and the factory system based upon the inventions, had brought it wealth and power. Agriculture, commerce, manufacture, and mining were in the wave of prosperity that accompanies the conquest of new fields. Everywhere the watchword was expansion.

Prior to about 1855 the interests of the North had been too sectional, competitive, and diversified to form the foundation of any common political action. Each little competing section had interests uniting it with the South. There was no widespread interest demanding control of the national government. Here we find the explanation of the sham fights between the Whigs and the Democrats, with their utter lack of any conflict of principles.[1]

There now arose a class throughout the North compact in its organization, definite and largely agreed in industrial interest, and having need of the national government to defend that interest. This was the little competitive bourgeoisie that had already overthrown feudalism in Europe. It was in the upper Mississippi Valley that this class ruled with fewest entangling alliances with other classes. Here old political ties were weak, and the new industrial interests keen. The new state governments commanded no such local and state patriotism as did the seaboard states, with their prerevolutionary traditions. The little capitalist mind possessed employers, wageworkers, and farmers alike. All hoped, and with better reason than at any time since, to become capitalists. The new and growing country about them apparently offered unlimited oppor-

[1] M. Ostrogorski, "Democracy and the Organization of Political Parties," Vol. II, pp. 40–41.

tunity to "rise" — the highest ideal of the bourgeois mind.

The members of this class wanted internal improvements built by the national government. They wanted a protective tariff. They favored immigration, — the manufacturer to cheapen labor, the landowner to raise real estate values, all to build up the country and bring "prosperity." They wanted a homestead law that should assure the remainder of the West to wage labor. They opposed any further extension of the slave power, and were determined to wrest the control of the national government from that power. All these desires found expression in the Republican party.

There was an idealistic element in the organization of the Republican party that should not be overlooked. There is always such an element in any revolutionary movement, and the Republican party was essentially revolutionary in many of its purposes. It was demanding that the control of government be transferred to a new social class, and that is the essence of revolution. It was the same in the days of the French Revolution, — in the time of the repeal of the Corn Laws in England, and in every time of great social and political change. Such an idealistic element was already in existence in the Eastern states. Its prophet was Horace Greeley, and its inspired message was found in the columns of the *New York Tribune*. Around this paper, with Greeley at its head, had been gathered Charles A. Dana, as managing editor, Albert Brisbane, the Fourierite, as the contributor of a column each week on Utopian Socialism, and Karl Marx as principal European correspondent.

The *Tribune* had taken up many of the reforms that had been demanded by the labor movement of the thirties. It had given an idealistic and labor turn to many bourgeois principles, which were now adopted by the Republican party. It advocated a protective tariff as a measure to increase wages instead of profits. In so doing it gave to the defenders of the tariff the only new argument since Hamilton. Greeley advocated the homestead law as a means of granting all an equal share in the earth.[1] This action of Greeley and the *Tribune* brought to the new Republican party the support of a large section of the working class. The idealism that accompanied the birth of the party also gained the allegiance of the college and school influence of the North. Whittier wrote its campaign songs. Lowell translated its doctrines into poetry, while Emerson, Bryant, Longfellow, Holmes, and Motley were some of the names high in American literature who were counted on its membership rolls.[2]

Seeing in the Republican party the incarnation of the ideals for which they had fought in Europe, the revolutionary German exiles of 1848 added their strength to the new political movement. This element included such men as Carl Schurz, afterward a cabinet officer, Weydemeyer, the Socialist and fellow-worker with Marx, and whole regiments like those who "fought mit Siegel" in the war that was already casting its shadow before.

---

[1] John R. Commons, "Horace Greeley and the Working Class Origin of the Republican Party," *Political Science Quarterly*, Vol. XXIV, No. 3.

[2] Wm. H. Smith, "A Political History of Slavery," Vol. I, pp. 233–234.

RISE OF NORTHERN CAPITALISM

The first railroad uniting Chicago with the East was completed in 1853, and the next year organizations bearing the name Republican party sprang up almost simultaneously in Wisconsin, Illinois, Michigan, Indiana, and Ohio.[1]

The first national convention of the new party was held at Pittsburg in February, 1856. The committee calling that convention submitted an address which gives the following reasons for forming a new party:[2] —

"The slaveholding interest cannot be made permanently paramount in the general government without involving consequences fatal to free institutions. We acknowledge that it is large and powerful; that in states where it exists it is entitled under the constitution, like all other local interests, to immunity from the interference of the general government; and that it must necessarily exercise through its representatives a considerable share of political power. But there is nothing in its position, as there is certainly nothing in its character, to sustain the supremacy which it seeks to establish.

. . . .

"The representatives of freedom on the floor of Congress have been treated with contumely, if they resist or question the right to supremacy of the slaveholding class. The labor and commerce of sections where slavery does not exist obtain tardy and inadequate recognition from the general government. . . . Thus is the decision of great questions of public policy, touching vast interests and vital rights, questions even of peace and war, made to turn, not upon the requirements of justice

---

[1] Francis Curtis, "The Republican Party," Chap. IV.
[2] Benjamin F. Hall, "The Republican Party," pp. 448-456.

s

and honor, but upon its relation to the subject of slavery — upon the effect it will have upon the interest of the slaveholding class."

It is plain that the indictment here is not of slavery, but of the rule of the slaveholding class.

John C. Fremont, the candidate of the Republican party in this first campaign, received more votes than the Whig nominee and within a half million of the number received by Buchanan, the successful Democrat. More than 90 per cent of this vote came from New England and the states that touch the Great Lakes. Wherever in these states commercial connections were close with the South the Republican vote was small.[1]

During the next four years every force that had created the Republican party grew stronger. To these steadily growing forces was added that sudden shock which seems always necessary to bring long developing revolutionary forces to a climax. This shock was furnished by two events — the Dred Scott decision and the panic of 1857. The panic had the effect of accentuating the need of expansion of capitalist territory and markets, of emphasizing the need of controlling the national government and in general of sharpening class consciousness and class antagonisms.

The panic having created a highly unstable social compound, the Dred Scott decision furnished the spark that led to the explosion. The Supreme Court had been

[1] James Ford Rhodes, "History of the United States," Vol. III, p. 227: "West of the Allegheny mountains the enthusiasm for Fremont was like that in New England, New York, and Ohio; but as one traveled eastward a different political atmosphere could easily be felt, and when one reached Philadelphia, which was bound to the South by a lucrative trade, the chill was depressing."

steadily usurping power since the days of Marshall. It had grown arrogant and isolated from popular sentiment. Years of Democratic control of the national government had packed the court with justices friendly to the slave power. Now it proceeded to enact into law things that the chattel slaveowners had never dared to ask of Congress.

Dred Scott was a negro whose master had taken him from Missouri into the free state of Illinois. When he was taken back to Missouri, he demanded his freedom on the ground that taking him into a free state had broken his master's right of property. The court not only decided against him, but, anxious to show its complete subserviency to the slavocracy, it proceeded to destroy all the carefully built up compromises by which politicians had sought to cover up the struggle between the North and the South. Chief Justice Taney, who has made his name infamous and the Supreme Court forever contemptible by this decision, went on to declare that slaves being property and not persons, neither Congress nor territorial governments could prevent the owner of slaves from going where he wished with his property.

This was telling the capitalists of the North that no matter what happened, while the slaveholders controlled the Supreme Court the powers of government were out of the reach of the society resting upon wage labor.

When the power of the slaveowner seemed strongest, when the Supreme Court had apparently placed him in complete command, it was inevitable that those who could not see that this was an act of desperation on the part of a falling class, rather than of bold defiance by an impregnable ruler, should also grow desperate. Such a one was John Brown, who now hurled a new mass of explosives into the midst of the conflagration. In as recklessly foolish "propaganda of the deed" as was ever suggested by the most fanatical defender of "individual warfare" he tried, with a handful of men, to capture the United States arsenal at Harper's Ferry, Virginia. He dreamed that by so doing he would place himself at the head of an uprising of negro slaves, who would cut their way to liberty over the bodies of their masters. He seems to have combined the dream of the abolitionist, the bloody visions of bleeding Kansas (where he had been a doer of bloody deeds), and the slave-insurrection nightmare of the South, and from these phantoms sought to build a new society. Of course Brown's little force was wiped out, he was hung, and the North almost unanimously joined with the South in denouncing his action. But before twelve months had passed away, troops were marching southward to the tune of "John Brown's body lies a-moldering in the grave, but his soul goes marching on."

It would be foolish to pass judgment on the deed of John Brown. It was inevitable that in the terribly electric atmosphere that preceded the coming social storm, there should be some individual who should seek to "short circuit" the social forces, and get burned up for his pains. Such a phenomena did little more than demonstrate the existence of these forces.

When the Republican party held its next convention in the summer of 1860, the forces that were to carry it to victory had already been crystallized along well-defined class lines. That convention was expected to nominate William H. Seward for President. He represented the idealistic, scholarly, antislavery element of New England. But the scepter had passed from the Northeast. The Great Lakes region was vigorously assertive in its right to be heard. This section put forward a young politician, whose fame rested largely upon the triumphs he had gained in a series of joint debates with Stephen A. Douglas. This man's name was Abraham Lincoln.

No man could better typify the class he represented than Lincoln. The product of the golden age of capitalism, he embodies all the best of that system. Strong common sense, marvelously keen judgment of men, shrewd insight into human relations, infinite patience and sterling honesty, — these were the ideal virtues of capitalism, and in Lincoln they reached their transcendent expression. He proved himself the "fittest to survive" in that fierce "struggle for existence" under those frontier conditions where the struggle was freer and fairer than the world has ever known elsewhere.

The days that produced Lincoln are gone. He will stand as the greatest American until some other social stage shall have produced its best. In some ways he stood above the system that produced him, but this is true of any man who incarnates the very best of any social system, because he must, perforce, incarnate something of the promise of that system.

To say that the Republican party was organized or that the Civil War was waged to abolish slavery, is but to repeat a tale invented after the war was almost over to glorify that party and the class it represented. No candidate was ever a better representative of his party than Lincoln. He repeatedly and emphatically denied any intention of interfering with slavery in the South. In his debate with Douglas he said: "We have no right at all to disturb it in the states where it exists, and we profess that we have no more inclination to disturb it than we have the right to do it." In his first inaugural he declared his purpose to be to "save the Union" and this either with or without slavery.

So eager was the North and the Republican party to maintain the Union, and so indifferent were they to the slavery question, that after the election of Lincoln, both houses of Congress passed a provision for a constitutional amendment and sent it to the states for ratification, providing that slavery should be forever guaranteed and that no future amendment to the Constitution should ever be submitted authorizing Congress to interfere with slavery in the states where it was then located.[1]

The South seceded because no industrial system can continue unless its ruling class controls the government. This is especially true of a system based on exploitation. The South had no need of the North. Its industrial system was barred by soil and climate from expanding in that direction. If it had a government it could control, there was the possibility of expansion to the South. Even at the price of surrendering the system of chattel slavery the Southern ruling class preferred a government which it could control. Numerous proposals looking to the abolition of negro chattel slavery were considered in the Confederate Congress, when it was thought

[1] J. Schouler, "History of the United States," Vol. V, p. 507.

that such action might possibly bring the support of France and England to the Confederate cause.[1]

The North, on the contrary, had a strong interest in maintaining the Union intact. Capitalism must expand, and it knows almost no limits of soil or climate. The South was largely in the nature of a colony of the North. Estimates of the debts of Southern planters and merchants to Northern capitalists in 1860 run from forty to four hundred million dollars.[2] These debts were promptly repudiated on the outbreak of war. The Confederate government authorized the payment of such debts to it instead of to the original creditor.[3]

When, therefore, the capitalist class came into power through Lincoln and the Republican party, secession by the South and Civil War to prevent that secession were inevitable.

[1] *American Historical Review*, Vol. I, p. 97.

[2] John C. Schwab, "The Confederate States of America," p. 110.

[3] *Ibid.*, pp. 112-121. London *Economist*, Jan. 12, 1861, p. 30, says: "Many voices have been heard clamoring for secession as an excuse for repudiating the debts, private and commercial, as well as public, which they owe to the wealthier classes of the North."

CHAPTER XXII

THE ARMED CONFLICT OF SECTIONAL INTERESTS

THE ruling class of the South having determined upon secession, and the rulers of the North being convinced that their interests demanded a united nation, the question of which set of interests should prevail was decided by an armed conflict.

Looking back upon that conflict through the lens of later knowledge, the South seems foredoomed to the defeat it met. When the Constitution was adopted and the nation began, the two sections were almost exactly equal in area, population, and wealth. The slight shade of advantage belonged to the South. This equality continued until the industrial revolution that followed the War of 1812. From that date on the North, borne by the new machine-driven industry, began to leave the agricultural South behind.[1]

[1] Ellwood Fisher, "The North and the South," in *DeBow's Review*, Vol. VII, p. 135: "When the constitution of the United States was adopted, the population of the two sections of the United States was nearly equal — each being not quite two million of inhabitants, the South including more than half a million slaves. The territory then occupied by the two was, perhaps, also nearly equal in extent and fertility. Their commerce also was about the same; the North exporting about $9,800,540 in 1790 and the South $9,200,500. Even the property held by the two sections was almost exactly the same in amount, being four hundred millions in value in each, according to an assessment for direct taxes in 1799. For the first quarter of a century of the present government, up to 1816, the South took the lead of the North in com-

By 1860 the South had a population of but nine million. Of these three million were negro slaves. The North had a population of twenty-two million, the industrial portion of whom were wageworkers, much more effective fighters in a military contest, — and this whether they carried guns or tools of production. In accumulated capital, in industrial productivity, in transportation facilities, in financial resources, commercial power, and all the other things from which modern militarism draws its strength the North was overwhelmingly the superior.[1]

merce; as at the end of that period the exports of the Southern states amounted to about $30,000,000, which was five millions more than the Northern. At this time, in 1816, South Carolina and New York were the two greatest exporting states of the union, South Carolina exporting more than $10,000,000 and New York over $14,000,000.

. . . .

"Even in manufactures, the South at this period excelled the North in proportion to the numbers of their populations. In 1810, according to the returns of the marshals of the United States, the fabrics of wool, cotton, and linen manufactured in the Southern states, amounted to 40,344,274 yards, valued at $21,061,525, whilst the North fabricated 34,786,497 yards, estimated at $15,771,724. . . .

"Since that period a great change has occurred. The harbors of Norfolk, of Richmond, of Charleston, and Savannah have been deserted for those of Philadelphia, New York, and Boston; and New Orleans is the only southern city that pretends to rival its northern competitors. The grass is growing in the streets of those cities of the South, which originally monopolized our colonial commerce, and maintained their ascendancy in the earlier years of the union. Manufactures and the arts have also gone to take up their abode in the North. Cities have expanded and multiplied in the same favored region. Railroads and canals have been constructed and education has delighted there to build her colleges and seminaries."

[1] John C. Ropes, "The Story of the Civil War," Vol. I, p. 99: "In material prosperity the North was far in advance of the South. In accumulated capital there was no comparison between the two sections. The immigration from Europe had kept the labor market of the North

In spite of these apparently self-evident facts, the organs of ruling class interests in the South kept up a strange sort of bombastic self-deception. This exaggerated self-confidence, and indifference to impending overthrow, together with a blindness to the strength of rising classes, has been an almost universal characteristic of ruling classes. An editorial in *DeBow's Review*, in 1862, when defeat for the South was already written plain upon her industrial and social life, is a striking illustration of this blind overconfidence: —

"The North is bankrupt. Her people must migrate to the West or starve. The census of 1860 will prove beyond the possibility of doubt that the states of New York and Pennsylvania and the New England states do

well stocked, while no immigrants from Ireland or Germany were willing to enter into a competition with negro slaves. The North was full of manufactures of all kinds; the South had very few of any kind. The railroad systems of the North were far more perfect and extensive, and the roads were much better supplied with rolling stock and all necessary apparatus. The North was infinitely richer than the South in the production of grain and meat, and the boasted value of the South's great staple — cotton — sank out of sight when the blockade closed the southern ports to all commerce.

"Accompanying these greater material resources, there existed in the North a much larger measure of business capacity than was to be found in the South. . . . The great merchants and managers of large railroads and other similar enterprizes, in the North were able to render valuable assistance to the men who administered the State and National governments. . . ." Page 101: "The Mercantile marine of the United States, which in 1861 was second only to that of Great Britain, was almost wholly owned in the North. It was chiefly in the New England states that the ships were built. The sailors, so far as they were Americans at all, and the greater part of them were Americans, were Northerners. The owners were nearly all merchants in the North Atlantic cities. Hence the government had no difficulty in recruiting the navy to any extent, both in officers and men, from a class thoroughly familiar with the sea."

not produce annually enough meat and bread to feed their population for six months in the year, and (except for a little wool) produce nothing with which to clothe them. Their soil is extremely sterile, and it would require many years manuring to make it capable of supporting the present population. They cannot produce their own food and clothing and will have nothing wherewith to purchase it. The cotton and tobacco crop of the South for a single year would sell for four times as much as all the specie currency in the States we have mentioned. They will require every cent of this specie for home use, at least during the war. Their manufactures will sell only in the Northwest, and there they can sell but a few of the cheapest and coarsest kind — not one quarter enough to supply the deficiency of food and clothing. Their coarse cottons were the only articles which they could sell in the markets of the world before secession. Now the raw cotton will cost them so much that they will no longer be able to sell cotton fabrics abroad. Their local wealth, derived from houses, factories, railroads, etc., ceased to exist the instant secession became an accomplished fact. Their mercantile marine is the only thing they can sell in foreign markets, and as they will have no further use for it at home, they should sell it as speedily as possible. The South will need it all, and would buy it, to carry on that very trade which secession has transferred to her from the North."

Some idea of the value of knowledge transmitted through class interests is gained when it is remembered that the writer of this was the Commissioner of the census in 1860 and was generally looked upon as one of the ablest students of economic and political conditions.

The Southern rulers did not believe that a united North would resist separation. Much dependence was placed upon the strong ties of commercial interest that bound whole sections of the North to the South. This dependence was by no means wholly misplaced. Throughout the war there were many sections of the North where the tide of Southern sympathy ran high. In every case it will be found that these sections were bound to the South and to the system of chattel slavery by economic ties.[1]

When broad class interests are sharply threatened, such exceptions become of small importance. In time of great class conflicts, the representatives of dominant class interests are ruthless in their suppression of divergent individual or group interests, whether these be of "Tories," "copperheads," or "scabs." If public opinion does not suffice to suppress all expression of revolt against the general class interest, then this opinion is at once reënforced by all the measures of group defense. This is the reason why the firing upon Fort Sumter caused such an instantaneous crystallization of "union" sentiment in the North and of "Southern patriotism" in the slave states.

As soon as the two systems of industry were definitely pitted against each other, the tremendous superiority of the wage-labor system appeared.

Chattel slavery in America was an historical atavism, and not a stage in social evolution. It came many generations after the disappearance of the era of which chattel slavery was an essential foundation. It came because of the great profits which the raising of one

[1] Brown, "The Lower South in American History," pp. 59–60.

crop in the midst of an otherwise capitalist society produced. This social reversion made the South industrially dependent upon the capitalist societies that were its workshops. When the access to these workshops was stopped, the South became almost helpless. It was not quite helpless. The first effect of isolation and war was, as always, to hasten industrial evolution, and especially to force artificially the growth of machine production.[1]

No opportunity was offered for even this accelerated evolution to produce any important results. Time was not given to construct mills and machines and to develop the skilled artisans and to organize the industrial and distributing machinery essential to capitalized industry. From the first the Northern campaigns were directed toward the disorganization and disintegration of all germs of industrial life.

The Mississippi was the great artery of internal Southern trade. When armies to the north and the blockade on the sea had stopped foreign trade, the possession of that river by the Federal forces prevented

[1] Walter E. Fleming, "Industrial Development in Alabama during the Civil War," in *South Atlantic Quarterly*, July, 1904, p. 267: "Both the state and the Confederate government encouraged manufactures by legislation. . . . Factories were soon in operation all over the state, especially in central Alabama. In all places where there were government factories there were also factories conducted by private individuals. In 1861 there were factories at Tallahassee, Autauganville, and Pottsville, with 23,000 spindles and 800 employees, which could make 5000 yards of good cloth a day. And other cotton mills were established as early as 1861. The federals burned these buildings and destroyed the machinery. There was the most unsparing hostility displayed by the Northern armies to this branch of industry. They destroyed instantly every cotton factory within their reach."

even the local circulation of commodities which would have maintained at least a semblance of industrial life.

The army of the West under Grant captured Vicksburg in July, 1863, and the Mississippi became a Union stream. This also separated the eastern and larger section of the Confederacy from its granary and provision supply — Texas.[1] With the essential foreign trade cut off and the principal channels of internal trade disrupted, the industrial destruction of the South was completed by Sherman's "march to the sea," which destroyed the beginnings of the factory system and the already imperfect railroad system.

Military strength rests upon an industrial base. The Civil War was decided far from the noise of exploding powder and blaring bands and flowing flags. In the South the industrial base was a miserable makeshift at the best, a crumbling hulk at the finish.

Modern industrial society is built upon an iron framework. Nothing is more characteristic of the weakness of Southern industrial life than the futile, frantic efforts made to secure iron.

"In a paper read before a railroad conference in Richmond," says Rhodes, "it is suggested that the government make a public appeal for all the cast and wrought iron scrap on the farms, in the yards and houses of the Confederacy, and that it establish a system for the collection from the country, cities, towns, and villages of 'broken and worn-out plows, plow points, hoes, spades, axes, broken stoves, household and kitchen utensils,' with promise of adequate compensation. The rails of the street railroad in Richmond were taken up

[1] Rebellion Records, Series I, Vol. IV, pp. 119, 122.

to be made into armor for a gunboat. The planters of Alabama, in the very regions where iron ore existed in abundance underground, could not get iron enough to make and repair their agricultural implements."

By the time of the Civil War the railroad had already become the most important tool of an industrially interdependent society. In railroads the South was at a miserable disadvantage in the beginning, and every day aggravated that disadvantage. Mileage, already too little, grew less before the ravages of Northern armies and the paucity of Southern resources. The war dissolved the loose beginnings of systems into their feeble isolated elements.[1] A defective and scanty equipment quickly deteriorated from its original low standard into almost complete uselessness.[2] The workshops for the manufacture and repair of equipment were in the North, and the South was unable to improve or even maintain the scanty rolling stock possessed at the time of secession.

The postal system of the North looks poor when

[1] Schwab, "The Confederate States of America," pp. 272-273.

[2] *Ibid.*, p. 274. Rhodes, "History of the United States," Vol. V, p. 384: "In 1861 the railroads had already begun to deteriorate, and as the years went on the condition got worse and worse. . . . An estimate in detail of the capacity of 34 railroads was made to the Secretary of War (in 1863) which showed on an average of the whole less than two freight trains daily each way, each train carrying 122 tons; and this estimate was undoubtedly too high to apply to regular operations throughout the year. From everywhere came complaints. Cities wanted food which the railroads could not bring. In January, 1864, it was said that corn was selling at $1 to $2 a bushel in southwestern Georgia and at $12 to $15 in Virginia. Another Richmond authority at the close of that year was sure that every one would have enough to eat if food could be properly distributed. The defective transportation was strikingly emphasized when Sherman's army in Georgia revelled in plenty while Lee's soldiers almost starved in Virginia."

viewed from to-day's vantage point. It was infinitely superior to that of the South. The Confederate constitution required the postal service to be always self-supporting. To meet this condition letter postage was placed at five cents per half ounce for less than five hundred miles and ten cents for greater distances. When even these rates failed to pay expenses, they were doubled.

In the financial resources which are drawn from industrial development the South was even more strikingly inferior. Although this section had the sympathy of the European industrial and commercial rivals of the North, England in particular, yet this sympathy did not lead them to purchase Confederate bonds in large quantities. There was no powerful banking class in the South to gain profits for its members and furnish resources to the government by great financial operations such as are essential to the conduct of a great war.

The one important Southern asset was cotton. Later writers, with that wise foresight that comes so clearly after the events are long past, have often pointed out that had the Confederate government seized all the cotton possible during the months after secession, and before the blockade was declared, and shipped it to England, that cotton could have been drawn against for many millions of much needed dollars. But Southern economic philosophy was as atavistic as its social system, and, with a strange revival of a long dead Mercantilism, the Confederates imagined they could compel the weaving nations to come to their relief by withholding the raw material for the looms. So the South fell into the trap of its opponent, and aided the Northern blockade by forbidding the export of cotton. By the time the foolishness of this policy had become apparent the tentacles of the Northern navy had tightened until the harbors of the South were closed save to the highly hazardous and expensive commerce of the blockade runners.

Since there was no class of profit-takers at home or abroad, both able and willing to purchase Confederate bonds, the government was soon compelled to fall back upon the forced loans of fiat money. Later this was supplemented by an economic reversion to the stage of barter and commodity currency. Bonds were exchanged for and taxes collected in commodities (especially cotton, of course), and the government accumulated great quantities of commodities whose market was barred by Federal gunboats.[1]

When defeat was seen to be inevitable the whole Confederacy collapsed. The currency lost all value, and nearly as many soldiers deserted and returned to their homes as remained to be surrendered to Federal generals. There are rumors that these general desertions were due to the spreading of the idea that "this is a rich man's war and a poor man's fight," and that non-slaveholding soldiers left because they had come to realize their non-interest in the war.[2] Unfortunately there seems to be little contemporary evidence of such intelligence. The South was defeated because its social life rested upon a lower, more undeveloped, less perfectly organized and more essentially atavistic industrial base than that of the North.

[1] "Cambridge Modern History," Vol. III, p. 610.
[2] James S. Pike's "The Prostrate State," p. 75.

T

There was one fact which, had there been any to read its significance in the light of historical evolution through class struggles, would have been seen to be darkly portentous for the negro. This was the fact that there were no slave revolts during the war.[1] The goblin that had kept the South in trembling terror for a half a century was seen to be the phantom created by a guilty conscience. The fact was more sinister in its significance for the black. His inaction in time of crisis, his failure to play any part in the struggle that broke his shackles, told the world that he was not of those who to free themselves would strike a blow.

Representatives of a ruling class, both North and South, have praised him for his "loyalty" and "fidelity" in a time of danger. At the same time this same ruling class has shown its contempt for him by taking from him many of the rights tossed him as incidental to the game of war. Among the rights so tossed him was freedom from chattel slavery. Emancipation was not granted to help the negro, but to hurt the South. That it came too late to have much effect even in that direction may be judged from the fact that the Confederate Congress long debated the question of freeing, and even arming, the slaves as a means of gaining European sympathy.

Not only were Northern resources vastly superior at the beginning of the war; but war under wage labor, unless pushed to a degree of exhaustion not attained even by the stupendous struggle of the Civil War, so far from impoverishing or weakening, actually enriches and strengthens the dominant class.

The panic that began in 1857 reached its most acute

[1] Rhodes, "History of the United States," Vol. V, pp. 460-464.

and depressing stage at the outbreak of the war. It is this fact that is largely responsible for the "hard times" that are associated with the first years of the war. At the very time when the military outlook was darkest for the North, industrial recovery began.[1] The momentum of the upward movement was much accelerated by the military operations. The vast armies in the field, averaging a million and a half men from the North alone,[2] and making no account of the large numbers indirectly connected with military operations and withdrawn from productive industry, created a tremendous market "foreign" to the direct industrial process. This unproductive mass absorbed such a quantity of the products of labor, that a surfeited market was almost impossible. Consequently the surplus value produced by the workers who remained in the fields and the factories, using the newly invented machinery with multiplied productive power, flowed in gigantic streams into the pockets of the Northern capitalists.[3]

The Civil War brought the era of great manufacturing plants. It made iron and wool the rulers of the industrial world, and therefore the political rulers, and the makers of tariffs and masters of appropriation bills for two generations. The demand for uniforms and blankets for the armies guaranteed an almost exhaustless market for cloth of an unchanging character. Mill after mill ran month after month exclusively upon goods for the armies in the field. Cotton mills were remodeled to enable them to weave wool. Hundreds of new establishments were built. All paid great dividends upon the capital in-

---

[1] Rhodes, *loc. cit.*, Vol. V, pp. 198–199.   [2] *Ibid.*, p. 186.
[3] David A. Wells, "Our Burden and our Strength."

vested. The following table shows the sudden increased consumption of wool by American mills during the Civil War :[1] —

YEAR	POUNDS USED
1840	45,615,326
1850	71,176,355
1860	85,334,876
1863	180,057,156
1864	213,871,157

The production of profits and the creation of new industries in connection with wool was not confined to the process of weaving. The necessity for making such great quantities of identical suits brought into existence the ready-made clothing industry. The mechanical foundation for this industry had been laid by the invention of the sewing machine, which had been in process since 1840, and been perfected to a practicable working machine by Elias Howe in 1849.[2]

The great profits in the production of genuine woolen goods could not fail to create a fraudulent imitative industry. The war, with its scarcity of cotton and high price for wool, created the great American "shoddy" industry.[3]

Iron and steel completed their conquest of the industrial field during, and largely because of, the Civil War.

[1] Statistical Abstract 1900; Bolles, "Industrial History," pp. 382–383; Census of 1890, "Manufactures," p. 8; Levasseur, "The American Workman," p. 26.

[2] Sewing machines using the "chain stitch" had been in use for many years and had been gradually improved. Howe's contribution was the "lock stitch" with two threads. See article "Sewing Machines" in "Encyclopedia Americana"; also Fite, "Social and Industrial Condition in the North during the Civil War," pp. 88–89.

[3] Census of 1890, "Manufacturing Industries," Vol. III, p. 38.

The demand for small arms and artillery, wagons, railroad supplies, and ironclads made this the Golden Age of profits in iron. Not only did existing mills find their capacities taxed at exorbitant prices; new ones were erected almost by the hundreds, and the earth was searched for ore supplies. In this search the great ore beds of Lake Superior, the possession of which insured the establishment of a world-wide steel trust in the future, were discovered and opened up on a large scale.[1]

The wage system gains much of its power from its ability to substitute machines for men. The armies taken from industry left an increased demand for labor power. This demand was met by increasing the productive power of those left behind through improved machinery. The records of the patent office show that a quick response was made to the premium that was thus placed upon invention. In 1861 there were 3340 patents granted. Four years later, when the patents from the inventions made during the war were reaching the patent office in large numbers, and while the Southern states were outside the Union and more than a million of the men at the North were in military service, the remnant left behind took out 6220 patents.[2]

---

[1] "One Hundred Years of American Commerce," p. 325; Bolles, "Industrial History," pp. 208–209; J. H. Kennedy, "The Opening up of the Lake Superior Iron Region," *Magazine of American History*, Vol. II, p. 357.

[2] David A. Wells, "Recent Experiences of the United States"; Report Commissioner of Patents, 1863, p. 47: "Although the country has been engaged in a war which would have seemed to tax to the utmost all its energies, the applications for patents for the last year have been equalled in only two former years; and yet one half of our territory, shrouded in the cloud of rebellion, has contributed nothing to invention or human improvement."

It was this power of the North to produce, this peculiarity of the wage system that draws strength from the murderous waste of war, that gave that section its power. The war, was won as much by the industrial workers who toiled in the shop (and whose death rate and percentage of injured was fully as high as that of the workers in the military ranks) as by those who carried guns. Yet pensions and glory are reserved exclusively for those who took up the trade of killing.

Perhaps the strongest battalions in this industrial army that fought for the North were on the farms. It has been said that "the war was won by the McCormick reaper," and the statement is more nearly true than most popular generalizations on history. It was not alone that the new horse-drawn machinery multiplied the power of the workers in the fields. It transformed the aged, the women, and the children, whom the marching armies had left behind, into producers more effective than strong men had been with the former tools. So it was that the wartime crops, raised by the weakest fraction of the industrial population, were greater than any raised by adult skilled farmers in former years.[1]

[1] Commissioner of Patents, Report for 1863, p. 21: "The most striking fact connected with this class (agricultural implements) is the rapid increase of applications filed. Notwithstanding half a million of our agriculturists have been withdrawn from the farm to engage in military service, still the number of applications for patents on agricultural implements (exclusive of reapers, beehives, horse hay-forks, and horse hay-rakes) has increased from 350 in 1851 to 502 in 1863. At first thought such a result would seem an anomaly, but it is this large drain upon the laboring classes which has caused a greater demand than usual for labor-saving machinery. The increased demand for farm products, and their higher price in consequence, have also doubtless helped to increase the number of labor-saving machines."

These bountiful crops found a ready market at high prices. To the increased demand from the unproductive armies in the field was added an extra call from Europe due to poor harvests. The farmer, like the industrial capitalist, drew prosperity from the war. His influence in government was still considerable, as is seen by the establishment in 1862 of a national department of agriculture and the subsidizing the state agricultural colleges.

The influence of the war, through its effect upon manufacturing, transportation, and agriculture, had far-reaching effects upon the movements of population and the relative strength of sections and cities.

That the states around the Great Lakes were not mistaken in deciding that their material interests united them with the system of wage labor is evidenced by the fact that to no other section did the Civil War bring such great material growth. When the Mississippi was completely closed to traffic and the South was cut off as a market, the lake ports became the only gateways for the tremendous commerce of the broad agricultural *Hinterland*.[1] Chicago and Cleveland leaped at once

[1] Fite, "Social and Industrial Conditions in the North during the Civil War," p. 67. Speaking of Chicago: "This city had the unique distinction among the growing western cities of possessing no railroad indebtedness, while her rivals, St. Louis, Milwaukee, Detroit, and some smaller cities, weighed down by debts to obtain the few railroads they had, were even compelled to call upon their respective states to issue many millions of dollars of bonds in their aid. The railroads created Chicago, not Chicago the railroads. It was a natural trade center to which in the short space of ten years seven new trunk lines from the South, West and North were built, and from which three trunk lines and the Lakes led eastward. As late as 1850 the city celebrated the arrival of the first train. In 1864 it was entered by over ninety trains daily." James F. Rhodes, in *American Magazine of History*, II, p. 337: "The turning point of the material development of Cleveland was reached in

from trade centers to great crude industrial centers. The flow of agricultural products called into existence the outline of that great radial system of railroads that now feed those cities, and has been responsible for their growth.

The manipulation of war finances poured such a golden flood into the vaults of a clique of New York bankers as to give them domination within the capitalist ranks.[1] Inflation of the currency with the accompanying opportunity to gamble in gold, the manipulation of internal revenue taxes, vied with corrupt military contracts and contraband trade in cotton in contributing to that "primitive accumulation," upon which American fortunes are based.[2]

So tremendous was the graft in connection with contracts for military supplies that most historians draw

1860. . . . In 1860 the coal and iron industries had only begun to be developed, and the war stimulated these manufactures at Cleveland as elsewhere. . . . The war found Cleveland a commercial city and left it a manufacturing city."

[1] A. S. Bolles, "Financial History of the United States," Vol. III, p. 20, tells of a meeting of New York bankers with the assistant Secretary of the Treasury, where the arrangements were made for the handling of the war bonds, by which these bankers controlled the sale of the securities.

[2] "United States Cobden Club Essays," Series 1871–1872, pp. 479–480 : "Prices rose rapidly with every increase in taxation, or additional issues of paper money; and, under such circumstances, the burdens of the war were not regarded by the majority of producers as oppressive. But, on the contrary, counting the taxes as elements of cost, and reckoning profit as a percentage on the whole, it was very generally the case that the aggregate profits of the producers were actually enhanced by reason of the taxes to an extent considerably greater than they would have been had no taxes whatever been collected. Indeed, it was not infrequently the case that the manufacturers themselves were the most strenuous advocates for the continued and rapid increase of taxation."

back in horror when they have lifted but a corner of the thick blanket of concealment that those who profited by the plunder have drawn over the mess. One Congressional committee, headed by Robert Dale Owen, son of Robert Owen the Utopian Socialist, uncovered frauds of $17,000,000 in $50,000,000 worth of contracts.

Graft rendered the very weapons of warfare as dangerous to those who held them as to those against whom they were supposed to be directed. Carbines, that before the outbreak of hostilities had been condemned by the War Department, and sold as condemned weapons at the almost nominal price of $3.50 each, were resold by the buyers to the very government that had condemned them for $22.00 each.[1]

Rivaling even the military contracts as a source of "primitive accumulation" by corruption, treason, and theft, was the contraband trade in cotton carried on by Northern merchants in illegal collusion with Federal army officers. To prevent the exportation of cotton was one of the main objects of the Federal campaign. To assist in the marketing of that cotton was treason, "giving aid and comfort to the enemy." But cotton was less than ten cents a pound in the South and more than fifty cents a pound in New England. Before such a profit capitalist patriotism has never yet stood unscathed. Soon "permits" began to be issued for cotton to pass through the Northern lines. Then the floodgates of corruption broke and the carnival of profit was on. Congressman Ten Eyck of New Jersey stated upon the floor of the House of Representatives: —

"We have . . . prolonged the rebellion, and strength-

[1] Rhodes, "History of United States," Vol. V, pp. 213–221.

ened the arm of traitors by allowing the very trade, in consequence of which not only union men and women, but rebels of the deepest dye, have been fed and have had their pockets lined with greenbacks, by means of which they could carry on the rebellion. Under the permission to trade, supplies have not only gone in, but bullets and powder, instruments of death which our heroic soldiers have been compelled to meet upon almost every field of battle in which they have been engaged in the South. . . . I am greatly afraid that in some quarters the movements of our armies have been conducted more with a view to carry on trade . . . than to strike down the rebels. . . . The whole valley of the Mississippi along the line of the permitted trade has been debauched; not merely the Treasury agents, . . . but men engaged in carrying our flag, not only upon the land but out upon the sea."

The financing of the war not only created a whole set of banking institutions [1] and placed them in the control of a small clique,[2] but an enormous national debt was contracted that was to maintain a class of bondholders for a generation and more to come. A. S. Bolles, in is "Financial History of the United States," estimates the total expenditures of the war at $6,189,929,908. At the close of the war the national debt was $2,773,236,174. The workers who had been fighting in the field were now compelled to join an army of industrial toilers engaged in producing the interest with which the class of bondholders were supported.

Workingmen made up the military armies and the industrial armies alike, but they obtained few benefits

[1] The present system of banking was established Feb. 25, 1863. See "Cambridge Modern History," Vol. VII, p. 571.

[2] Bolles, "Financial History of the United States."

from the war. Some of the few organized workers of the time saw this and protested against the war.[1]

The "antidraft riots" that took place in many cities, and especially in New York, partook of many of the characteristics of a labor movement.[2] They began with a general strike, or an attempt at such a strike. The spokesmen of the movement were insistent in their denunciation of the "exemption clauses" that enabled rich men to escape the draft. There were many who demanded that "money as well as men should be drafted."[3]

On the other hand, the more far-seeing and consciously revolutionary element among Northern workers realized that chattel slavery stood in the way of progress. The German immigrants, especially, who were filled with the "spirit of '48," enlisted in the Union army almost *en masse*. The presence of large numbers of these men at St. Louis is commonly recognized as being responsible for the defeat of secession in Missouri.

In Europe the Socialists, and nearly the whole wage-working class, were with the North. It was the cotton spinners of Lancashire who, believing that the war would

[1] Jas. C. Sylvis, "Biography of Wm. H. Sylvis," p. 42: "Among the workingmen, a few choice spirits, North and South, knowing that all the burdens and none of the honors of war are entailed upon labor, were engaged in an effort to frustrate the plans of those who seemed to desire, and whose fanaticism was calculated to precipitate hostilities."

[2] See "The Volcano under the City," by "A Volunteer Special."

[3] In the scrapbooks collected by William Sylvis, now in the Crerar Library, Chicago, there is a clipping (Vol. 12) of an article by C. Ben Johns, Corresponding Secretary Pennsylvania State Labor Union, discussing a plank in the platform of the National Labor Union, from which the following is taken: " There is a resolution . . . in which we demand that in time of war, money shall be drafted as well as men."

end chattel slavery, starved rather than see work come through lifting the cotton blockade. When the capitalists of England, more eager to defend their immediate profits than even the broad interests of their class, would have interfered in behalf of the Confederacy, it was these workers who stood in the way of such action, and not the least of those who were responsible for this steadfast position of the English workers was the founder of modern scientific Socialism — Karl Marx.[1] He worked tirelessly to this end, and as a result of his efforts the International Workingmen's Association (the "Old International") sent a resolution of sympathy to President Lincoln. When we remember the strength of this organization at this time, its widespread influence in Europe, and the critical moment at which that influence was exerted, it seems probable that it had as much to do with the outcome of the Civil War as many factors to which historians have given much greater weight.

Out of the Civil War was born the elements of present society. It created the great capitalist and the great industry and the mechanical foundation upon which these rest. It placed these in control of the national government, and for the next generation capitalism was to find its greatest development in the nation the war had maintained as a unit.

[1] John Spargo, "Life of Karl Marx," pp. 268–270.

CHAPTER XXIII

RECONSTRUCTION

DURING armed conflict the commercial and industrial capitalist skulks in the background, fattening upon the offal of war. When even the low virtues that war demands were no longer necessary to social rulership, these vultures came from their retreat and ruled and rioted in plunder. Part of that ruling and rioting made up what is called the Reconstruction Period.

The conquest of the South was complete and crushing. The old ruling class, and the social system upon which it lived, were gone, and none could be foolish enough to expect its restoration. The attitude of the ruling spirits of the South may be judged by the announcement in the first number of a new series of *DeBow's Review*, appearing in January, 1866, and which reads as follows: —

"My purpose in the future is to give it [the Review] a *national character*, and to devote all of my energies and resources to the development of the great material interests of the Union. . . .

"Regarding the issues of the past as dead, about which a practical philosophy will not dispute, and those of the present as living and potential, it is the part of the Review to accept in good faith the situation and deduce from it all that can be promotive of the best interests of the whole country."

Northern generals who were stationed in the South at the close of the war were almost unanimous in reporting that the former Confederate soldiers and officers were willing to accept the results of the defeat they had suffered.

The passage of sectional hatred would, however, have thwarted the plans of a small but powerful division of the Northern capitalists. The group of great capitalists created by the war was still composed of too few persons, and was too highly competitive, to be able to control the national government under normal conditions.

This group of great corporations, whose influence was so feared by Lincoln, was helpless to combat the small bourgeoisie which was still dominant in much more than a majority of the states. The abolition of slavery raised the same small bourgeoisie into power in the South. Had the South been permitted to return to the Union in the simple natural manner desired by Lincoln,[1] there would have been a vast fairly uniform body of voters throughout the South and the upper Mississippi Valley who would have been hostile to the interests of the great capi-

---

[1] "Complete Works," Vol. II, p. 674. Last public address: "We all agree that the seceded states, so-called, are out of their proper, practical relation with the Union, and that the sole object of the government, civil and military in regard to those states is to again get them into that proper practical relation. I believe that it is not only possible, but in fact easier, to do this without deciding, or even considering, whether these states have ever been out of the Union. Finding themselves safely at home, it would be utterly immaterial whether they had ever been abroad. Let us all join in doing the acts necessary to restoring the proper, practical relations between these States and the Union, and each forever after innocently indulge his own opinion whether in doing the acts he brought the States from without into the Union, or only gave them proper assistance, they never having been out of it."

talists. The Greenback movement, the Union Labor party of the early 70's, and the widespread antagonism to the clique of bondholders, great steel and woolen manufacturers, and government contractors, show how real was this danger to great capitalist interests.

If, on the other hand, a way could be found to keep alive and aggravate sectional hatred, and to keep the Southern states from the Union until a powerful plutocracy could seize upon all the strategic points of social control, then the interests of rapidly concentrating wealth would be conserved. It is not necessary to conceive that all this was clearly foreseen and made the basis of conscious social action, by those responsible for the program of Reconstruction. There were plenty of immediate material advantages for individual members of the class whose more distant interests were to be conserved which led to the same end.

There were still prodigious possibilities of plunder in the stricken South. There were hordes of picayune political camp followers hungry for pelf. The fanatical abolitionist, to whom the chattel slaveholder had been a demon, and the purchaser of wage slaves a public benefactor, was a willing tool in the orgy of Reconstruction. To these could be called the support of all that flock of vultures that was to glut itself upon the desolation of the Southland.

At first glance there would seem to have been little left in the South worthy the attention of vandals. Seldom has the desolation of war been more terrible, for seldom has war swept over as complex a society, where its destruction could be so terrible. For compared with the societies of other centuries that of the South was complex, however simple it appears when contrasted with that of to-day or with the contemporaneous North.

Almost all of the industrial life that belonged to recent times was wiped out by the war. It would be hard to paint an exaggerated picture of the conditions that prevailed. One such picture has been given by James W. Garner, in his "Reconstruction in Mississippi." This will hold good for the entire South save that in many states where the operations of the armies had been more general, the devastation and social disintegration was much greater. He says of Mississippi: —

"The people were generally impoverished; the farms had gone to waste, the fences having been destroyed by the armies, or having decayed from neglect; the fields were covered with weeds and bushes; farm implements and tools were gone, so that there were barely enough farm animals to meet the demands of agriculture; business was at a standstill; banks and commercial agencies had either suspended or closed on account of insolvency; the currency was in a wretched condition; . . . there was no railway or postal system worth speaking of; only here and there a newspaper running; the labor system in vogue since the establishment of the colonies was completely overturned; . . . worse than all this was the fact that about one-third of the white bread-winners of the state had either been sacrificed in the contest or were disabled for life, so that they could not longer be considered as factors in the work of economic organization. . . . The number of dependent orphans alone was estimated at 10,000."

Into this industrial and social chaos came a horde of mercenary Goths and Vandals. They were released upon this desolated land as a part of the political *coup d'état*, by which the present ruling class attained to power.

Had President Lincoln lived, it seems probable that his powerful personal following, his political shrewdness, and keen tactful insight into human motives might have enabled him to rally the interests from which he sprung,— the pioneer, farmer, and small manufacturing and trading class,—and joining these with the new-born factory wageworking class, carried through his policies. But he was dead, and there is no small amount of evidence tending to show that the shot that killed him came from the direction of Wall Street rather than Richmond.

It would be hard to find a man more unsuited to take up Lincoln's task than Andrew Johnson. Tactless, stubborn, abusive, quarrelsome (aggravated by occasional intoxication), lacking in political skill, suspected of Southern sympathies and of general mediocre ability, he was the very opponent which best suited the purposes of the followers of Thad Stevens, the Pennsylvania ironmaster.

By a skillful use of sectional animosities and political alliances the great capitalist element had gained control of Congress. The war it had waged secretly against Lincoln, was made openly and boastingly upon Johnson, who was trying to continue Lincoln's policies. That he was so following Lincoln, though in a blundering, tactless manner, no historian of to-day would deny.

As fast as the rebellion had been crushed, Lincoln had set about reorganizing the state governments in a simple, practical manner. This was a natural action since the whole war had been waged upon the theory that a state cannot secede, and that therefore the Southern states had never been outside the Union. The national government had been conducting the war under the clause of the constitution giving power to "suppress domestic insurrection" in any state.

While the states were *de facto* out of the Union, therefore, Congress, courts, and army had declared them firmly inside.[1] When the "domestic insurrection" was suppressed, and the state governments were recognizing the authority of the national government, it became to the interest of the class that controlled Congress to proceed upon the theory that these states were now outside the Union.

This theory was translated into action by another *coup d'état*. When the regularly elected representatives of the former Confederate states presented their credentials at Washington, the clerk of the House of Representatives under the instructions of the so-called "Radical," or Stevens wing of the Republican party, refused to read their names when calling the roll of the new House.

A law was then forced through by this same element (March 2, 1867, nearly three years after the war had closed), entirely contrary to all constitutional provisions, and therefore strictly revolutionary in character. This law wiped out state governments and even ignored state

[1] The Crittenden Resolution, adopted by large majorities of both houses of Congress in July, 1861, gives the theory upon which the war was waged. In part it read as follows: "That this war is not waged on their part in any spirit of oppression, or for any purpose of conquest or subjugation, or purpose of overthrowing or interfering with the rights or established institutions of those states, but to defend and maintain the supremacy of the constitution, and to preserve the union with all the dignity, equality and rights of the several states unimpaired; and that as soon as these rights are accomplished the war ought to cease." — "Documentary History of Reconstruction," Vol. I, p. 118.

lines, and divided the South into five military districts. The military officers in charge of these districts were given absolute power over life, liberty, and property, save only that death sentences required presidential sanction.

No such power had been exercised while war existed. It was conferred now long after peace had been restored as one of the methods by which the present capitalist class captured and held the control of the national government.

Lest it may be denied that such was the purpose of these actions, I will let the man who was directing this legislation speak for himself. Whatever else may be said of Thad Stevens, friend and foe alike admit his brutal frankness. Speaking of the Southern states on the floor of the House of Representatives, December 18, 1865, he said:—

"They ought never to be recognized as capable of acting in the union, or being counted as valid states, until the constitution shall have been so amended as to make it what its framers intended; and so as to secure permanent ascendency to the party of the union."

Again on January 3, 1867, he said, speaking for the passage of the Reconstruction legislation:—

"Another reason is, it would assure the ascendency of the union party."

By the "party of the union" and the "union party" he meant, and intended to be understood as meaning, the "Radical" wing of the Republican party.

Having eliminated President Johnson by well-nigh successful impeachment proceedings, after he had almost eliminated himself by his foolish actions, the Stevens faction proceeded to work its will upon the South in such a manner as "to secure permanent ascendency to the party of the union."

Cotton was still king in the South. Prices were still phenomenally high, although four years of war had brought about a great increase of cotton-growing in India. In the twelve months after the close of the war the value of cotton exports reached $200,000,000.[1] Here was a prize worth grabbing, and the hungry "Reconstructionists" did not overlook it. During the war the Confederate government had contracted for some cotton, hoping to smuggle it through the blockade. All so contracted for was declared confiscated for the benefit of the United States treasury. How that confiscation was carried out is thus described by Professor Walter L. Fleming, editor of the "Documentary History of Reconstruction": —

"The territory of the former states was invaded by swarms of treasury agents, or those who pretended to be, searching for confiscable property. No distinction appears to have been made by them between property legally subject to confiscation and property that was not. These agents often united with native thieves and plundered the country of the little that was left in the way of supplies, cotton, tobacco, corn, etc."[2]

We learn of one agent in a small town in Mississippi who cleared $80,000 in one month "confiscating cotton."

The great instrument of class rule, exploitation, expropriation, and accumulation is always the state. Here rests the power of taxation and of conferring special privileges. This was the next instrument grasped and used by the Reconstructionists in plundering the South.

---

[1] "Cambridge Modern History," Vol. VII, p. 697.
[2] "Documentary History of Reconstruction," Vol. I, p. 4.

Four means were effective in this capture of the power of the states: military force, negro suffrage, the Freedmen's Bureau, and widespread secret conspiratory organizations, like the Loyal League.

The national troops in the South were the pliant tools of the politicians. They intimidated voters, protected ballot-box stuffers, or assisted in the stuffing, and when these methods failed to obtain a majority suitable to the political camp followers, regularly elected officials were thrown out that defeated candidates might take their place.[1] An extensive state militia, composed of black and white "Radical" Republicans, was later added to the national troops. Ninety-six thousand such "soldiers" were supported by the Reconstruction government of South Carolina at one time. Their only duty was to draw money and supplies from the state treasury and see that the elections went for the proper Republican candidates.[2]

The trump card of the Reconstructionists was negro suffrage. This was advocated as a benevolent measure for the protection of the negro, and was accompanied by acts disfranchising nearly the whole white population in the South. Had freedom and the vote been achieved by the negro, they would have been powerful defensive and offensive weapons. But they were thrust into his hands as tools with which to do the work of his industrial and political exploiters. Like the hoe with which he "chopped cotton," they were but instruments with which to bring profit to his masters.

[1] "Documentary History of Reconstruction," Vol. II, pp. 148-156, tells how this was done in New Orleans.
[2] *Ibid.*, Vol. II, p. 79.

Lincoln had favored an educational test, and also, apparently, some proof of individual initiative, as a condition of suffrage.[1] It should be unnecessary to say that I do not raise the question of the "rightness" or "wrongness" of universal negro suffrage, but am only discussing the forces which led to its being conferred at this time and the results which flowed from it. Several Northern states, controlled by the Republican party, refused the negro the ballot by referendum vote during the very years when that party was philanthropically thrusting that same ballot into the hands of the negro in the South.[2] A possible explanation of this action may be found in the greater average intelligence and individual initiative of the Northern negro.

The immediate excuse for forcing suffrage upon the negro without any request for it being preferred by him, and indeed for much of the hypocritical "protective" legislation, was found in the "black codes" and "vagrancy laws" enacted by some of the Southern states immediately after the war.[3] These laws sought to introduce a sort of modified serfdom for the negro. They were much like those enacted by capitalist nations to compel the natives of tropical colonies to work.[4] In some cases, with a shrewd cunning, they were copied almost verbatim from the "vagrancy laws" of Northern states, with

[1] Letter to Gov. Hahn, Nicolay and Hay, "Complete Works," Vol. II, p. 496.

[2] Hilary H. Herbert, "Reconstruction at Washington," in "Noted Men of the South," p. 13.

[3] J. G. Blaine, "Twenty Years of Congress," Vol. II, pp. 93-104; Lalor's "Encyclopedia of Political and Social Science," article on "Reconstruction."

[4] Paul S. Reinsch, "Colonial Administration," Chap. IX.

the exception that instead of leaving the competitive struggle to decide to whom the law should apply, they described the persons aimed at by the color of their skin. The same laws, with slight change, have been reënacted in most Southern states in recent years, along with measures disfranchising the negro, and no protest has been raised from Republican sources.

There was no question of the pitiable predicament of the negro at the close of the war. Cut off from his former master and unable to adjust himself to the new social organization in whose coming he had played no part, the football of all contending factions, with a death rate far higher than in chattel slavery days, one is not surprised to learn that many of them longed for the "good old days."[1]

[1] Albert Phelps, "New Orleans and Reconstruction," in *Atlantic Monthly*, Vol. LXXXVII, p. 125: "Under the institution of slavery he had developed from a state of lowest savagery to a condition of partial civilization; but this development had been due to wholly abnormal conditions, and had not been at all analogous to the slow process and weeding-out struggle through which the white races had toiled upwards for thousands of years. . . . The peculiar institution of slavery, however, protected him, not only from this competition, but also, by artificial means, from those great forces of Nature which inevitably weed out the weaker organisms, and which operate most unrestrainedly upon the ignorant savage. For the first time, perhaps, in the history of the world, human beings had been bred and regulated like valuable stock, with as much care as is placed upon the best horses and cattle." *Montgomery Advertiser*, Aug. 13, 1863; quoted in "Documentary History of Reconstruction," Vol. I, p. 89: "Nine hundred of [the negroes] assembled (near Mobile) to consider their condition, their rights and their duties under the new state of existence upon which they have been so suddenly launched. . . . After long talk and careful deliberation, this meeting resolved, by a vote of 700 to 200, that they had made a practical trial for three months of their freedom which the war had bequeathed to them; that its realities were far from being so flattering as their

Those who had forced the ballot into his hands now set about driving and deceiving him into doing their work. One of the means to this end was the Freedmen's Bureau, one of those strange combinations of cant and crookedness, philanthropy and profits, piety and plunder, that are peculiar to capitalism.

The form of the law creating the Bureau was cast in terms of philanthropy. It was to be the most gigantic piece of paternalism ever attempted by any government. The most intimate details of the lives of the negroes were confided to its care. Their marriages, their business transactions, their food, homes, clothing, wages, education, and religion were to be supervised, regulated, and adjusted by the agents of this benevolent institution.[1] The War Department issued supplies for the destitute, and vast sums from various sources were placed at the disposal of the Bureau. That suffering was relieved, schools established, many impositions prevented, and much general charitable work done by the Freedmen's Bureau is indisputable.[2] But that such work was its main object after the first year of its existence none but the most prejudiced of its friends could claim.[3]

imagination had painted it . . . and finally that their 'last state was worse than their first,' and it was their deliberate conclusion that their true happiness and well-being required them to return to the homes which they had abandoned in the moment of excitement, and go to work again under their old masters." Garner, "Reconstruction in Mississippi," p. 124: "The black population of Mississippi decreased 56,146 between 1860 and 1866. . . . The Southerners said they had died from disease and starvation resulting from their sudden emancipation, and the explanation was not wholly without foundation."

[1] "Documentary History of Reconstruction," Vol. I, pp. 319–340.
[2] W. E. B. DuBois, "The Soul of Black Folk," chapter on "Freedmen's Bureau"; also in *Atlantic Monthly*, Vol. LXXXVII, p. 360.
[3] Rhodes, "History of United States," Vol. VI, p. 185.

RECONSTRUCTION

With its hundreds of agents possessed of the power to grant or withhold nearly all the necessities, comforts, and luxuries of life from the enfranchised blacks, it constituted a perfect machine for the control of the negro vote.[1] It was so used to the extreme limit of that power. The agents elected themselves and their friends to office everywhere.[2] Bureau funds were used directly for political corruption, and its whole far-reaching influence was always openly used as a political asset.[3]

Interwoven with the Freedmen's Bureau and the military organization in the work of controlling the negro vote were several secret oath-bound conspiratory organizations, the chief of which, and the pattern for the rest, was the Union League. The Bureau agents were the organizers of this society. "By the end of 1867 nearly the entire black population was brought under its influence."[4] Solemn oaths bound the members to vote for the League nominees. All the methods of secret terrorism, boycotts, and personal violence were used to enforce this political obedience.[5] The organizers of these societies did not overlook any opportunities for petty graft in the form of dues and fees that could be dragged from the deluded and terrorized blacks.[6]

All sorts of despicable swindles were perpetrated upon

---

[1] Hilary Herbert, "Why the Solid South," p. 17.   [2] *Ibid.*, p. 18.

[3] Minority Rept. Howard Investigation; House Rept., No. 121, 41st Cong., 2d Sess., pp. 47-53.

[4] "Documentary History of Reconstruction," Vol. II, p. 3.

[5] *Ibid.*

[6] *Ibid.*, p. 20. The Freedmen's Bureau commissioners in Florida organized a Lincoln Brotherhood, charging "an initiation fee of from one to two dollars and fifty cents per month." John Wallace, "Carpet-Bag Rule in Florida," pp. 28-29.

these "wards of the nation" by their grasping guardians. The story that Congress had voted "forty acres and a mule" to every former slave was almost universally circulated and believed among the negroes. Red-white-and-blue pegs were peddled to the confiding blacks, with the tale that any land marked with them would belong to the owner of the pegs.[1]

The army of men that were thus marshaling the negroes for the Republican party, organizing, voting, and robbing them, was made up in part of Northern adventurers ("carpet-baggers") and so-called Southern "Union men" ("scalawags"). These took the spoils of office, and made the state government simply means for private profit.

It is probably impossible to exaggerate the corruption of these Reconstruction governments. They voted enormous issues of bonds, and coolly pocketed the money for which they were sold. They doubled, quadrupled, and multiplied state debts twenty fold, and this without creating a single public improvement.[2] They raised the taxes until, in Mississippi, 20 per cent of the acreage was sold to satisfy the tax collector.[3] Legislatures voted fabulous sums for "supplies" for their members.[4]

All this was inflicted upon a land devastated by war and in most desperate need of every resource available for the establishment of the most elementary social needs. All this was part of the "original accumulation"

---

[1] "Documentary History of Reconstruction," Vol. I, pp. 359–360.
[2] Daniel H. Chamberlain, "Reconstruction in South Carolina," in *Atlantic Monthly*, Vol. LXXXVII, p. 477.
[3] Woodrow Wilson, "History of American People," Vol. V, p. 47.
[4] "Documentary History of Reconstruction," Vol. II, pp. 59–72.

of the political and profit-making power of the present ruling class.

The character of these Reconstruction governments is sometimes offered as a proof of the evils of negro suffrage. It should never be forgotten that it was not the black, but the white, man who maintained these governments, by military force, conspiracy, and chicanery, and that the white alone profited from them.[1] At the first signs of independence by the negro, even though that independence found no further expression than a demand for a share of the plunder,[2] interest in negro suffrage by the Reconstructionists waned. When some of the negroes joined with a remnant of decent whites, the Northern philanthropists withdrew the military support, and the Reconstruction governments collapsed.[3]

A parenthetic word is here necessary before discussing the further reasons for the fall of Reconstruction governments and policy. It would be as foolish to follow those Southern historians who would have it that the evils of the Reconstruction governments were due to the immorality and vindictiveness of the carpet-baggers and politicians, as to follow those Northern writers who make of the whole thing a benevolent action on behalf of the negro, alloyed only by a patriotic ambition to "save the Union."

Even the Congressional leaders were but instruments working in the interest of newly enthroned capitalism, — that royal heir whose birth we celebrated in the War of 1812. The way to that throne led through four

---

[1] "Documentary History of Reconstruction," Vol. II, p. 33.
[2] Wallace, "Carpet-Bag Rule in Florida," p. 105.
[3] "Documentary History of Reconstruction," Vol. II, p. 35.

bloody years of Civil War, followed by three times as many more years of political anarchy, bribery, oppression, conspiracy, hypocrisy, violent disregard of law and order, and the creation of a murderous race and sectional hatred, the terrible depths of which we have not yet sounded.

These words imply individual moral judgments and responsibility. This is necessary until a new industrial basis of society shall develop a vocabulary based on social responsibility.

Yet it would be false to assume that a majority, or even the leaders of the dominant faction in Congress, were consciously moved by a desire to place the great capitalists in power. Some were fanatically sincere abolitionists, earnestly and intensely believing that they were helping the negro. Even Thad Stevens seems to have been to some extent controlled by this motive.

They were "good" men when judged by individual standards of morality and responsibility. Looked at from a little broader social point of view, the vocabulary of denunciation and abhorrence seems inadequate when applied to their actions. Viewed with a still wider social and historical vision, they are seen to be instruments in the process by which the capitalist class attained to a power without which it could not have worked out its destiny and prepared the way to the better things that are still possible.

One of the obstacles to the carrying out of the Reconstruction program was the Supreme Court. This body was still dominated by a combination of small capitalist and chattel slave interests and ideas. Because that power generally safeguarded the interests of the exploiting class, this Court had been permitted to retain its usurped power to declare laws unconstitutional. It now became evident that this power would be used to nullify some of the Reconstruction legislation. Another "palace revolution" was necessary.

Accordingly on the 27th of March, 1868, Congress passed a law threatening the members of the Supreme Court with fines and imprisonment if they interfered with the carrying out of such legislation, and notifying that body that this legislation was not subject to review as to its constitutionality.

The Supreme Court at once recognized the right, or rather the power (which in class government is the same thing), of Congress to so curb the judicial department of the government, and dismissed the cases which were already before it.[1]

The Court and Congress by this action completely punctured the bubble upon which the autocratic power of the Supreme Court rests, and demonstrated that the Supreme Court only declares laws unconstitutional when it is to the interest of the ruling class to permit it to exercise that power.

Several years later, when powerful class interests had no further use for such legislation, the Court was permitted to receive another case involving these laws, and to then declare them unconstitutional (October, 1875).[2]

By the time the negro became dissatisfied with the rôle of a blind and dumb political tool, the great capital-

---

[1] Rhodes, "History of the United States," Vol. VI, p. 74; *Cong. Globe*, Jan. 13, 1868, p. 476. See especially the speech of Frederick T. Frelinghuysen, Jan. 28, 1868.

[2] U. S. *vs.* Reese, 92 U. S. Reports, p. 214.

ists of the North had gained such complete domination over the national government and political machines that they could afford to relax their violent rule in the South. The troops were withdrawn, and military rule was ended by Hayes in 1876, and the whole Reconstruction society crumbled and fell. The negroes were disfranchised, at first by force and fraud, and then later by laws. Meanwhile their erstwhile Republican defenders, who had once thrust that ballot into their hands at the point of the bayonet, now passed by on the other side without protest.

These interests could well afford to ignore the South. They had found a richer field of plunder. A saturnalia of corruption now centered around the national government, and had extended to state and municipal administrations. It was not simply that the powers of taxation were used to convert the national treasury into a mammoth widow's cruse, from which the privileged few stole almost countless sums. The national government was also used to bestow empires of land and piled up millions of dollars upon railroad corporations, who in turn were to use this national plunder only as a base for still further and greater frauds. In the stock and bond market it was the time of the Tweed Ring in New York and the Credit Mobilier in the West. To merely enumerate the more flagrant frauds of this time, when the fortunes of to-day were being founded, would fill the pages of a larger volume than this one.

Out of this corruption the great capitalist class drew the funds that enabled it to control the machinery of politics. The horrors of Reconstruction had engendered a sectional hatred so fierce as to render impossible any political combination across the line that divided the North from the South. The Republican party had made itself the object of a peculiar sort of patriotism, based on its claim to have saved the Union, and this made possible its dominance for a generation.[1]

Great and complex political machines had been built up throughout the country, resting on political patronage and illicit favors of government, which controlled nominations and directed elections. In the South a race war had been fostered that embittered and strengthened sectional antagonism, and helped to maintain the divisions among the voters so valuable to a ruling class.

By such methods and measures did the present ruling class obtain its industrial and political power.

[1] Ostrogorsky, "Democracy and the Origin of Political Parties," Vol. II, pp. 126–127.

CHAPTER XXIV

THE TRIUMPH AND DECADENCE OF CAPITALISM

EVENTS since the days of Reconstruction are still too close to afford that perspective view necessary to isolate the historically important from the sensationally striking. Only the length and vision of years, or the foresight of the prophet, can determine with certainty the events and the forces that form institutions and shape society, and thereby constitute the stuff of which history is made.

The one great fact of these years has been the stupendous development of concentrated capitalism. This has been based upon a continuous rapid transformation of the tools with which society does its work. Invention has crowded fast upon invention. The whole wonder-working cabinet of the electrician has been unlocked and its contents put at the service of man. Almost every department of industry has been revolutionized over and over again in this period, and every revolution brought greater power of production.

The network of railroads begun at the close of the war has been extended until it has covered the nation as with a web, whose radiating threads of steel mark the industrial centers. To the building of these railroads an empire of land, larger than the territory of any nation of western Europe (about five times as large as the state of Ohio) has been given. To this imperial graft the same paternal government added cash subsidies and guarantees of bonds amounting to hundreds of millions more. To this has still been added piled up millions of bounties and bonuses by state and local governments until it is well within the truth to say that such funds, so given, have been sufficient to build and equip every railroad in the United States as they were built and equipped in the early eighties.

These roads were then permitted by the government to become instruments of private profit.

In those years steel displaced iron, owing to the introduction first of the Bessemer and then of the open hearth process. The development of the Lake Superior ore deposits, the cheapening of lake transportation, and the shifting of the market for iron westward, with the growth of the railway systems and the building of great cities, caused the center of the steel trade to move from Pittsburg to the point where these sources of demand and supply found an equilibrium. This point now seems to be located near the southern end of Lake Michigan.

With the United States as a leading factor in the international steel trade an international steel trust was inevitable.

More and more the population drifted cityward. As industry after industry — weaving, shoemaking, manufacturing of clothing, preparation of meat, and a host of others — left the rural household for the city factory, the workers perforce followed their work. At first the rural population was merely outdistanced in rate of growth. But the census of 1910 shows a positive decline in rural population in the predominant agricultural states.

This growth of the cities was accelerated by the mighty flood of immigration. There was a succession of waves in this coming of the peoples of other countries. Irish, Germans, and Scandinavians formed the first battalions. These, like those that had been coming since colonial days, pressed forward to the frontier and were swiftly amalgamated. Later came a series of waves from southern and eastern Europe, Italians, the mixture of nationalities from within Austrian boundaries, and a great army of exiles from the Russian ghettoes.

When these reached America, the frontier was gone. Free land was no more. Agriculture, instead of swiftly expanding, was already declining. This new army of colonists was caught up in the internal currents of population already flowing strongly toward the cities, and settled in ever growing colonies that resisted amalgamation and endured a degree of exploitation and misery hitherto unknown in America.

Not even the Homestead Law, creating its millions of small freeholders, could prevent the forces of concentration producing their result. The census of 1910 again shows that even this wholesale apportionment of land by the government, the division into small farms of great sections of railroad holdings, and the breaking up of the Southern plantation, were unable, for more than a generation, to check the effect of the law of concentration of ownership in this, the slowest of all industries to respond to the pressure of social forces.

From the beginning the farmer of the Western prairies formed a less self-sufficient industrial unit than the small pioneer farmer of the earlier and more eastern stage. The Western farmer was a grower of staple crops for

TRIUMPH AND DECADENCE OF CAPITALISM 307

the market. Railroads, elevators, and marketing facilities were essential instruments in the production of these commodities. These instruments became the means of his exploitation, and against them he turned his wrath. In three great uprisings, — the "Granger Movement" of the late seventies, the Populist uprising of some ten years later, then the Bryan Democracy of 1896, — the farmers, aided by an incoherent mass of discontented members of the crumbling small-capitalist class, sought to capture the powers of government. In each of these uprisings the old cry of the debtor class for cheap money that had been heard ever since colonial days was brought to the fore; but these later movements in their demands for governmental action in fields of industry emphasized the importance of the industrial changes that had taken place.

Each of these efforts went down to defeat. The class of great capitalists was in control of nation, state, and municipalities, and of the executive, legislative, and especially the judicial departments of each and all. At no other time in this country, and never in any other land, has this class enjoyed such complete domination. Its ideas and ideals made and modeled social institutions. It created a society after its own image, and looked upon its work in bombastic spread-eagleism and pronounced it good. As the final triumph of capitalist evolution, its institutions deserve analysis.

It was the time when the American dollarocracy of beef, pills, soap, oil, or railroads became the worldwide synonym for the parvenu and the upstart. In literature it produced the cheap, wood-pulp, sensational daily, the *New York Ledger* type of magazine, the dime novel, and the works of Mary J. Holmes, Laura Jean Libby, and "The Duchess." In industry its dominant figures were J. Gould and Jim Fiske. In politics it evolved the "machine," the ward heeler, and the political boss, with Tweed as the finished sample. Its religious life found expression in sensational revivals upon the one hand, and a cheap negative atheism upon the other. In public architecture it erected the hideous piles that now disfigure our cities, and for private homes it added the type of the "Queen Anne front" and the "Mary Ann back." Its triumphs in sculpture were the bronze and cast-iron dogs with which the millionaire decorated his front lawn. It moved forward to the music of Moody and Sankey hymns and ragtime bands, while its one contribution to the pictorial art of the world was the chromo.

There was a steady progress in industrial concentration, but there are certain distinct stages worthy of notice. The ten years following the Civil War might be properly designated as the period of the domination of the "large industry," the next fifteen years as that of the "great industry," in contrast with the monopolistic stage prevailing since that date. These phrases are indefinite, and do not fully express the qualitative as well as the quantitative differences that distinguish these periods.

Until the panic of 1873, the dominant industrial unit (not the most numerous, but the one of which the ruling portion of industry was composed) had a capitalization of between fifty and five hundred thousand dollars. The number of firms was increasing quite rapidly in all but a few lines. There was still room at the top, and a host struggling upward.

When in 1873 the "mad gallop" of industry ended once more in the ditch of an industrial crisis, with Jay Cooke and Sons, the great bankers and governmental agents of the war period, at the bottom of the mess, it was the last general panic of capitalism. Henceforth there were to be those who were to stand outside industrial crises.

In 1873 the average capitalization of the firms failing was forty-four thousand dollars. Twenty years later, with the average industrial unit fully three times as large, there came another crisis, and the average capitalization of the firms failing was less than twenty thousand dollars. In the five years from 1893 to 1897 only five firms, with a capitalization of five hundred thousand dollars or over, failed.

The gods of our industrial world were now safe upon a monopolistic Olympus above the storms that had once overthrown them. A few years later, in 1908 and 1909, they were able to largely direct the tempest, and even to hurl its lightnings at those who had presumed to dispute their divinity.

The panic of 1873 marked the climax and collapse of expanding and competitive industry. This is shown most graphically by the table on the following page.

Forty years of the most rapid growth in production, the doubling of the population, and the conquest of the international markets were accompanied with a decrease in the number of firms in the leading industries.

Even these figures give but little idea of the tremendous concentration of power that has taken place within the capitalist class itself. The periodical press is now filled with descriptions of "inner circles," "spheres of interest," and all the multitude of methods by which a little group completely dominate the financial and industrial life of a nation.

NUMBER OF ESTABLISHMENTS

	1850	1860	1870	1880	1890	1900
Agricultural Implements	1333	2116	2076	1943	910	715
Carpets and Rugs	116	213	215	195	173	133
Cotton Goods	1094	1091	956	1005	905	1055
Glass	94	112	201	211	294	355
Hosiery and Knit Goods	85	197	248	359	796	921
Iron and Steel	468	542	726	699	699	668
Leather	6686	5188	7569	2628	1787	1306
Paper and Wood Pulp	443	555	677	742	649	763
Shipbuilding	953	675	694	2188	1006	1116
Silk and Silk Goods	67	139	86	382	472	483
Slaughter'd & M't P'kg.	185	259	768	872	1367	1134
Woolen Goods	1559	1260	2891	1990	1311	1035
Malt Liquors	431	1269	1972	2191	1248	1509
Totals	13,514	13,616	19,349	18,405	11,617	11,193

The period between the panics of 1873 and 1894 was still fiercely competitive, but it was the beginning of the competition of cannibalistic absorption, not for the conquest of new fields. It was the war to determine who should survive and dominate within the national market. When all industries, including railroads, were in a tooth and claw fight for survival, some rather startling weapons were discovered and brought into play. These were the palmy days of rebates, secret rates, and the various devices that gave rise to a whole system of repressive legislation after they had accomplished their purpose and were of no value to the ruling powers.

After the panic of 1894, the industrial battle entered into another phase. The field was now filled; the number of really effective competitors in each industry was so small that the imminence of possible destruction and deglutition became evident to all. So the profit seekers decided to hunt in packs instead of as individuals, and the trust appeared as a dominant figure of industry. The creation and filling to repletion of the national market brought about a situation similar to that existing in the South before the war. There was a demand for expansion. The Spanish American War, the invasion of China, the Panama Canal, the ransacking of the dark corners of the earth for trade opportunities, followed.

The century-long march across the continent was ended. The frontier of unoccupied land was no more. With the birth of the factory system at the close of the Napoleonic wars, American society turned its face inward. Now having conquered the continent and arisen to another stage of development, the curve of the ascending spiral swung once more outside of national boundaries and became involved in the sweep of international forces. That this movement was that of a spiral rather than of a pendulum is shown by the fact that this second entry into international politics was with a wholly different attitude than that which had been left behind when American capitalism broke loose from Europe.

In these earlier days American society was but a plaything of forces outside its own boundaries, owing its existence as a nation as much to conflicts and jealousies between other nations as to its own power of assertion.

Now it returned to become one of the most powerful factors in the struggle for worldwide commercial domination.

The Rise of Labor

When the multitude of workers were released from military service, and returned to industrial life, they were confronted with a transformation that had been wrought while they fought. The individual employer had largely given way to the corporation. Great masses of workers were selling their labor to a common master. The railroads especially were creating and demanding a body of fluid labor power drawn hither and thither in search of employment.

The Civil War had abolished the system by which the master hunted down the slave. Those who had fought that war returned home to find a society, one of whose new and most striking features was a body of workers hunting for masters.

These new conditions affecting men so many of whom were familiar with the effectiveness of military discipline could not but produce an organized labor movement. Many of the powerful "International" unions of to-day were born in the decade following the surrender at Appomattox.

These first unions were soon drawn together in the National Labor Union, that held its first convention in September, 1866.[1]

After a couple of years of growth this party was weakened by being drawn into a "Labor Reform Party,"

[1] "Documentary History of American Industrial Society," Vol. I, p. 227.

TRIUMPH AND DECADENCE OF CAPITALISM 313

which was seeking to represent the interests of the small capitalist and the working class, without any very clear understanding of the interests of either.

The "hard times" of 1873, therefore, found the working class almost completely unorganized. The first move of the employers, affected by the crisis, was to reduce wages. The unorganized workers could offer no effective resistance, and the return for labor was forced lower and lower until in 1876, when the Centennial of American Independence was celebrated, the American workers were suffering beneath an industrial tyranny worse than any imposed by English kings, and, in many ways, worse than that endured by the negro slaves in the South before the Civil War.

So helpless were the workers that when, in 1877, the Pennsylvania railroad announced a still further reduction of 10 per cent in the already less than living wage, there was no organized body to resist. While there were grumblings and threatenings of revolt, the day set for the reduction came and went with no action on the part of the workers. Another day came and went, and the crew of a train running into Martinsburg, West Virginia, left their posts as they drew into the division end and walked out, declaring it to be no worse to starve idle than to starve working. Then one of those strange waves that seizes those on the verge of desperation swept across the country. The spirit of revolt leaped along the telegraph wires from city to city, until from the Mississippi to the Atlantic the wheels of industry were almost paralyzed. Then Labor learned one more reason why great capitalists wish to control a powerful, unified national government. For the first time in American history workers in uniform shot down workers in the grimy garments of toil that profits might grow and wage slaves be kept in submission.

The slaves had not yet learned the uselessness of violent resistance to organized power, and for a time they fought back. In Pittsburg they momentarily overcame some companies of militiamen, but the battle quickly ended. The workers were shot and bayoneted and clubbed back to defeat and submission. But Labor is born of the earth, and when crushed to earth draws new strength and new weapons from its very defeat.

In 1869 a little band of workers, having discovered that open organization only invited the vengeance of the new form of outlawry, — the blacklist, — met at Philadelphia, and under the cover of secrecy, formed a society whose very name was never written, but was indicated by five stars whenever it was necessary to refer to it with pen or type. This society grew slowly, but steadily, until the strike of 1877, but it was not large enough at that time to play any important part in that struggle. The strike and its momentary defeat so suddenly and dramatically impressed the need of organization upon the workers that vast numbers flocked to this new organization. This sudden influx of members rendered the extreme secrecy of earlier years both impossible and unnecessary, and the mystical five stars were discarded and replaced by the words "Knights of Labor."

At this time the spirit of the American labor movement was as thoroughly filled with the great revolutionary tendency of the times as that of any country in the world. The pioneers in its organization were largely German refugees of 1848 and the succeeding years. Many had been connected with the International Working-men's Association (the "Old International" founded by Marx). The whole ritual, literature, and spirit of the "Knights of Labor" was permeated with vague socialism. This spirit now found expression in the eight-hour crusade that swept the laboring masses of the country with a sort of religious enthusiasm. This movement, like the "Knights of Labor," had started shortly after the close of the Civil War, and had remained dormant until about 1880. Then it gathered momentum until by 1885 it had become nation-wide and taken on more and more the character of a religious crusade.

In some way the impression became general that the first of May, 1886, had been fixed upon as the day of the millennial dawn of the eight-hour heaven on earth. No organization of any importance fixed this date. The "Knights of Labor," whose members had grown so rapidly that its general officers were refusing to charter new locals, lest the organization become unmanageable, especially disavowed this date as being set for any action.

Yet the movement grew, and reached such proportions as to threaten a serious reduction in the share that Capital was taking of Labor's product. Something like a panic seized upon the ruling class. Men elected to office by laborers were deliberately counted out in Chicago. This caused some of the leaders of labor to lose their heads and talk vaguely of violence. Then some one, whether fool, fanatic, or police spy, we shall probably never know, threw a bomb into a detachment of police who were breaking up a meeting on Haymarket Square in Chicago — a meeting that the mayor of that city but an hour before had declared to be wholly peaceable.

Then all the fiends of vengeance, controlled by the powers of plutocracy, broke loose. Few would deny to-day that evidence was manufactured by wholesale by the Chicago police and newspapers, or that even class law was stretched to the breaking point that the leaders of labor might be brought to the scaffold. They were brought to the scaffold, and the exploiters of labor rejoiced that resistance to exploitation was crushed. There was more reason for rejoicing than ever before. The appeal to violence and anarchistic individualism set back for many years the intelligent defense of Labor's interest. The American labor movement, hitherto inspired and largely dominated, even if in a somewhat indefinite manner, by the spirit of intelligent class revolt, now fell largely under the control of its most reactionary and short-sighted element.

Organized labor in the United States became separated from all political action or social philosophy save that of expediency and opportunism, and the road was thrown wide for corruption and confusion. There were many causes for this, but it is doubtful if this period of isolation and partial sterility in the broader fields of action would have come, had it not been for the opportunity for judicial murder and popular prejudice created by those who appealed to anarchy and condoned violence.

But no power on earth can permanently crush Labor. Gradually its revolt has grown conscious. Gradually it has evolved its philosophy in common with those of other nations. Slowly at first, but with ever increasing speed, it has been translating its economic interests into political and industrial action.

Like the commercial and plantation interests that brought about separation from Great Britain and formulated the Constitution, like the chattel slave owners that controlled the government and molded it for two generations, like the capitalist class that rode into power amid the blood and fraud and terror of civil war and Reconstruction, the working class has become in its turn the embodiment of the spirit of social progress, and is fighting for victory with a certainty of success before it.

Every class that has controlled the powers of government has used these powers to create a society after its own image. The workers will do the same. While history may appear to have nothing to do with the future, it is impossible to draw the lines of social forces through all the perspective of the past and then stop them short at the present.

The same forces that have operated in the past will continue in the future. New and more effective machines will be invented and hitched to more powerful and yet undiscovered sources of energy. Concentration and ownership of these instruments and forces will proceed while they remain private property. Labor will grow farther and farther away from the possibility of ownership of those things to which the lives of laborers are attached.

Out of these facts the workers of the world in pursuit of their class interests have evolved a line of action that leads to organization for the attainment of political power. Labor, like the merchant class, chattel slave owners, and capitalists, is fighting for political power. It will use that political power to obtain control of the instruments essential to the lives of the workers. That ownership cannot be individual. Industry cannot be disintegrated back to the stage of individual ownership. It must be still further integrated into common ownership by a democratically controlled government of the workers.

Labor is certain of victory in this last struggle. All other classes have gained power only as they have persuaded, bribed, or terrorized workers into fighting or voting for them. Now that the working class is fighting its own battles, there is no possibility of defeat.

INDEX

Abbot, Willis J., 38.
Abolitionism, 218–219.
Adams, Henry, 104.
Adams, Herbert B., 65.
Adams, John, 61, 218.
Adams, Samuel, 73–74, 92.
Agricultural machinery, 248, 278.
Agriculture, 49–51; at formation of the Union, 102; mother of industry, 121; on frontier, 136–137; on eve of Civil War, 248; during Civil War, 278–280.
Alien and Sedition Laws, 120.
Alvord, H. E., 103.
Ames, Fisher, 88.
Anarchists, Chicago, 315–316.
Annapolis convention, 94.
Arnold, S. G., 91.
Astor, John Jacob, 159.
Austrian Succession, War of, 57.

Babcock, K. C., 146, 157.
Back-country, struggle with coast, 46, 53, 56; opposition to constitution, 98.
Bacon's Rebellion, 47–49.
Bagnall, W. R., 37.
Baker, Kames, 234.
Baltimore, 102.
Bank of United States, first, 161; second, 162–163, 205–208; and Daniel Webster, 205.
Bankers and Civil War, 280.
Bankruptcy, 167.
Bassett, J. S., 112, 124, 230.
Benton, Thomas H., 160, 165, 172, 203, 204, 206.
Berkeley, Governor, 47.
Bishop, Leander J., 88, 96, 122, 159, 195.
Blaine, James G., 294.
Bogart, Ernst L., 195, 223, 246, 247.

Bolles, Albert S., 35, 37, 238, 239, 245, 246, 247, 276, 277, 280, 282.
Boston, 76, 102, 179.
Boston Tea Party, 63–64.
Brisbane, Albert, 214, 255.
Brown, John, 260.
Brown, William G., 222, 230, 237, 239, 268.
Bruce, Phillip A., 46.
Bryant, W. C., 256.
Burr, Aaron, 125.
Byllesby, L., 188.

Cabet, Etienne, 214.
Cairns, W. B., 169.
Calhoun, John C., 157, 162, 202, 226.
California, discovery of gold in, 253.
Cambridge Modern History, 10.
Campbell, 18.
Capitalist class, rise of, 254–255.
Capitalist society, characteristics of, 307–308.
Carey, Matthew, 148, 154, 156.
Carlton, Frank T., 177.
Cattle in New England colonies, 35.
Cavaliers, 45–46.
Chadwick, Frank E., 226.
Chamberlain, Daniel H., 298.
Chamberlain, Mellen, 70.
Channing, E., 214.
Channing, William E., 169.
Charity, beginnings of, 166.
Charleston, 102.
Chattel slavery, atavism in America, 268–269; concentration of ownership in, 224; inferior in productive power to wage system, 228–230; industrial effects of, 232; movement to South, 233–234; demand for more territory, 236; security for social peace, 225.
Cheney, Edward P., 4, 5.
Chevalier, Michael, 174, 178.

319

INDEX

Chicago, 191; grain shipments from, 249.
Child labor in early cotton factories, 172-173.
Chittenden, H. M., 205.
Church and Merchants, 3.
Cities at formation of Union, 101; growth of population, 250; struggle for market, 199-200.
Civil War, corruption during, 280-282; cotton speculation during, 281-282; effect on industry, 275-277; financing of, 282; patents during, 277.
Clay, Henry, 153, 202, 212.
Cobb, Elkanah, 149.
Cobb, Thomas R., 226.
Columbus, Christopher, 1, 10, 11.
Coman, Katherine, 44, 246.
Commerce, in 1810, 130; in 1846, 246; progress of, 120.
Commercial interests and constitution, 88.
Committees of Correspondence, 73, 83.
Commons, John R., 256.
Commonwealth, English, 70.
Communism, primitive in colonies, 31.
Concentration in chattel slave ownership, 224.
Concentration in industry, 309-310.
Confederation, Articles of, 99.
Constitution, adoption of, 97-98.
Constitution and Bill of Rights, 98.
Constitutional convention a conspiratory body, 92-93; secrecy of, 95.
Continental Congress, 83, 84, 94-95.
Continental currency, 86.
Corn, importance of, 137.
Cornwallis, surrender of, 80.
Corruption during Reconstruction, 298.
Cotton, and blockade, 272-273; and negro slavery, 192, 219-220; in Reconstruction, 292; trade during Civil War, 281-282.
Cotton gin, 123.
Cotton, Joseph P., 126.
Cotton mills, 122, 149.
Courts created by Federalists, 125-126.
Coxe, Tenche, 155.
Crime in 1820, 168.

Crisis, of 1819, 160-168; of 1837, 199; of 1873, 309; of 1894, 309; of 1908, 309.
Crittenden Resolution, 290.
Cromwell, Oliver, 36, 47.
Crusades, 6.
Cumberland Road, 158.
Cunningham, William, 8.
Curtis, Francis, 257.

Dana, Charles A., 255.
Davis, John P., 239, 240.
Debow, J. D., 225, 227, 231, 252, 253, 266-267, 285.
Debt, imprisonment for, 86-87, 176.
Debt, national, 111-115.
Debtor class and constitution, 89.
Debts, assumption of state, 112-115.
Demands of early labor movement, 183-186.
Depew, Chauncey M., 201.
Dewey, D. R., 118.
Dexter, Edwin G., 177, 187.
Dickens, Charles, 210.
Diffenderfer, Frank R., 17.
Dodge, 104.
Domestic Animals, 102-104.
Donaldson, Thomas, 204, 208.
Douglas, Stephen A., 191, 217.
Doyle, J. A., 31, 141.
Draft riots, 283.
Drake, Charles D., 137.
Dred Scott decision, 258-259.
DuBois, W. E. D., 296.
Dutch West India Co., 50.
Dwight, Timothy, 251.

East India Company, 63.
Education, demands of labor movement concerning, 181-183.
Education, public, 177.
Ellis, George E., 72.
Emancipation of negro, 274.
Embargo, 145-146.
Emerick, C. F., 161.
Emerson, Ralph Waldo, 214, 256.
Erie canal, 158, 195-197, 251.
Evans, Oliver, 122, 171.
Excise tax, 117.
Express, beginning of, 242-244.

Factory system, beginning of, 105, 147;

INDEX

efforts to encourage, 148; evolution of, 170; in the West, 152.
Factory workers, misery of early, 172–174.
Farmers', Mechanics' and Workingmen's Advocate, 182.
Farrand, M., 96.
Faux, W., 103.
Fish *vs.* Western Meat, 204.
Fisher, Ellwood, 264.
Fisher, S. G., 73.
Fisheries, 25; as cause of Revolution, 62–63; after Revolution, 86.
Fiske, John, 41, 42, 43, 45, 46, 50, 52, 53, 83.
Fitch, John, 106.
Fite, Emerson D., 252, 276, 279.
Fitzhugh, George, 234.
Fleming, Walter E., 269, 292.
Flick, A. C., 72.
Flint, Timothy, 159, 161, 193, 194, 196.
Ford, Ebenezer, 181, 184.
Ford, H. J., 94.
Forests, influence of, 25.
Fourier, Francois C. M., 214.
Franklin, Benjamin, 53, 57, 116.
Freedman's Bureau, 296.
Free Enquirer, 182.
Frelinghuysen, Frederick T., 301.
Fremont, John C., 258.
French and Indian War, 57, 60, 66.
French Revolution, 151.
Frontier, influence in American history, 134–142; and Jackson, 209; and laborers, 178; meaning of, 139.
Fur-trade, 26, 49, 205.

Gannett, H., 142.
Garrison, William Lloyd, 217.
Geiser, Karl F., 17.
German immigrants, 15–16.
Gibbins, H. de, 160.
Goode, John Paul, 21.
Goodloe, Daniel R., 232.
Gordon, Charles, 194.
Gouge, William H., 160, 163, 164, 168, 206.
Granger movement, 307.
Grant, William, 200, 252.
Great Lakes, commerce on, 257; region during Civil War, 279; settlement of, 249.

Y

Greeley, Horace, 255.
Greenback movement, 287.
Greene, E. B., 44.
Gregg, William, 230.

Hall, Benjamin F., 257.
Hamilton, Alexander, 61, 96, 98, 109–119.
Hammond, M. B., 223, 233.
Hancock, John, 61, 62, 63.
Hanseatic League, 8.
Harrison, William H., 212–213.
Hart, Albert Bushnell, 219.
Haymarket riot, 315.
Heath, David, 171.
Helmholt, 5.
Helper, Hinton Rowan, 228–230.
Herbert, Hilary H., 294, 297.
Hildreth, Richard, 129.
Hill, Rowland, 244.
Holmes, Oliver W., 256.
Homestead Law, 306.
Hosmer, J. K., 73, 92.
Howe, Elias, 245, 276.
Howe, William, 76–79.
Hulbert, A. B., 200.

Immigration, 250, 306.
Imprisonment for debt, 176.
Indians, 27–29, 53–54.
Ingle, Edward, 231, 235.
International capitalism, 311–312.
Inventions, 2–3, 195, 245.
Iron, colonial, 37; industry, 106, 305; inventions in, 195; changes in, 245–246; in Civil War, 277; in Confederacy, 270–271; rails, 245; shipbuilding, 246.
Irving, Washington, 90.

Jacksonian Democracy, 209–211.
James I of England, 43.
Jay, John, 124.
Jefferson, Thomas, 113, 124, 133, 145, 153.
Johnson, Andrew, 289.
Johnson, Emory R., 238.
Johnson, James F. W., 234.

Kennedy, J. H., 277.
Kentucky, settlement of, 152.
Kettel, Thomas P., 231, 233.

Kindergartens, demanded by Labor, 183.
Knights of Labor, 314-315.
Kuhns, Oscar, 16.

Labor, final triumph certain, 317-318.
Labor movement, results of early, 184-187.
Labor unions, 312-316.
Lalor, J. J., 294.
Land grants to Confederation, 84.
Land speculation, 58.
Legislatures, colonial, 68.
Leisler, Jacob, 53, 59.
Levasseur, E., 276.
Lewis and Clark exploration, 159.
Libby, Orin G., 98.
Library, Congressional, 153.
Lincoln, Abraham, 217, 261, 286, 289, 294.
Lodge, Henry Cabot, 2, 42.
Logan, John A., 138.
Longfellow, Henry W., 256.
Louisburg, capture of, 57.
Louisiana, purchase of, 128-129.
Lowell, Francis C., 149.
Lowell, W. R., 256.
Luther, Seth, 174.

Macaulay, Thomas B., 16.
Macgregor, John, 193, 194, 198.
Madison family, 46.
Madison, James, 94, 95, 98.
Maize, 136-137.
Man, The, 180.
Mann, Horace, 187.
Manufactures, 194-195; and Civil War, 275-277; Hamilton's Report on, 115-116; and Revolution, 64; at close of Revolution, 87; in the South, 230, 269.
Marshall family, 46.
Marshall, John, 126, 164.
Martineau, Harriet, 210.
Marx, Karl, 189, 255, 284.
Mason and Dixon's Line, 55.
Mason family, 46.
Massachusetts, 90; education in, 177; manufacturing in, 37.
McCarthy, Charles, 200.
McCormick, Cyrus, 245.
McCullough *vs.* Maryland, 164.

McMaster, John Bach, 40, 86, 87, 90, 92, 129, 130, 131, 132, 133, 146, 148, 152, 158, 162, 163, 165, 174, 182, 204, 205, 207, 209.
Meat-packing, 193.
Mechanics' Free Press, 180, 182.
Mercantile domination in government, 154.
Mercantile System of economics, 60, 64.
Merchant class, 2, 4, 108.
Michaux, F. A., 137.
Minot, G. R., 91.
Mississippi, State, condition after War, 288.
Mississippi River, 124, 247, 252.
Mob methods in Revolution, 74.
Monroe family, 46.
Moonshining, 117-118.
More, Sir Thomas, 13-14.
Morse, J. D., 94.
Moseley, Edward A., 201.
Motley, J. L., 256.
Myers, Gustavus, 187, 205, 206.

Nail industry, 106.
Napoleon I, 108, 144.
National Labor Union, 312.
Navigation laws, 61.
Negro, condition after emancipation, 295; submissiveness, 274; suffrage, 293-294, 299; swindling during Reconstruction, 298.
New England, 33-40, 129, 146, 159.
New Orleans, 159.
New York city, 101; influence of Erie Canal, 200; trade unions in, 179.
Niles, Henry, 163, 167.
Niles' Weekly Register, 122, 132, 157, 160, 166, 174; founded, 149.

Ogg, Frederick A., 58.
Ohio River, influence in settlement, 158.
Ordinance of 1787, 84-85, 128.
Oriental trade, 5.
Ostrogorski, M., 125, 132, 168, 211, 254.
Owen, Robert, 189.
Owen, Robert Dale, 281.

Pacific railway, 239.
Palatinate Germans, 15-17, 51.

INDEX

Paper money, 54, 66.
Parkinson, 137.
Parkinson's Tour, 103.
Patents, 149; for scythe, 37; during Civil War, 277.
Pauperism in 1819, 167.
Peck, Charles H., 204, 212, 219.
Peck, J. N., 193, 194.
Penn, William, 59.
Pennsylvania, early education system of, 182; manufactures in, 148.
Philadelphia, 101; early union movement in, 180.
Phillips, U. B., 145.
Phillips, Wendell, 217.
Piedmont Plateau, influence on settlement, 45.
Pike, James S., 273.
Pine Tree Shillings, 39.
Pioneers, various stages, 135–136.
Piracy, in New York, 51–52.
Pittsburg, 58, 195.
Plantation interest, and constitution, 88–89; War of 1812, 145.
Plantation system, origin of, 43–44; changes in, 223.
Platforms of early Labor Party, 184–186.
Political machines, 210–211.
Pollard, Edward A., 217.
Poor whites, 227–230.
Population in colonial times, 56; movement toward cities, 305.
Populists, 307.
Portuguese explorations, 9.
Postal system, of Confederacy, 271–272; establishment of, 57; at formation of Union, 101; service of, 241–244.
Property qualifications for voting, 175.
Public land, and crisis of 1837, 208; Foote resolution on, 203; grants of, to railroads, 239; in formation of Union, 84.

Rabbeno, Ugo, 116.
Railroads, beginning of, 197–199; in Confederacy, 271; commerce on, 247; grants to, 239, 304–305; Pacific, 239; progress prior to Civil War, 238.

Ranching stage, 138; in Illinois, 194.
Randolph family, 46.
Randolph, John, 153.
Rebels, hereditary pioneer, 140.
Reconstruction, 285–303.
Reinsch, Paul S., 294.
Religious changes in New England, 168–169.
Renaissance, relation to discovery of America, 2.
Republican Party, 255–258, 261.
Revolution, American, boycott in, 74; mob violence in, 74; smuggling as cause of, 61–63.
Revolution of 1848 and emigration, 250.
Rhode Island, 91, 99.
Rhodes, James Ford, 258, 270, 274, 275, 279, 281, 296, 301.
Rice industry, 104.
Ringwalt, I. L., 32, 158, 197, 198.
Ripley, George, 214.
Risson, Paul, 3.
Roosevelt, Theodore, 136–137.
Ropes, John C., 265.
Rotation in office, 210.
Rum-molasses-slave trade, 38–39.

Salisbury, J. H., 137.
Salt tariff opposed by West, 204.
Santa Fe Trail, 205.
Sawmill, first, 38.
Schaper, W. A., 222.
Schouler, J., 65, 94, 117, 206, 262.
Schulte, Aloys, 5.
Schurz, Carl, 256.
Schwab, John C., 263, 271.
Scotch-Irish, 18.
Secession, cause of, 237; and Civil War, 216–217.
Semple, Ellen, 142, 193, 196.
Sentinel, The Daily, 180.
Shaler, N. S., 137.
Sharpless, Isaac, 54.
Shays' Rebellion, 90–92.
Simons, May Wood, 67.
Simpson, Stephen, 188.
Skidmore, Thomas, 188.
Slater, Samuel, 105.
Slaves, chattel, 55–56, 104; and cotton gin, 123; and Civil War, 218; conditions of, 223; foreign trade in, 234–

235; price of, 233; and tobacco, 42; and wage-workers, 96.
Slavery, negro, in Illinois, 192.
Slavery of colonial whites, 18–19.
Smith, J. Allen, 96.
Smith, William H., 104, 256.
Smugglers and Revolution, 73.
Smuggling as cause of the Revolution, 61–63.
Socialists and Civil War, 283–284.
Soil, effect on settlement, 23; on cotton raising, 222.
South, industrial inferiority, 265.
Spargo, John, 284.
Stamp Act, 68.
Stanwood, Edwin, 122, 157.
State governments and Reconstruction, 289–290.
Steamboat, first, 106; in Western waters, 159; on Great Lakes, 197; on ocean, 246.
Steam in cotton mills, 171.
Stedman, Charles, 62.
Stevens, Thaddeus, 290, 291, 300.
Stickney, 137.
Stimpson, A. L., 243.
Strikes, 313, 314, 315; as conspiracies, 131.
Sumner, William G., 65.
Supreme Court and Dred Scott decision, 258–259; and Reconstruction, 300–302.
Swank, James M., 245.
Swank, M. D., 195.
Sylvis, James, C., 283.
Sylvis, William H., 283.

Tammany, 125, 210.
Tanner, H. S., 199.
Tariff, 109–110, 115–117, 149; and chattel slavery, 235–236; labor argument for, 256.
Tea-tax and Revolution, 63–64.
Telegraph, 230.
Texas, as granary of Confederacy, 270, 271.
Textile industries, 122.
Thatcher, Samuel, 169.
Thoreau, Henry D., 214.
Thwaites, R. G., 56.
Tobacco, 41–43, 104.
Tocqueville, Alexander De, 210.

Tories in Revolution, 71–72.
Transcendentalism, 214.
Transportation, in colonies, 31; at formation of Union, 100.
Tribune, New York, 255–256.
Trumbull, Jonathan, 61.
Turner, Frederick J., 142, 152, 153, 164, 165, 168, 202, 205.
Tyler, John, 213.
Tyler, M. C., 72.

Unemployed in 1819, 166.
Union, plans for colonial, 59.
Unions, first, 179–180.
Utopian communism, 214.
Utrecht, treaty of, 56.

Van Buren, Martin, 211.
Virginia, colonial, 41–49; decline of industry in, 153; dynasty, fall of, 153; House of Burgesses, 43.
Von Holst, Herman E., 94, 129, 225, 226, 235.

Wages, 130–131; in 1819, 173.
Wageworkers and constitution, 89.
Wampum, 35.
War, effect on manufactures, 147.
War of 1812, 143–147.
Warden, D. B., 148, 161.
Washington family, 46.
Washington, George, 58, 76, 100; as land speculator, 65.
Watson, Thomas, 65, 94, 153.
Webster, Daniel, 157, 202, 203; and Bank, 205–206; and tariff, 168.
Webster, William C., 3, 88, 96, 120.
Weeden, W. B., 32, 34, 35, 36, 37, 39, 40.
Wells, David A., 275, 277.
Wells, David H., 61.
West opposes Bank, 164.
Western immigration, 152.
Weston, George M., 227.
Westphalia, Peace of, 15.
Weydemeyer, Joseph, 256.
Whig Party, 212.
Whiskey Rebellion, 118.
White, Horace, 165, 206.
Whitney, Eli, 123.
Whittier, J. G., 256.
Williamson, Captain, 103.
Wilson, Henry, 237.

INDEX

Wilson, Woodrow, 48, 86, 129, 204, 237, 298.
Winden, Julius, 200.
Winsor, Justin, 65, 70, 72, 96.
Woolen, industry, 105; effect of Civil War on, 276.

Women, labor of, in early cotton mills, 172–173.
Workingmen's Advocate, The, 178, 183.
Workingmen's ticket, 181.
Wright, Carroll D., 171.

Printed in the United States of America.